The Picaresque

CENTER FOR RENAISSANCE AND BAROQUE STUDIES

Director: S. Schoenbaum
Executive Director: Adele F. Seeff

Advisory Board

Susan Amussen
Connecticut College

Shirley Strum Kenny
Queens College

Howard Mayer Brown
The University of Chicago

Max Palevsky
Los Angeles, California

Esther Coopersmith
Potomac, Maryland

J. G. A. Pocock
Johns Hopkins University

David Driskell
University of Maryland

William Rearick
University of Maryland

Jeanne Roberts
American University

Robert L. Gluckstern
University of Maryland

Ellen Rosand
Rutgers University

Werner L. Gundersheimer
Folger Shakespeare Library

Betty S. Travitsky
Brooklyn, New York

Jay Halio
University of Delaware Press

G. Thomas Tanselle
John Simon Guggenheim
Memorial Foundation

The Center for Renaissance and Baroque Studies at the University of Maryland, College Park, sponsors programs in all disciplines of the arts and humanities as well as in such allied fields as the history and philosophy of science. Designed primarily for faculty and graduate students, the Center's scholarly programs include an annual Scholar-in-Residence program, conferences and colloquia, lectures, an annual interdisciplinary symposium, and a series of summer institutes for secondary school teachers. Programs in the arts include concerts, lecture-demonstrations, and exhibitions. The Center is administered by its executive director and its director in conjunction with an advisory board of outside consultants and a faculty advisory committee.

The Picaresque

A Symposium on the Rogue's Tale

Edited by
Carmen Benito-Vessels
and Michael Zappala

Newark: University of Delaware Press
London and Toronto: Associated University Presses

© 1994 by Associated University Presses, Inc.

All rights reserved. Authorization to photocopy items for internal or personal use, or the internal or personal use of specific clients, is granted by the copyright owner, provided that a base fee of $10.00, plus eight cents per page, per copy is paid directly to the Copyright Clearance Center, 27 Congress Street, Salem, Massachusetts 01970. [0-87413-458-7/94 $10.00 + 8¢ pp, pc.]

Associated University Presses
440 Forsgate Drive
Cranbury, NJ 08512

Associated University Presses
25 Sicilian Avenue
London WC1A 2QH, England

Associated University Presses
P.O. Box 39, Clarkson Pstl. Stn.
Mississauga, Ontario
L5J 3X9 Canada

The paper used in this publication meets the requirements of the American National Standard for Permanence of Paper for Printed Library Materials Z39.48-1984.

Library of Congress Cataloging-in-Publication Data

The Picaresque : a symposium on the rogue's tale / edited by Carmen Benito-Vessels and Michael Zappala.
    p. cm.
  Papers delivered at a symposium held Apr. 21–22, 1989, sponsored by the Center for Renaissance and Baroque Studies, the Department of Spanish and Portuguese, and the College of Arts and Humanities.
  Includes bibliographical references and index.
  ISBN 0-87413-458-7 (alk. paper)
  1. Picaresque literature—History and criticism—Congresses.
I. Benito-Vessels, Carmen. II. Zappala, Michael O., 1948–1991.
III. University of Maryland, College Park. Center for Renaissance and Baroque Studies.
PN3428.P48 1994
863.009′351—dc20
                                                                  91-51136
                                                                       CIP

PRINTED IN THE UNITED STATES OF AMERICA

To the memory of
Michael Zappala

February 10, 1948–March 4, 1991

Contents

Director's Preface
  S. Schoenbaum   9

Preface
  Carmen Benito-Vessels and Michael Zappala   11

Discursive Parameters of the Picaresque
  Marina S. Brownlee   25

Classicity in the Spanish Golden Age: Gonzalo Pérez's
Translation of *La Ulyxea* and the Origin of the Spanish
Picaresque Novel
  Joseph V. Ricapito   36

La Lozana andaluza as Precursor to the Spanish
Picaresque
  Bruno M. Damiani   57

The Picaresque and Autobiography
  Randolph D. Pope   69

Richard Head and Origins of the Picaresque in England
  Calhoun Winton   79

Translation and Cultural *Translatio*
  Jerry C. Beasley   94

From Duplicitous Delinquent to Superlative Simpleton:
Simplicissimus and the German Baroque
  Gerald Gillespie   107

A Latin American Enlightenment Version of the
Picaresque: Lizardi's *Don Catrín de la Fachenda*
  Nancy Vogeley   123

Don Picaro: Lord Byron and the Reclassification of the
Picaresque
  Jerome Christensen   147

The Brazilian Picaresque
 MÁRIO M. GONZÁLEZ 163

Notes on Contributors 176
Selected Bibliography 179
Index 185

Director's Preface

Established in 1981 through the vision of Dr. Shirley S. Kenny, provost of arts and humanities at the University of Maryland, and the beneficence of the Maryland legislature during an all-too-familiar period of retrenchment in high education, the Center for Renaissance and Baroque Studies held its Inaugural Conference on 11 and 12 March 1982. From the outset the university has envisaged the center as multidisciplinary. Music and the visual arts, literature in several modern European languages, philosophy, and history—indeed all the appropriate disciplines in the humanistic pantheon—come within our sphere. Throughout the academic year the center reminds staff and students of its presence with a continuing program of interdisciplinary symposia, scholars-in-residence, public lectures, and musical recitals.

On 21–22 April 1989, the Center trafficked—as it was no doubt destined to do—in roguery. Happily the encounter was entirely respectable, as scholars gathered in College Park for a symposium sponsored by the Center for Renaissance and Baroque Studies, the Department of Spanish and Portuguese, and the College of Arts and Humanities, to consider "The Picaresque: A Symposium on the Rogue's Tale." Among the papers delivered and discussed were "Translation and Cultural *Translatio*," by Professor Jerry C. Beasley of the University of Delaware, "Don Picaro: Lord Byron and the Reclassification of the Picaresque," by Professor Jerome Christensen of The Johns Hopkins University, and "Richard Head and Origins of the Picaresque in England," by Professor Calhoun Winton of the University of Maryland at College Park. The participants—classicists, humorists, Hispanists, comparatists, and yes, some graduate students—considered a field "roiling with problems of definition and method" as Michael Zappala puts it in the Preface to this collection. Thus did the assembled scholars go about re-evaluating their canon of received texts. Thus did the Spanish Golden Age live again in College Park.

S. Schoenbaum

Preface

I

To provide a framework for the diversity of approaches to the picaresque genre, these introductory pages will present well-known facts aimed at a general audience. This overview of the picaresque genre is based mainly on the selected works of experts in this subject and cited in this preface.

When the picaresque novel appeared in Spain, the country was suffering from a sharp decrease in population and a lack of public funds. Acute impoverishment affected all social classes and was dramatically highlighted by the extraordinary number of beggars that populated Spanish cities. Royal decrees were pronounced in 1599, 1603, and 1605 in order to eliminate mendicity, but their failure was proved by the need to formulate four subsequent decrees appearing in Spanish law before 1699.

It is Alberto del Monte's (1971) opinion that social desperation and its immediate consequence—moral abjection—contributed to the forging of the rogue as a literary character.[1] In *Los pícaros en la literatura española*, Alexander Parker has written that organizations of rogues in all of Europe were notorious and even quite sophisticated: in Germany, the *Liber vagatorum* (c. 1520) distinguished twenty-eight kinds of beggars and in Italy Giacinto Nobili identified thirty-four of them in his *Il vagabondo* (1627).[2]

The study of picaresque literature underscores the meaning of the word *pícaro*, which identifies the literary rogue as a character without dignity, without a stable job, and dedicated to humble activities that barely allowed him the satisfaction of his basic needs. The rogue does not have a defined occupation; he is a vagabond, related to the underworld and to begging, and his destiny is generally dismal. Above all, the rogue is a socially marginalized and uprooted character who is conditioned by his own genealogy to which he refers in a shameless manner in his autobiographical narrative.

Picaresque literature was immersed in a cultural ambience in clear contrast to the artificiality of chivalric novels. It has repeatedly been said that the picaresque novel is a realistic genre that depicts the reality of Post-Tridentine and Counter-Reformation Spain of the second half of the sixteenth century. Nonetheless, according to Paul Julian Smith (1988),[3] the so-called picaresque realism is an invalid postulate. Smith defends the idea that, with its basic autobiographical form, picaresque novels share the same principles of fiction as chivalric novels, differing only in a matter of degree or in the mode of fictionality (82). The paradoxical similarity between picaresque and chivalric novels has been briefly and clearly expressed by Juan Bautista Avalle-Arce.[4] In this scholar's opinion, the determinism of Amadís de Gaula and of Lázaro are two manifestations of the same phenomenon, although located on opposite poles. According to Avalle-Arce (1975) "el determinante del *Amadís* es la gloria (lo heroico), mientras el determinante del *Lazarillo* es el éxito (lo humano)" (221), but this success is based on deception, on an alteration of perception, and, therefore, it represents a pathetic failure perceived as such by the reader, although not by the protagonist of the novel. If Lázaro goes from bad to worse, Amadís goes from good to better (Avalle-Arce 1975, 223). Lázaro, the prototype of the rogue according to some critics and its precursor according to others, was marked *ab initio* by a negative determinism that radically contrasts with the positive determinism that characterizes Amadís and chivalresque heroes. Lázaro was born of a mistress and he considered himself successful in life when he married the mistress of the archpriest. On the other hand, in his article included in this volume, Bruno Damiani defends the realist aspect of the picaresque in contrast to the fanciful chivalric novel. Damiani affirms this in the case of the polemic novel, the *Lozana andaluza*, which, although it "may not be properly called a picaresque novel, . . . does exhibit several traits characteristic of the later novel of roguery." The freedom of the character, and not her determinism, is the factor that leads her to an unorthodox sexual life. These two conflicting points of view highlight the vitality of the controversy related to the characterization of the picaresque.

Much has been written on the episodic fragmentation of the picaresque novel, especially in *Lazarillo*. Instead of fragmentation, however, we should refer to what Paul Julian Smith (1988) has called a "non-pictorial" vision of the entourage. The artistic value of the text, and not the breaking of continuity, includes the "refusal (or inability) to conceal the labour or process of writing, [and this] is itself a defining characteristic of the picaresque as a genre" (80).

The aesthetic presuppositions of the picaresque novel emerge, according to Edward Friedman (1988),[5] from what he calls an autobiographical impulse directly related to confession (and confessional literature); in Friedman's opinion "the picaresque has as its focal point a 'life' recounted in the first person. Not only is the teller in the tale, but he is the tale; the narrative act becomes both form and substance of message production" (120).

The already mentioned social, individual, and aesthetic points are fundamental to an understanding of the picaresque novel, but they also provide a large dose of ambiguity that Maurice Molho (1985) suggests to analyze in light of the ideology that dominated the atmosphere: "el picarismo español es un discurso antiseñorial que se enuncia desde un enfoque y mediante un lenguaje claramente señoriales."[6]

The merely economic explanations and those used to justify the origins of the picaresque as the result of the literary and cultural atmosphere of Erasmian humanism or of the Spanish Counter-Reformation (Parker 1967, 62) have given way to studies about the effects that the nature of the narrative and autobiographical fiction have upon the receptor. At the present time, the receptor is viewed as the explicit addressee of the picaresque text who plays a crucial role because the narrator continually speaks directly to the reader, revealing the reasons for the story and the expected effects of this speech, all the while laying bare the process of writing fiction (Smith 1988, 85). Even though the rogue receives literary accolades with the work *Lazarillo*, it is possible to identify his origins with characters that belong to earlier folkloric traditions. The author as well as the first editions of *Lazarillo* have been polemic, but today the anonymity of the text and the independence of the first three editions of *Lazarillo*—the Burgos, the Ambers, and the Alcalá de Henares—are generally accepted. The date of the first of them was in all likelihood 1552 or 1553. The fulfillment of basic needs and the lack of honor dominate the personality of Lázaro.

Guzmán de Alfarache by Mateo Alemán, published after *Lazarillo*, inherits and outgrows the principal theoretical delineations of its ancestor. The contribution by Marina Brownlee included in this volume refers to this work as "paradigmatic of the genre," in contraposition to the *Buscón*, which is considered "parodic of the genre," even though it is true that, as Brownlee has written, "the criteria that have been used in the past to determine canonical inclusion or exclusion may be ultimately arbitrary." The *Guzmán*, concluded around 1597, was published in Madrid in 1599. That same year it was republished three times, twice in Barcelona and once in Zaragoza. Twenty-five subsequent republications followed, with the majority of them pirate editions. Translations of the work into English, French, and German made it extremely popular throughout Europe. Guzmán is a cosmopolitan rogue whose life becomes increasingly degraded. In this work, according to Smith (1988), it is the reader and not the author or the narrator who confers unity to the text: "The *Guzmán* contains within itself a constant ever-changing projection and representation of the public to whom it is addressed" (105). It is well known that autobiography acquires new dimensions in the *Guzmán* due to the close relationship between the fictitious character's experiences and those of the real author.

La pícara Justina (1605) by Francisco López de Ubeda presents the theme of lineage in a sarcastic manner. Justina even ridicules her literary genre and is considered to be the more immediate literary antecedent of the German rogue, Courasche. However, this work is admitted into the canon only as a marginal work. Also dubiously picaresque is *La vida de Marcos de Obregón* (1618) by Vicente Espinel. This work combines autobiographical features with elements characteristic of the Byzantine novel. Two years after the publication of Vicente Espinel's work, a new edition of *Lazarillo* was published in Paris. It was later translated into English by Juan de Luna, who also penned the *Segunda parte del Lazarillo*. The latter work is generally considered the representation of the maximum degradation of the rogue. Before the end of the sixteenth century, another continuation of the *Lazarillo de Tormes*, *Lazarillo de Manzanares* (1590) by Juan Cortés de Tolosa, was published. The reading public of the beginning of the seventeenth century was acquainted with an archrogue in the masterful work by Francisco de Quevedo, the *Buscón*.

Alberto del Monte considers that after Quevedo the agony of the rogue begins with a series of works: *Alonso mozo de muchos amos* (1624) by Jerónimo Alcalá Yáñez; *El castigo de la miseria* (1637) by María de Zayas y Sotomayor; *El Proteo de Madrid* (1625), *Aventuras del bachiller Trapaza*, and the *Garduña de Sevilla* by Alonso de Castillo Solórzano. The picaresque novel written in the Spanish language enjoys a large following on the American continent. As Nancy Vogeley has written in her essay included in this volume, the *Periquillo Sarniento* and *Don Catrín* reflect "the colonial ideological dilemma . . . [between] the teachings of the church on faith and morality . . . [and] the foolishness of such views." Vogeley defines the American colonial "picardía" as "the result, not of naiveté or rebelliousness or willful disregard of authority, but of the conflict, felt personally and collectively, between opposing language constructs and inner needs, between sound and silence."

In contrast to the importance of the genre in the rest of Europe, picaresque literature is scarcely represented in Portugal. The most important works are the *Tercera parte de Guzmán de Alfarache* by Felix Machado da Silva Castro e Vasconcelos, Marquês de Montebelo; the *Vida de Dom Gregório Guadanha* by António Enrique Gómez; *O desgraciado amante Peralvilho* by Father Gaspar Pires Rebelo; and *Vida de Peralvilho de Córdoba* by M. Silva Cabral. A detailed history of the life of the rogue in Portugal is found in *Do pícaro na literatura portuguesa* by João Palma Ferreira.[7] But picaresque literature in the Portuguese language enjoys a tremendous success on the South American continent. In this volume, Mário M. González defines the Brazilian picaresque, which he calls "neopicaresque," as "a narrative mode which, originating in sixteenth-century Spain, projects itself through the centuries in permanent transgression of previous modes, obeying historical circumstances that contextualize its different manifestations." According to González, some of the most outstanding picaresque works in Brazil are well-known novels, for example, *Memórias de um Sargento de Milícias* by Manuel Antônio de Almeida, and *Macunaíma o herói sem nenhum caráter* by Mário de Andrade. González concludes that:

> These texts—among possible others—suffice to show the symptomatic presence in contemporary Brazil of a narrative based on the antihero. The obstacles to social ascent, a result of the concentration of wealth and the loss of prestige of labor, impose marginalization and generate parody. The novelty in these neopicaresque works seems to lie in the relatively explicit formulation of alternative social projects that substitute for the contradictory eagerness, traditional in the classic picaresque, to integrate into the corrupt society being denounced.

Besides that written in the Spanish and Portuguese languages, picaresque literature appears in other modern European countries as well. The novel *Der abenteuerliche Simplicius Simplicissimus* was published in Germany in 1668 and *Die Landstörtzerin Courasche* and *Der seltsame Springinsfeld* by J. J. C. Grimmelshausen were published in 1700. In the *Simplicissimus*, according to Parker (1967), it is said that Grimmelshausen achieves an originality previously unknown in the Spanish picaresque, mainly because its plot shows more affinities with contemporary history than those of the Spanish novels and because it incorporated in the work his personal experiences, which give the narrative a personal approach otherwise nonexistent in the picaresque genre (148). Parker says that Grimmelshausen was much more original when he created the feminine rogue, Courasche. In *Die Landstörtzerin Courasche*, the protagonist was unavoidably forced by the Thirty Years' War into a morally degrading and hated life-style. Grimmelshausen is said to contrapose clearly Courasche's character with Simplicissimus's, the former being a hardhearted sinner and the latter a converted delinquent.

Even though the picaresque genre was also known in Italy and Holland, the genre did not take root in these countries. In contrast, England and France embraced and adapted this tradition to their own likings. During the seventeenth century France was the European country that most enthusiastically received the Spanish picaresque. La Geneste's translation into French of the *Buscón* is one of the high points of the Spanish picaresque tradition in France. In his *Histoire de Gil Blas de Santillane* (1715), Lesage gives the rogue a more sophisticated origin, a superior education, and good manners. Also published in seventeenth-century France were the *Histoire comique de Francion* by Charles Sorel, the *Roman comique* by Paul Scarron, *Les adventures tragicomiques du Chevalier de la Gaillardise* by Oudin Préfontaine, and the *Roman bourgeois* by Antoine Furetière.

The English picaresque, which is deeply related to criminal life, is defined by Calhoun Winton in his essay as a narrative whose origins "are to be found for the most part not in book-length narratives but in shorter works: in pamphlets, in chapbooks, and, especially during the early eighteenth century, in periodicals." *The Unfortunate Traveller, or the Life of Jack Wilton* (1595) by Thomas Nashe, *Piers Plinnes Seaven Yeres Prentiship* (1559) by Henry Chettle, and *The Life and Death of Mr. Badman* (1678) by John Bunyan were all written in a sui generis picaresque tone well outside the Spanish parameters of the genre. The number of translations of picaresque works into English, as Jerry Beasley proves in his essay included in this volume, is yet another proof of the great acceptance of the genre in England. James Mabbe translated the *Guzmán* under the title *The Rogue* (1622). *The English Rogue described in the Life of*

Meriton Latroon appeared later in print, begun by Richard Head in 1665, continued by Francis Kirkman in 1668, and finished by both men in 1771. Latroon is depicted more as a criminal than as a rogue in keeping with the tastes of the English public of the era. In spite of the originality of the British picaresque, there are numerous similarities between *El Guzmán* and *The Life and Death of Mr. Badman* (1680) by John Bunyan. Both works focus on delinquency with a religious point of view. Also, it is said that *Moll Flanders* is directly related to the Spanish picaresque because of the humble background of the heroine, her ambition to climb the social ladder, and finally her fall and conversion at the end of the work.

To summarize, the picaresque as a literary genre was consolidated in Spain in the sixteenth century and diffused throughout Europe and America in the form of translations, continuations, or sui generis creations. As a genre, it offers an extensive range of at times conflicting social and literary perspectives.[8] Taking into consideration the plurality of analytic perspectives and the diversity of the picaresque canon, Michael Zappala organized the symposium whose proceedings are here edited. The conference at the University of Maryland focused on the individuality and plurality of the picaresque. A short time before falling ill and subsequently passing away, Professor Zappala wrote the pages in the second part of this preface, giving ample evidence of the many successes of this conference. Respecting Michael Zappala's work, I have minimized the corrections and annotations to the text that follows.

CARMEN BENITO-VESSELS

II

The canon of the body of picaresque texts is undergoing intense revision. Underlying and previously unexamined conception are being challenged. Paul J. Smith's (1988) critique of "pictorialism" and of the unreflecting, implicitly Platonic evaluations of terms such as *unity* and *symmetry* in the criticism of Francisco Rico or Claudio Guillén and his questioning whether it can be assumed that "point of view" is "benevolent" or whether the critics' enterprise is to resolve apparent discontinuities redraw the previous critical landscape.[9] The chronological limits of picaresque are also being debated. Critics are also staking out radically different maps in regard to questions of origins and the terms in which development is discussed—whether the picaresque is limited to a period or whether it is, as Stuart Miller claims, an "ideal genre type."[10] The traditional view of the picaresque as a social document of an exhausted society is taken up with clearly different theoretical bases, for example, by Alan Francis.[11] Finally, a polemic about the most basic issue of all is currently being waged: are these texts in some way a window onto a human profile and society—antihero, delinquent, or rogue—or are the humanistic assumptions of criticism, founded until recently on the "myth of 'Man' as founding father of the text and as integrated, active subject within that society which the text is thought to reflect" outmoded and no longer useful for understanding this family of texts.[12]

Not even this methodologically crowded landscape and the Gadarene rush from historicist and universalizing to aesthetic and particular studies exhaust the possibilities of method. There has been, for example, no adequate description of the rhetoric of picaresque texts in the Spanish Golden Age. A tropological register—the kind that would serve in another genre to delimit Góngora's rhetoric from Sor Juana's—would be highly illuminating. The constant function, for example, of antithetical tropes in *Lazarillo de Tormes*—polarities identifying the rift between pragmatism and ethics—clearly distinguishes that text from the sliding, reversible antitheses of *Guzmán de Alfarache*, which figure the oscillation of conversion–deconversion–reconversion. A study to isolate "master tropes," like Thomas Mermall's recent investigation of chiasmus in Unamuno, is in order.[13]

The field of picaresque, then, is roiling with problems of definition and method. The different and at times conflicting approaches to picaresque studies are a challenge within the field of Golden Age studies. To study these texts and to address critical issues, a group of scholars of international reputation gathered for two days of lively exchange at the University of Maryland at College Park on 21–22 April 1989, under the auspices of the Center for Renaissance and Baroque Studies and the Department of Spanish and Portuguese, to reassess picaresque texts and critical tradition. The meeting demonstrated the continuing power of these texts to catalyze central critical concerns. The studies contained in this volume were first presented as papers during this symposium.[14]

The results of this symposium can be summarized as follows: Opening the first session, "Picaresque Antecedents and the Nature of Source," Barry Baldwin offered a free-wheeling review of picaresque, relating phenomena as disparate as Petronius and contemporary television sitcoms to this family of texts. Joseph Ricapito expanded the literary landscape within which *Lazarillo* is viewed in his study of Gonzalo Pérez's *Ulyxea* as a "textual incitement" of the *Lazarillo*. Ulysses' *zozobras* as victim of fate, the self-conscious presentation of a biography "for viewing and appreciation by readers," and the hero's role as "artisan of the conversion of experience into word" establish this text—like the *Momus* of Alberti, I add—as part of the literary constellation within which the *Lazarillo* appears in the mid-sixteenth century. Bruno Damiani's study of the *Lozana andaluza*, squarely and substantially positioned in the tradition of humanist criticism as precursor to the picaresque, forges an important link between the *Celestina* and the *Lazarillo* through an investigation of traits common in the later novel of roguery: the philosophy of the protagonist, realism, milieu of delinquency, and humor.

In the second session, "The Picaresque and Autobiography," Randolph Pope, taking a fresh look at a traditional polemic (Castro [1957] versus Parker [1967] on the essential or accidental role of autobiography in picaresque literature), investigated the split, "bicephalous" vision of autobiography in Golden Age picaresque, and the reconciliation of the "spliced" self in a text that oscillates between writing as rejection and as recovery. Marina Brownlee, in "Discursive Parameters of the Picaresque," asks whether there is an "essential feature, configuration, or environment which determines the presence of a picaresque text." Discarding criteria formerly used to determine "canonical inclusion or exclusion" as arbitrary, Professor Brownlee looks into the relationship of novelistic discourse to genre. The session closed with Harry Sieber's "Society, Genre and Invention of the Picaresque in Spain," an investigation of the radical shift in court culture—epitomized in the different realities communicated by the term *caballero* in the Spain of Philip II and Philip III.

In the third session, "The Picaresque beyond the Pyrenees," Jerry Beasley studied the questions of the translation of picaresque texts and spoke on the impact of this family of texts on novelistic discourse throughout Europe. Studying translators' "improvement" of received texts, a standard practice of the period, Beasley illustrated the range of possible "new" picaresque texts recreated through translation and the relationship of this transferral to cultural *translatio*. In "Richard Head and Origins of the Picaresque in England," Calhoun Winton looked into the rise of the picaresque novel "in that murky swamp which is seventeenth-century London printing and publishing practice." Unlike the Spanish picaresque, the English picaresque literature of this period is virtually without canonical text, with the exception of Head's *The English Rogue*. After studying pamphlets, chapbooks, and periodicals, Winton posed the question, by whom were these examples of the picaresque mode in English written, for what expectation of reward, and with what audience in mind? Investigating the figure of Meriton Latroon and examples of "nugget fiction" in Head's *Rogue* and in the papers of Steele and Addison, Winton traced the "domestication" of picaresque in England. In his study of Grimmelshausen's *The Adventurous German Simplicissimus*, the "hero with a thousand faces," Gerald Gillespie contextualized this text in French comic and satiric and Spanish disillusionistic modes. He looked into Grimmelshausen's "pilfering of contemporary encyclopedias to organize the baffling diversity of reality" in this work, and studied the mechanics of the text (motive network, closure and reoverture, "polyphony") to situate in the literary history of the German Baroque the protagonist's pilgrimage "from duplicitous delinquent to superlative simpleton."

In the final section, "Continuity and Redefinition," Nancy Vogeley presented Lizardi's *Don Catrín de la Fachenda* in the context of the Enlightenment redefinition and politicization of the concepts of vice and virtue, and discussed how these changing thought patterns, "inversions of terms required by Machiavellianism or utilitarianism," facilitated the task of American writers who were then rethinking their political and moral landscape. Vogeley investigated the contribution of the picaresque in this struggle between Christian and Enlightenment philosophy, and how picaresque convention—the role of fortune, the importance of appearances—permitted Lizardi "an imaginative channel for dialogically exploring the Enlightenment sets of terms, an alternative language of vice and virtue" in the public discourse space of the colony. Jerome Christensen's paper on "Don Picaro: Lord Byron and the Reclassification of the Picaresque" investigated with primary and secondary textual sources the meaning of picaresque in *Don Juan*, established the vitality of the genre in this work of Byron, and looked into the distinction of *tuum* and *meum* in this work. The last paper was Professor González's overview of the picaresque in Brazilian literature. Professor González affirmed the existence of a Spanish "nucleus" of texts and studied the figure of the *malandro*. Using the term *neopicaro*, González set out analogues of Spanish and Brazilian picaresque (the "carnivalization" of literature, the rhapsodic and parodic nature of picaresque, the cunning protagonist) and studied a group of novels from *Macunaíma* (1928) to *O cogitário* (1984), indicating the appropriations of picaresque convention in these works and how picaresque convention is itself delimited by its new context.

As in any gathering of this kind, the diversity of approaches to the study of picaresque opened up new questions concerning the picaresque canon and its criteria for the definition of parameters that include elements from classic antiquity (Barry, Ricapito, Damiani) to contemporary literary theories (Brownlee, Winton, Beasley). The validity of the canon can be further explored through the studies of Gillespie and Vogeley.

Finally, I wish to thank the Center for Renaissance and Baroque Studies and the Department of Spanish and Portuguese for their generous support and Adele Seeff, executive director of the center, for her indefatigable efforts and continuous help in bringing this project to birth.

MICHAEL ZAPPALA

Notes

1. Alberto del Monte, *Itinerario de la novela picaresca española*, trans. Enrique Sordo (Barcelona: Lumen, 1971), 70.

2. Alexander Parker, *Los pícaros en la literatura. La novela picaresca en España y Europa (1599–1753)*, trans. Rodolfo Arévalo Mackry (Madrid: Gredos, 1971), 45–46.

3. Paul J. Smith, "The Rhetoric of Representation in Picaresque Narrative," in *Writing in the Margin: Spanish Literature of the Golden Age* (Oxford: Clarendon Press, 1988), 78–127.

4. Juan Bautista Avalle-Arce, "Tres comienzos de novela (Cervantes y la tradición literaria. Primera perspectiva)," in *Nuevos deslindes cervantinos* (Barcelona: 1975), 213–45.

5. Edward Friedman, "The Picaresque as Autobiography: Story and History," in *Autobiography in Early Modern Spain*, ed. Nicholas Spadaccini and Jenaro Taléns (Minneapolis: Prisma Institute, 1988), 119–129.

6. Maurice Molho, "El pícaro de nuevo," *Modern Language Notes* 100 (1985): 100-223, 207.

7. João Palma Ferreira, *Do pícaro na literatura portuguesa* (Lisboa: Biblioteca Breve, 1981).

8. See Américo Castro, "Perspectiva de la novela picaresca," in *Hacia Cervantes* (Madrid: Taurus, 1957), 83–105; Alan Francis, *Picaresca, decadencia, historia* (Madrid: Gredos, 1978); Claudio Guillén, "Toward a Definition of the Picaresque," in *Literature as System* (Princeton: Princeton University Press, 1971), 71–106; Stuart Miller, *The Picaresque Novel* (Cleveland: Case Western Reserve University Press, 1967); Francisco Rico, *La novela picaresca española*,

I. (Barcelona: Planeta, 1967), and *La novela picaresca y el punto de vista* (Barcelona: Seix Barral, 1970).

9. Smith, "The Rhetoric of Representation," 78–127; Rico, *La novela picaresca española* and *La novela picaresca y el punto de vista*; Guillén, "Toward a Definition of the Picaresque," 71–106, and *Anatomies of Roguery: A Comparative Study in the Origins and Nature of Picaresque Literature* (New York and London: Garland, 1987).

10. Miller, *Picaresque Novel*.

11. Francis, *Picaresca, decadencia, historia*.

12. Smith, "The Rhetoric of Representation," 78–127.

13. Thomas Mermall, *Publications of the Modern Language Association (PMLA)* 105 (1990): 245–55.

14. It has not been possible to include Professor Barry Baldwin's presentation nor Professor Harry Sieber's—"Society, Genre and Invention of the Picaresque Novel in Spain." The collection of symposium papers also includes the contribution of Mário Miguel González on the Brazilian picaresque. Professor González was originally scheduled to speak at the symposium but was unable to attend.

The Picaresque

Discursive Parameters of the Picaresque
MARINA S. BROWNLEE

I

Despite the diversity of its expression, postmodern criticism constitutes a unified enterprise in that it seeks to explore cultural authority and its articulation. It is no wonder, therefore, that genre studies—especially in the principles of canon formation—have of late become the focus of intense scholarly investigation. Genre is not conceived as ahistorical, typologically hermetic categories, but rather as temporally specific and mutable manifestations of particular cultural climates. The concept of genre, we now realize, is practical, empirical, and heuristic, not theoretical, prescriptive, and absolute.

As a rule, critics engage in genre studies well after the literary texts in question have been produced—witness the influential work of Aristotle, the sixteenth-century participants in the *romanzi* polemic, or Boileau. In periods of strict literary codification, however, notions of genre may serve a prescriptive function. Thus, as Cesare Segre concludes: "Genre, therefore, will sometimes have a nomenclative function, sometimes a projectural, or even normative, function."[1]

The subject of the picaresque is a particularly intriguing topic in the context of genre and canon formation given the heterogeneity of even those works that by critical consensus have been deemed "canonical": *Lazarillo de Tormes* (1554) is considered to be not the first true picaresque composition but protopicaresque primarily because the first best seller of the genre (*Guzmán de Alfarache*) did not appear until nearly fifty years later, after which there followed a number of other narratives that are consistently differentiated from these first two manifestations of the genre by literary critics. Despite its notable discursive differences with the anonymous *Lazarillo*, Alemán's text is viewed as paradigmatic of the genre. And, in a sense, the tradition ends there. Quevedo's *Buscón* (1626) is referred to not as picaresque but rather as a parody of that form. Likewise, Cervantes is credited with writing not picaresque fiction, but an incisive exploration and critique of that form (a metanarrative) in a number of his works.[2]

In other words, there seems to have existed virtually no normative picaresque. Of the thirty-seven works identified as picaresque by Petriconi,[3] only *Guzmán de Alfarache* Part I is universally viewed as such. Still worse is the fate of those texts that appear after *Guzmán*, for they tend to be collectively viewed by and large as belated, decadent expressions of the genre—as part of "el proceso de desgaste evidente en todos los autores picarescos del siglo XVII."[4] In an article provocatively entitled "Does the Picaresque Novel Exist?" Daniel Eisenberg points out that "Francisco Rico would exclude Part II of the *Guzmán* [from consideration], A. A. Parker, and others before him, the *Lazarillo*, and Edmond Cros would study the *Guzmán* and exclude all others."[5]

By contrast with this reductively taxonomic attitude, we find the occasional notable exception, such as José Montesinos's study entitled "Gracián o la picaresca pura," in which he discerns deep-structure affinities between *El Criticón* and Alemán's text: "Coincide Gracián con los picarescos en su visión desolada del mundo y de la vida, como coincide en muchos aspectos de su técnica. Novela de peregrinación es la suya, novela de camino, de andanzas incesantes remansadas en pocas peripecias. Novela en que el camino determina la marcha, y de la que está ausente la libertad."[6] Montesinos is not attempting to argue that *El Criticón* is a picaresque narrative, but he perceptively understands that "ni siempre que aparecen pícaros hallamos picaresca, ni al contrario."[7]

II

What, then, is the essential feature, configuration, or environment that determines the presence of a picaresque text?

In attempting to answer this question, we should consider the relationship of discourse to genre. *Discourse* is defined in two primary senses: either as "the exposition of a given argument," be it written or oral; or as the "act of language communication."[8] As such, entire texts as well as the individual speech acts inscribed within them constitute examples of discourse. Discourse then differs from language per se in that it assumes a "common horizon between speaker and listener."[9]

Unlike other discourses, however, literary discourse is "a very special kind of speech act, for it is without any immediate communicative aim (in fact it will still be found valid by readers who are distant in space and time)."[10] By contrast, genre is "the object, the goal, and the context of the discourse."[11] Genre offers a selective representation of reality, only one of whose component parts is discourse. A particular spatiotemporal configuration (what Bakhtin terms the "chronotope") is also characteristic of any given genre.[12] Thus, hagiography deals with the space of this earth and the heavenly realm as they pertain to the temporal coordinates of mortality and eternity. Clearly, a characteristic axiology accompanies any particular chronotope. The atemporal, oneiric space of romance, for example, is guided by a fundamental belief in the eventual triumph of good over evil. A particular attitude toward language is also essential to any genre. Epic is predicated on the unassailable truth of a transcendent religious discourse, of Scripture, whereas at the other extreme, the novel is predicated upon the decomposition of stable verbal and ideological systems. Closer to epic, romance, on the other hand, never doubts the power of language, only the hero's personal fortitude—and even that is merely a provisional doubt. This attitude toward language is, in my opinion, the most basic feature of genre, since it determines and reflects the place of the individual not only within the boundaries of any given text but within the cosmos as a whole. Questions of social context, style, diction, and so on, are further dimensions of the literary process we call genre.

Focusing selectively on one or another of these features, various critics have posited four principal model texts or authors for the *Lazarillo* and its progeny. The first two—Apuleius and Lucian—are related, and the reason for their selection as analogues to the picaresque is clear. That is, they both offer a first-person journey, a critique of society in the Menippean mode. Yet satire aims to expose, not to edify, and edification is an essential component of picaresque literature (at least of the *Lazarillo* and the *Guzmán*). Speaking of Lucianic literature, but in terms equally applicable to Apuleius, Robert Scholes draws an important distinction between satire and mimesis: "Employing a first-person, peripatetic narrator in his *True History*, Lucian developed the form of the mock-journey designed for an intellectual and satiric purpose rather than a mimetic or fictional one."[13]

The picaresque is—beyond its undeniably satiric dimension—as a rule mimetic, didactic, intended to convert the reader to the narrator's and/or implied author's point of view.

A third paradigm that has been offered is that of romance. Whereas picaresque used to be viewed as the antiromance form par excellence, it is now also viewed as reflecting a pervasive longing for romance wish fulfillment. Ulrich Wicks articulates this phenomenon in the form of an interrogative: "Is not the essential pattern [of the picaresque] a quest for 'home'—home in the sense of social and material success (as in *Lazarillo*), or the spiritual sense of union with God (as in *Guzmán* or *Simplicissimus*), or even in the mythic sense of a return to Paradise?"[14] Yet, aside from the fact that romance is third-, not first-person narrative, and that it is clearly not concerned with critiquing society, it does not evince the instability of language that is a hallmark of the picaresque. Obviously, the picaro does wish for an ordered cosmos. That is why we often follow him from his naive belief in its possibility, as a child, to his adult realization of its nonexistence. But such a realization is fundamentally antithetical to the world of romance.

The fourth and most recent model to be proposed for the picaresque is the *Libro de buen amor*. Yet here too, the parallels, while suggestive, are, in my opinion, insufficient. The world of the archpriest—replete with its talking animals who debate traditional fables, allegorical figures, epic mice, and so on—offers us a decidedly fictional world, one that is not intended as a realistic panorama of fourteenth-century society into which a marginal figure will attempt to integrate himself. The office of archpriest is, after all, a mark of the protagonist's comfortable integration into society. In an admirable recent study of the figure of the picaro, Edward Friedman writes that: "The *Libro de buen amor* depicts the tension caused primarily by an inflexible social code acting on man's flexible nature."[15] However, it is, in reality, Juan Ruiz's insatiable *luxuria*, not societal intolerance, that is at issue. At another juncture in his argument, Friedman concludes that the *Libro* is an "anti-confessional work, because words state and negate its message, and because the author will not sacrifice fictional creation to convert sinners. The moral frame strives to create order from chaos, but the text responds ambiguously to the professed intention."[16]

Language is ostentatiously polysemous in this text—*buen amor* signifies both allegiance to the Christian love of God and the pagan God of Love. However, the *Libro* is nothing if not an extended confession. More importantly, it is a confession without definitive conversion since the Archpriest repeatedly yields to temptation. Nonetheless, he consistently attempts to convert to the idealizing Christian world view, the societal norm. He is not a marginal member of society nor does he attempt to cynically expose it as hypocritical, as a situation that leaves him no alternative but deception. Rather, he represents the Adamic figure who is constantly prey to temptation, in spite of his good intentions.

Finally, because of its place in literary history, its status as an originary discourse, Augustine's *Confessions* is occasionally mentioned in the context of picaresque narrative, by Hans-Robert Jauss, for example. The fact that the *Confessions* is the first example of autobiographical discourse—generated from the tension between the present time of writing and the past time of narration—an affinity between it and the picaresque is routinely acknowledged.[17]

This fundamental narrative configuration that unites all examples of the genre known as autobiography is the first of three discursive features that both the Augustinian text and most picaresque narratives exhibit. The second has to do with the ontological status of the text itself. That is, the picaresque narrative, like the *Confessions*, often offers a confession of an individual life, a spiritual autobiography that is designed to justify the author's approach to the world. The third recurring feature is that, like the Augustinian autobiography, the picaresque text is often calculated to elicit the reader's conversion to a particular cognitive perspective. For Augustine, this perspective involves an understanding of the transcendent order and its relationship to earthly existence. For Lázaro, the issue is the same, but the conclusion is the opposite: namely, a conversion to the materialistic pleasures of this world after having understood that the *caritas* he initially believed in and sought as a child is inoperative. At the end of his own confession, Guzmán overtly speaks of his conversion, which is, nonetheless, highly debatable. And, despite its fragmentariness as narrative, the subject of the *Buscón* is, similarly, the justification of a particular axiology—in this case a poeticization of worldly chaos—a conversion not to any transcendent spiritual values, but to the cynicism that results from personal experience.

The fourth feature that links Augustine's enterprise to many picaresque narratives is the problem of linguistic referentiality. In the case of Augustine, it is the relationship of pre- and postlapsarian language. As Eugene Vance remarks: "Rhetorician that he was, Augustine was aware that in the limited and imperfect sphere of human speech, there are multiple alternatives in the choice of reality that one wishes to understand, and multiple alternatives in the mode of expressing reality."[18]

With the picaresque the issue is very often the same—namely, whether there exists any viable relationship between fallen and redeemed language. For Augustine, there clearly does exist a meaningful relationship between the two. For the picaresque there does not. Ginés de Pasamonte, we recall, offers one of the most densely patterned examples of such nominalistic skepticism in part 1 of the *Quijote*. Acknowledging the paramount importance of this linguistic dimension, Harry Sieber insightfully speaks of Lázaro's discovery of

> language as the basis of social reality: From the blind beggar [Lazarillo] learns the magic quality of words: they produce money from unsuspecting alms-givers. From the priest . . . Lazarillo perceives that his 'sacred' words bring forth money as well as food. From the squire he learns that honour is as 'real' as the language used to create it. But the most important lesson he learns is from the pardoner. . . . His ecclesiastical rhetoric is so polished that . . . his congregation is totally deceived.[19]

If viewed in this light—as rewritings *in malo* of the Augustine paradigm—we discern in several (but not all) picaresque narratives a certain coherence that is otherwise obscured. We are left with the misperception that the genre—its canonical texts— flourished primarily in one incongruously brief six-year period (1599–1605) corresponding to the publication dates of the *Guzmán*, with a subsequent group of texts that constitute decadent examples of the form.[20] This latter attitude represents a limited understanding of the way that genre and discourse (particularly novelistic discourse) behave.

III

Reception of the *Lazarillo* and its three sequels is illustrative of the problem. As literary histories repeatedly indicate, Golden Age Spain, especially the twelve-year period between 1548 and 1560, was an era of intense literary innovation. In 1548 the first epistolary novel in Europe (the *Processo de cartas*) appeared; in

1552 the first Greek romance in Spanish was published (*Clareo y Florisea*); in 1554 the first picaresque (namely, *Lazarillo de Tormes*); between 1550 and 1560 the first Moorish romance (*El Abencerraje*); and finally, in 1559 the first Spanish pastoral romance (*La Diana*) was written. All of these new forms, with the exception of the *Processo* and the *Lazarillo*, were widely read and spawned multiple imitations of themselves within a short period of their appearance.

From our twentieth-century, pan-European perspective, it is remarkable that the *Lazarillo* (clearly the most influential of the texts I have just mentioned) had to wait half a century before it gained a wide readership, a fact that has been directly attributed to the appearance of the second picaresque narrative, *Guzmán de Alfarache*, in 1599. Although these two texts are markedly different in axiological terms, in terms of what Lukàcs calls the "utopia of self-knowledge,"[21] they are seen by Claudio Guillén and others as forming a small but essential "critical mass" that created an audience for this type of literature—hence the notable increase in the *Lazarillo*'s popularity fifty years after its production.[22]

I would challenge a conclusion based on this circumstantial evidence, however, First of all, as we know, a continuation of the *Lazarillo*—the anonymous *Segunda parte*—appeared in 1555, only one year after the original. In addition, as the reception of the other works mentioned attests, a new literary form does not need to be replicated in other texts in order to establish an enthusiastic reading public.

Instead, we should look elsewhere for an explanation of the hiatus in readership undergone by the *Lazarillo*. The critical difference that determined the reception of this text, I would argue, is not quantitative but discursive. And discourse cannot be analyzed outside the time frame in which it was produced (Guillén implicitly ignores this fact when he assumes that the "horizon of expectations" for readers separated by half a century would be the same.) It is, moreover, this awareness of the diachronic specificity of discourse that makes Michel Foucault's notion of "literary archeology" a useful heuristic tool, for it tries to articulate rules of discursive formation in order to understand the conditions necessary for their realization.[23]

If we consider the texts produced during that remarkable twelve-year period, we see that the potential for semantic ambiguity that the *Lazarillo* author cultivated was alien to the climate of the times. It was an age of romance (pastoral, Moorish, Greek, and chivalric)—hence a time that had a taste for linguistic referentiality. Given the inherently diachronic nature of discourse, it is, therefore, not surprising that the *Lazarillo* did not enjoy much success beyond the immediate time of its publication. It would take roughly fifty years—and a variety of sociohistorical changes—for Spain's linguistic positivism to turn to referential skepticism. What this literary reception corroborates is the validity of Foucault's view that the author is an "ideological" expression of his culture: "If we are accustomed to presenting the author as a genius, as a perpetual surging of innovation, it is because in reality, we make him function in exactly the opposite fashion."[24]

In the intervening years—in fact just one year after the original *Lazarillo* of 1554 appeared—another anonymous author decided to exploit the vogue of romance by rewriting the original picaresque text in romance terms. It is important to note, moreover, that this impulse constitutes an amplification of romance constructs already present in the original. Numerous readers have aptly remarked that the original *Lazarillo* from the heroic diction of its prologue throughout the text proper may be read as a parody of romance. And yet, despite this generic association, the *Segunda parte* still tends to be dismissed as an aquatic aberration that bears virtually no resemblance to the model text. As I have argued elsewhere, however, the sequel foregrounds this parodic quality without destroying the axiology of the original.[25]

Laurent Jenny identifies three possible ways in which a model text may be rewritten either as representation, transformation, or transgression.[26] The *Segunda parte*, I would suggest, constitutes a transformation. In an inversion of his earlier situation, Lázaro finds himself in the service of a just master—one of a multitude of fish who populate this submarine fantasy. As a result, he is no longer obliged to act opportunistically, yet he does so because he has definitively internalized the picaresque values that had earlier conditioned his behavior.

This continuation offers a mock picaresque that criticizes the superficiality of society with which picaresque narrative concerns itself. Yet the author does not stop there, for clearly the parody is double-edged: while presenting a fundamentally romance environment, he is simultaneously offering a parody of that genre by grafting the heroic motives and elevated discourse of romance onto a community of fish. Nonetheless, this parodic romance discourse is sustained by and subsumed under the discursive configuration of the original—faithful to its consistently bivalent narrative tone: an ironic, anonymous authorial figure who implicitly comments on the self-complacent Lázaro. Because the sequel maintains Lázaro's conversion to the negative utopia he had attained at the end of the original text, it remains faithful to the spirit of its model—that is, to the subversion of the Augustinian paradigm in a secular, societal register, which I have posited as the most prevalent distinctive feature of picaresque narrative. At the same time, a significant generic expansion has been effected by the incorporation of the fantastic setting of Lucianic satire into the picaresque framework. Thus, to my mind, the *Segunda parte* is not only a subtle picaresque narrative, but in addition, one that reveals a lot about genre as literary process. Luna's 1620 continuation of the *Lazarillo* offers an appreciably different Lázaro, whom Francisco Rico terms a "preposterous Lázaro [who is] metamorphosed into a whole series of different characters, connected only by bearing the same name."[27] Rico is even more critical of Cortés de Tolosa's Lazarillo de Manzanares, whom he terms "the most non-descript individual it is possible to conceive, devoid of any distinguishing human feature."[28] To my mind, Rico is indicative of critical consensus of a fundamental error of picaresque scholarship in expecting the continuations and rewritings of the original picaresque novel to conform strictly to it.

It is important to recognize that the picaresque is a novelistic enterprise. And, like any novelistic enterprise, it exhibits two features that differentiate it from all other canonical genres. Firstly, the novel may circumscribe within itself a plurality of disparate discourses. Indeed, as Bakhtin has shown, it is precisely such discursive tension that is at the root of any novelistic production. For, by definition, novelistic discourse enacts the decomposition of stable verbal and ideological systems.[29] But, more important for the purposes of understanding picaresque "genre" and discourse, we must bear in mind the Bakhtinian observation that "the novel is a genre like no other, because each of its instances is ultimately irreducibly individual (a contradiction, indeed, of the very notion of genre). The essential point is that, unlike other genres, the novel has no canon: only particular examples play a role in history, but not the canon of the genre as such."[30] The novel, then, is an antigenre. Yet if we accept this singular status for the novel—that each text exhibits a different chronotope—what is the quality that accounts for novelistic progeny, for continuations and rewritings? As Walter Reed explains,

> The term "genre," as applied to the picaresque in particular and the novel in general, is misleading. . . . It implies a more stable set of rules than in fact ever pertained, and a greater commitment to the idea of such rules that can be discerned from the texts. As the spurious sequels to *Lazarillo*, *Guzmán* and *Don Quixote* attest, the novel was from its inception a particularly open invitation to other authors; it encouraged expropriation more than imitation, a cashing in on the marketable material rather than an observation of literary decorum.[31]

The novel, in other words, is iconoclastic of the very notion of genre. It actively seeks to be a discontinuous form. "Faced with the problem of the novel," Bakhtin explains, "genre theory must submit to a radical re-structuring."[32] We should not expect to find a series of constant principles of codification for the picaresque novel—or any other novelistic form.

To conclude, I would suggest that as we reconsider the various examples of picaresque narrative, we must bear in mind that many of the criteria that have been used in the past to determine canonical inclusion or exclusion may be ultimately arbitrary—vestiges of an era that exhibited an imperfect appreciation of the singular relationship of novelistic discourse to genre.

Notes

1. Cesare Segre, *Introduction to the Analysis of the Literary Text*, trans. John Meddemmen (Bloomington: Indiana University Press, 1989), 199.
2. For example, *La ilustre fregona*, *Rinconete y Cortadillo*, *Coloquio de los perros*, and *Don Quijote*.
3. Helmut Petriconi, "Zur Chronologie und Verbreitung des Spanischen Schelmenromans," *Volkstum und Kultur der Romanen* 1 (1928): 324–42.
4. Giuseppe Sansone, ed., *Juan Cortés de Tolosa* (Madrid: Espasa Calpe, 1974), xxix.
5. Daniel Eisenberg, "Does the Picaresque Novel Exist?" *Kentucky Romance Quarterly* 26 (1979): 201–19.
6. José Montesinos, "Gracián o la picaresca pura," *Cruz y Raya* 4 (1933): 52.
7. Ibid., 41.
8. Segre, *Literary Text*, 151.
9. Hans Robert Jauss, "Littérature médiévale et théorie des genres," *Poétique* 1 (1970): 79–101.
10. Segre, *Literary Text*, 217.
11. Ibid.
12. See in this context, Mikhail Bakhtin, *The Dialogic Imagination*, ed. Michael Holquist (Austin: University of Texas, 1981), and Tzvetan Todorov, *Mikhail Bakhtin: The Dialogical Principle*, trans. Wlad Godzich (Minneapolis: University of Minnesota Press, 1984).

13. Robert Scholes and Robert Kellogg, *The Nature of Narrative* (London: Oxford University Press, 1966), 77.

14. Ulrich Wicks, "The Romance of the Picaresque," *Genre* 11 (1978): 40.

15. Edward Friedman, *The Antiheroine's Voice: Narrative Discourse and the Transformation of the Picaresque* (Columbia: University of Missouri Press, 1987), 5.

16. Ibid., 9.

17. See Hans Robert Jauss, "Ursprung und Bedeutung der Ich-Form im Lazarillo de Tormes," *Romanistisches Jahrbuch* 8 (1957): 290–311, and Peter Baumanns, "Der *Lazarillo de Tormes* eine Travestie der Augustinischen *Confessiones*?" *Romanistisches Jahrbuch* 10 (1959): 285–91.

18. Eugene Vance, "The Functions and Limits of Autobiography in Augustine's *Confessions*," *Poetics Today* 5 (1984): 399.

19. Harry Sieber, *The Picaresque* (London: Methuen, 1977), 16.

20. Having reviewed the major critical assessments of the picaresque genre, Eisenberg concludes by saying that: "There is, in fact, only one work which all agree to be picaresque novel, Part 1 of the *Guzmán de Alfarache*, for Francisco Rico would exclude Part 2 of the *Guzmán*, Parker, and others before him, the *Lazarillo*, and Edmond Cros would study only the *Guzmán*, excluding all others. This is for a reason that is logical, consistent, and dramatically simple: the work contains a *pícaro*. Mateo Alemán used the word in the work, and the *Guzmán* was to contemporaries the *Libro del pícaro*. Since the book is a novel, what better reason could there be for calling it a picaresque novel?" ("The Picaresque Novel," 207).

21. See Georgy Lukàcs, *Die Theorie des Romans* (Berlin: Spandau, 1963), 74.

22. Claudio Guillén, *Literature as System: Essays toward the Theory of Literary History* (Princeton: Princeton University Press, 1971), 142ff.

23. Michel Foucault, "What Is an Author" in *Textual Strategies*, ed. Josué Harari (Ithaca: Cornell University Press, 1979), 141–60.

24. Foucault, "What Is an Author?" 159.

25. Marina S. Brownlee, "Generic Expansion and Generic Subversion: The Two Continuations of *Lazarillo de Tormes*," *Philological Quarterly* 61 (1982): 317–27.

26. Laurent Jenny, "La stratégie de la forme," *Poétique* 27 (1976): 257–81.

27. Francisco Rico, *The Spanish Picaresque Novel and the Point of View*, trans. Charles Davis with Harry Sieber (London: Cambridge University Press, 1984), 84.

28. Ibid.

29. See note 12.

30. Todorov, *Bakhtin*, 86.

31. Walter Reed, *An Exemplary History of the Novel* (Chicago: University of Chicago Press, 1981), 56.

32. Bakhtin, *The Dialogic Imagination*, 8.

Classicity in the Spanish Golden Age: Gonzalo Pérez's Translation of *La Ulyxea* and the Origin of the Spanish Picaresque Novel

JOSEPH V. RICAPITO

The *Ulyxea* was published in 1550 in Salamanca by Andrea de Portinariis; it was also published the same year in Antwerp by Juan Stelsio. In 1553 it appeared in Venice published by Gabriel Giolito; again in Antwerp by Juan Stelsio (Jan Steels) in 1556; and in Venice in 1562 by Francesco Rampazeto. In 1767 it was published in Madrid by Francisco Javier García.[1]

Although there was some question about the authorship of the translation, later studies by Iriarte, Menéndez y Pelayo, González Palencia, and others showed that in spite of this confusion, the author was Gonzalo Pérez.[2]

González Palencia gave a good description of the life and work of this courtier who flourished in the courts of Charles V and Philip II. Pérez was protected by the secretary Francisco de los Cobos, an influential member of the court, and had a close friendship with other court figures such as Alfonso de Valdés,[3] Pérez was a clergyman who practiced statecraft, held various religious offices, and, despite his vows of celibacy, had a son by María Tovar whom we now know as the humanist and writer Antonio Pérez.[4]

Anyone familiar with the court life of the time should not be surprised to find an individual interested enough in Classical studies to translate the *Odyssey*. Humanistic studies abounded, and no individual could claim to be *culto* without a proper Classical formation.

Commentators of the *Ulyxea* believe that Pérez worked directly from the Greek, and by and large he receives good marks from modern Hellenists for his translation.[5]

My essay will study the *Odyssey* in Pérez's translation and its link with the Spanish picaresque genre, specifically with *Lazarillo de Tormes*. Such a comparison may be undermined by chronology, and I wish to acknowledge in advance some of these difficult questions. Yet I believe that readers of *Lazarillo de Tormes* who were familiar with Pérez's translation (or with the *Odyssey*) could not help but recognize, if not influences, certainly intertextual resonances that made for a deeper reading of *Lazarillo de Tormes* and the *Ulyxea*.

Clearly, the publication of the *Ulyxea* (1550) precedes that of the *Lazarillo* (1554). We do not know when Pérez began his translation or whether it circulated in manuscript form, a very common practice at the time. Opinions about the date of composition of the *Lazarillo* range from shortly after 1525 to slightly before the publication date, 1554.[6] Francisco Rico recently spoke of an edition of 1553, a date suggested earlier by Brunet.[7] The Cortes alluded to at the end of chapter 7 could be those of 1525 or 1538, in which case the composition of *Lazarillo* may have preceded the writing and publishing of the *Ulyxea*.[8] The text of *Lazarillo de Tormes*, with its various dating lacunae, offers certain difficulties, and the specialist may be diverted from his critical task if he or she tries to formulate a purported influence of one on the other *in sensu stricto*.[9]

The study and comparison of these texts, then, rejects a rigorous cause-and-effect relationship and finds richer satisfactions in seeing these texts independently, as works that illuminate and reflect each other.

I

For the reader of *Lazarillo* the initial statements in the prologue regarding profitable reading were a convention inherited from the Middle Ages.[10] Erasmian literature of the time also spoke of a didactic principle in writing, a level above the profitable one. Speaking of Homer's *Odyssey*, in the introduction Pérez says:

> y que en aquella obra tratando de sus peregrinaciones y viajes, scrive muchas cosas, en que quitada la corteza se descubren muy grandes secretos de que no sólo V. Alteza [Philip II] con su excellentíssimo juycio, mas aun otro qualquier príncipe que no lo tuuiesse tan esmerado, podría sacar mucho fructo, he querido prouar a ver como hablaría en nuestro romance Castellano.[11]

The possibilities in each text to "sacar mucho fructo" could be as limited as they are limitless, but even as a mere convention both texts express the need to offer this possibility. These texts, created between fact and fiction, folklore and imagination,[12] ultimately invite the reader to speculate upon whatever profit is to be reaped from the adventures of each character.

II

The title of the Spanish work bears noting: *Vida de Lazarillo de Tormes y de sus fortunas y adversidades*. *Adversidades* is quite clear, but *fortunas* may be ambiguous, although I believe the sixteenth-century reader understood this to mean the *peripeteia*. Lazarillo and Ulysses have lives that are not soft and easy, but are full of suffering, and travail. The Spanish word *zozobras* conveys excellently the quality of both lives.[13] Odysseus is hampered in his return to Penelope by numerous events, each one subjecting the hero to various forms of suffering. Likewise, Lazarillo goes from master to master, suffering indignities and difficulties. In several cases in each text the characters are presented as innocent victims of capricious fate. In the case of Odysseus "Mas *quiso la ventura* [emphasis mine] que era ydo / A ver los Ethyopes" (2b).[14]

Lazarillo often speaks of his bad luck dealing with the blindman or the priest of Maqueda, or questions why he should be so unlucky as to fall in with the squire, only to realize later that ill luck once again has subverted his attempts at enjoying a good life.[15]

Ulysses, like Lazarillo, is cast in the role of sufferer: "Que naveg[ó] por mar tan largo tiempo / Passando mill trabajos y fortunas" (B).[16]

Ulysses' life is part of a greater scheme never free from cares. Even in his own home, he suffers, "enojos y renzillas, / Con sus propios amigos y allegados" (2a).[17]

His woes are not reserved to himself as a form of self-pity but are viewed through a pitying lens by others. We read: "Oyendo pues lo que padesce Vlyxes / ¿O padre como no se te enternece, / Y mueve el coraçon?" (4a).[18] Ulysses' woes are not without some rationale, for the narrator observes, "Desde entonces a Vlyxes le persigue [Poseidon], / Y no quiere que muera, sino que [Ulysses] ande / Perdido, y de su patria dulce tierra / Ausente, perseguido, y desterrado" (4b).[19] Pallas refers to this aspect of Ulysses, "Mill penas y trabajos" (39b),[20] and Nestor refers to "peligros y trabajos / En la guerra" (55a).[21] Similarly, the *Viejo*, in the fourth canto, keeping in mind perhaps the basic view of the ill luck that burdens Ulysses, remarks, "Que tus hados no quieren, ni permiten / Que puedas ver a tus amigos dulces" (86b).[22] Calypso senses the tragic and painful wanderings of Ulysses when she notes, "lo que el hado / Inevitable te amenaza, y quantos / Trabajos y fortunas te conviene / Vencer, primero que a tu casa llegues" (112a,b).[23] *Casa* here can also be understood in terms of the "buen puerto" at which Lázaro is aiming.[24] "Poniendole delante las viandas / A Ulyxes, y del vino muy suave / El qual comio y beuio con harta prissa / Como aquel que auia estado tantos dias / Ayuno, y de trabajos fatigado" (136b).[25]

But Ulysses' *penas* are not to be seen as merely occasional but part of the larger picture of punishment that the gods mete out to their victims. Ulysses sees his punishments, whether divinely inspired or not, as part of a basic experience of life, for he says, "Que no soy semejante yo a los Dioses, / . . . / Sino a los hombres frágiles mortales, / Los quales, como sabes, son subjectos / A padecer trabajos y fatigas" (149b).[26]

Lazarillo's life experiences are lived on the forge of pain and punishment, and his woes are comparable with those of Ulysses as part of a negative world view that sees life as struggle and pain. Gods intervene strongly in Ulysses' life, "Porque los grandes Dioses inmortales / Me han hecho passar males estraños" (151a).[27] Ultimately, what may be of greatest value for the purposes of this essay is the final communication of these woes and pain, their adoption within a literary, poetic frame, for viewing and appreciation by readers: "Mas a ti según veo, ha te movido / Tu ánimo a querer que cuente agora / Mis dolores tan llenos de sospiros, / Para que se renueue mi gran pena, / Y con llorar más gima, ny más sospire. / ¿Por do començaré yo mis trabajos? / ¿Quál será lo primero, o lo postrero?" (182a).[28]

Ulysses, like Lazarillo, is throughout his journey the cantor, the reciter, of his own life and woes, and the artisan of the conversion of experience into words.

The experiences of the Homeric hero make of him an individual punished by forces beyond his control for offenses he has committed in the name of the return to Ithaca. He is emblematic of a difficult and hard-lived life.[29] Similarly, Lazarillo in his climb to respectability feels the full power of adversity in the form of evil and malicious masters who exploit him, of individuals fueled by self-interest and gain, of persons who hide behind various guises but cannot face the realities of their everyday living. The combined threads of these experiences, none of which provides the character with any respite, join to form his own picture of his life as "fortunas y adversidades," and the final accommodation the hero makes with his own honor is an eloquent statement of his defeat by a life whose blows are greater than what he can honorably absorb.

III

At the forefront of the action in the *Odyssey* is kinship, the awareness of family and related persons as an identifiable unit. The structure of *La Ulyxea* revolves around Laertes, his son Ulysses, his wife Penelope and their son Telemachus. Ulysses' absence has brought numerous suitors to his home in search of Penelope's hand. She keeps the faith in Ulysses' return and finds ways to postpone the choice of a suitor. The family nucleus is endangered, and the actions of both Penelope and Telemachus are intended to maintain that unit. Telemachus's voyage in search of his father is similar to Lazarillo's unconscious quest for either a father or a father figure as substitute.[30] When Telemachus leaves, the description of Penelope is "Llorando de sus ojos agriamente" (97b).[31] She is concerned about the safety of her son because she senses the suitors' nefarious intention of destroying that family unit. As she says, "Pensando, en si su hijo escaparía / De la muerte cruel, o por ventura / Sus servidores malos y importunos / Le matarían, estando en acechança" (100b).[32] Her maternal feelings concerning the safety of her son (and husband) are a part of a basic concept in Homer. In one instance Ulysses says, "Hallele [Eolo] que coma con sus hijos / Y su muger muy casta, y en entrando / Sentamonos en parte que nos vieron" (209a).[33] The sanctity of the family unit, especially breaking bread, is observed. As Alcinous says, "Y vosotros que estays aquí comigo / En mi real palacio, y a mi mesa / Beuiendo alegremente el fuerte vino / Y oyendo este cantor dulce y suaue" (275b).[34] This basic unity is derived from the notion of parental union of Ulysses and Penelope. Ulysses notes, "Que la mayor merced que ellos dar pueden, / Es quando dos casados muy conformes / De vn ánimo y querer biuen contentos" (134a).[35] *Lazarillo de Tormes* begins with a union, its family unit, and ends with Lazarillo's forming of his own family unit.

But Ulysses' is not the usual family. It is endowed with special characteristics that separate it from the mere run of Greek life. He is, after all, king of Ithaca, and Homer endows his line, if not with godlike features, certainly with superior human ones. Lineage becomes a basic concern of the action as focused on Ulysses' immediate family.

Lineage in this poem is related to superiority, and qualities are passed down from one generation to the other. Menelaus says of Telemachus, "De tal padre eres hijo que no puedes / sino hablar con gran prudencia y seso" (75a).[36]

An unconscious undercurrent, a substratum of Lazarillo's life, is the emulation of his hardly imitable forebears. In the Homeric poem the idea of resembling someone appears and reappears throughout.[37] Mentes says to Telemachus "Harto paresces serle semejante / Que yo me acuerdo bien que tales eran" (10b).[38] Here *Parece*, as is the case in *Celestina*, involves lineage.[39] Minerva says, "Tú, hijo mío, pues eres de hermosura / Tan rara, y juntamente tan dispuesto, / Procura de ser fuerte y esforçado: / Porque los por venir que en ti hablaren / Te bendigan, y tengan por dichoso" (15a).[40] The play between father and son is accentuated by Pallas when she reminds the reader, "Que pocos hijos salen semejantes / A sus padres, y muchos se empeoran, / Y pocos, o muy raros son mejores" (35b).[41] Lineage as power and value is stressed by Menelaus when he says, "Antes paresce bien, y se conoce, / Que soys hijos de Reyes valerosos, / Nasçidos de Dioses sempiternos, / Porque viles nunca nascen tales" (68b).[42] It is, moreover, illustrious lineage that identifies this basic family unit. Minerva says, "No creas que han perdido ya los dioses / De tu linaje illustre la memoria, / Antes de aquí adelante yrá cresciendo / Tu gloria y nombre con eterna fama, / Porque tal madre tal le huuo parido" (11a, b).[43] Qualities of individuals stand out and remain as signifiers not easily erased, "Pues no ay hombre en el mundo que su nombre / No se le ponga en siendo a luz salido / Por bueno, o por astroso en si sea" (179b).[44] Lineage in the *Odyssey*—"los que por la sangre, o por linage / Deuen de dar cuydado y ser amados?" (180b)[45]—is the basic ingredient to noblesse oblige.

Lineage carries its prerogatives, and caste travels from one generation to the next. Yet another feature of this concept is the heroic and superlative nature of the characters. Homer's central characters in this poem are close to an ideal. They are heros in the basic, classical definition of the term, and their conduct corresponds accordingly. Telemachus acts "qual convenía / A su persona illustre y generosa" (22b).⁴⁶ Elsewhere, he is described, "con vn semblante / Al pareçer diuino mas que humano" (22b).⁴⁷ Nestor says of Telemachus, "Y tú, hijo, pues eres hermoso, / Y tan dispuesto ten muy grand cuydado / De ser en tus hazañas muy valiente. / Porque los por venir todos te ensalçen / Y de echar benediçiones nunca acaben" (52a).⁴⁸

For the critic of *Lazarillo de Tormes*, the superstructure of heroism and moral and physical idealism in the *Odyssey* must be seen in the Spanish work as another example of recoil: heroism/antiheroism; ideal/counterideal. Lazarillo in his everyday plainness is the complete opposite of the heroes of the *Odyssey*. Ulysses in this sense is rather the equal of Amadis of Gaul. The author of *Lazarillo de Tormes* creates a world redolent of everyday happenings narrated in a *sermo cotidianus*.⁴⁹ The Homeric world for the author of the *Lazarillo* is turned more toward the Stoic rather than the Platonic. The rest is quite alien to the novelistic conception of the *Lazarillo*. The ideal world and the idealistic matrix of the *Odyssey* function as intensifiers of the nonidealistic, dishonorable one of *Lazarillo*.

IV

Ulysses enters modern literature in part as a symbol of deception. His great-grandfather was Hermes. He is referred to as "Mañoso Ulyxes" (112a), and is seen by Nestor as "Ulyxes el diuino, que sabía / Vençerlos con astuçia y con sus mañas" (48b).⁵⁰ He himself will claim that, "por mi astuçia y mañas tienen cuenta / Comigo los mortales, y mi fama / Allá a los altos cielos ha llegado (181a).⁵¹ Tiresias says of Ulysses, "Pero despues que ya a los amadores / De Penelope huuieres despachado, / O por engaño, o con tu aguda espada / Tomando vn remo" (235a).⁵² Yet Ulysses is also as sinned against as sinning, for he says, "pues vsaron / comigo esta crueldad y falso engaño" (284b).⁵³ Ulysses, like Lazarillo, lives in a difficult world where one must be aware of being deceived and be ready to deceive others (which is the typical picaresque social response). Of Ulysses it is said, "Muy astuto, engañoso y muy doblado / Auía de ser por cierto el que pensasse / Poderte a ti vencer en ser mañoso / Aunque fuesse algun hobre más que humano. / Malo, falso, sagaz, ¿aun no has querido / Estando ya en tu tierra oluidar algo / De las astuçias falsas y doblezes / En que desde tan niño te has criado? / Mas quiero dexar esto, pues que entrambos / Sabemos en engaños lo que basta" (287b).[54]

The first three chapters of Lazarillo de Tormes (as well as the fifth) are based on a succession of deceptions and counterdeceptions. The action in fact is propelled by this oscillation of deception and counterdeception. In the Hispanic world, the figure of young Lazarillo becomes the symbol of trickster and deceiver. In this he is a perfect Ulyssean character.

The Odyssey, however, as we can see, has more than one trickster. The work is filled with various and sundry deceits. Penelope also complements her husband in deception. Like the narrator of A Thousand and One Nights, Penelope, hoping for the arrival of her husband in Ithaca, must find a means to put off the suitors.

Antinous says Penelope uses "mill astuçias engañosas" (26b).[55] Elsewhere, Antinous describes her trick of weaving and unweaving her "Prolixia tela" (27b).[56] Even gods are capable of deceit. Antinous refers in particular to a moment "en que Dios quiso / Sacarnos del engaño en que nos tuuo" (27b).[57]

The episode with Polyphemus shows Ulysses at his very best. Before blinding the cyclops, Ulysses impishly calls out, "Yo me llamo Ninguno, este es mi nombre" (197a).[58] The giant answers, "Amigos accorredme, que Ninguno / Me ha muerto con engaño no con fuerças" (198b).[59] For the reader of Lazarillo several verses have particular meaning, "Agora vn hombre malo y tan pequeño, / Y de ningunas fuerças, me ha cegado / Después que me venció con dulce vino" (203a).[60]

The first chapter of Lazarillo, involves several burlas dealing with wine. Lazarillo manages to have the blind man jump unknowingly into a stone post, the final vengeance of the young Lazarillo against his mentor. Arturo Marasso compared this dashing of the blind man with the blinding of the Cyclops.[61] The astute tricks Ulysses uses with the Sirens are indeed impressive (e.g., plugging the ears of his sailors and his use of the herb moly). The gods' inclination to deception and the resort of "Egisto engañador" ("deceitful Aegistus") (54b) to kill Agamemnon confirm that deception is as much a key to action and behavior in the Homeric world among humans and gods as it is in the picaresque novel, which would be inconceivable without it. In the Lazarillo the deceptions are not major, do not go beyond petty theft, and are done out of necessity. In later picaresque antiheros like Guzmán de Alfarache and Pablos el Buscón, the deceptions are far meaner and more cruel, but Ulysses as a model or parallel example, whether for petty theft or major malice, could not be clearer.

V

An important feature of Greek life, according to Finley, is the concept of hospitality. Guests are treated like members of an extended family. The *Odyssey* offers the readers several views of this principle.[62] There is throughout the poem a great concern for the presence of the suitors in Ulysses' house. While waiting to receive Penelope's decision regarding which of them she will choose, they manage to eat and drink heartily at the expense of Ulysses and his family. The concern for this effect on Ulysses' wealth is considerable and is noted when Minerva suggests that Telemachus "diga a los que siguen a su madre / Su caro matrimonio procurando, / Que le comen sus bienes y carneros, / Y gastan y destruyen su hazienda, / Que a sus casas se vayan a la hora" (5a,b).[63]

It is obviously a negative reflection on the sensitivity of the "descomedidos amadores" ("insolent suitors") that they are so heedless of the expense incurred by their presence (6a). This complaint is echoed throughout the text.[64] While wealth and substance were to be enjoyed, they were not meant to be trampled on, nor, to judge from the text, was a person's estate to be dealt with in such a careless and discourteous manner. Since Ulysses is not present to defend his own home and purse, and Penelope, within the purview of the Homeric view of women, would not do so,[65] and since Telemachus was either too young or too powerless, and Laertes too old and powerless, the home of Ulysses becomes a site of heedless enjoyment by the suitors. Its repeated mention displays the author's concern for wealth and status. The presence of the suitors signifies an all-out assault on this material side of Ulysses' life.

The suitors' vulgar display is only one side of the coin, although an important one structurally for the resolution of the poem, Ulysses' return and vengeance upon the suitors.[66] Their constant presence and their eating and drinking habits intensify in reverse one of the most, if not the most, important aspects of the *Lazarillo*. The Spanish novel has been referred to as the "epic of hunger." Its central point has been seen by Croce, among others, as the satisfaction of the *primum vivere*.[67] Lazarillo in the first three chapters literally has to battle his masters for food.

The blind man withholds food from him, so that Lazarillo has to resort to the ingenious trick of perforating the wine jug and sealing it with wax, or of replacing the sausage with a turnip. In his stay with the niggardly priest of Maqueda, Lazarillo is reduced to consuming pieces of stale bread. This of course culminates in the episode with the squire, who even less than the other masters can provide Lazarillo with sustenance. Lazarillo woefully concludes the episode by noting that while servants are usually supported by their masters, in this instance he supported the squire with whatever food he could beg.

In the poem, the reader finds a constant allusion to food. For the Renaissance mind and spirit, food represented the great cornucopia of nature and the blessings of the earth. The countryside in *Ulyxea* is described as a bountiful nature proffering its fruits to the Greeks (145). The great abundance of food is also linked with the concept of companionship, hospitality, and kinship.[68]

Gestures of motherly concern such as those of Penelope and Antoña Pérez could not have been missed by early readers of the *Lazarillo de Tormes*. Lazarillo's early years are marked by the struggle for existence punctuated by brief moments of respite (e.g., the arrival of Zaide). Afterward Lazarillo and his mother struggle to keep alive in various ways until she gives her son up to the blindman, knowing they will never see each other again. Penelope's persistent care and attachment are emphasized by their relative absence in the Spanish novel.

The stay at Menelaus's house appears as a feast with nothing spared.[69] This *cena* could easily represent the myth of plenty for any humanist who sought examples of the good life in antiquity. In the *Lazarillo*, food is represented, when it is present, by wine, a sausage link, a lonely string of onions, the broiled sheep's head, crusts of bread and bread crumbs, "uña de vaca," and in the last chapter gifts from the archpriest's store of food, presented to Lazarillo and his wife.

In the first three chapters, food and survival are main themes. In the Homeric poem, food and drink are plentiful. Animals are slaughtered without hesitation (60b, 69a, 148a, 181b, 213b). Eating is a social act, which is narrated with the author's own *regusto*, "Todo aquel día entero hasta la tarde, / Ya que el Sol se ponía, muy de assiento / Passamos en comer y en beuer vino / Suave, en gran plazer y regocijo" (225b).[70] Homer's concern about food reveals culinary subtleties aimed at satisfying the readers' sensuality, "Yendo ya cerca, diome en las narizes / El buen olor de aquello que se assaua" (271a).[71] The enjoyment of eating is a consequential pleasure of the myth of plenty, "Comieron d[él] las piernas, que se auian / Assado a muy gran fuego, y aun contentos / Hizieron vn combite sumptuoso" (276b).[72] The pleasures of life, identified with eating and drinking, could not find a better example than in the *Ulyxea*.

Even the hunger theme in the *Odyssey* is framed in a satisfying reference. Ulysses says, "Dexadme ya cenar, porque no ay cosa / Peor que vn vientre hambriento y fatigado" (149b).[73] Food is such an important part of the work that the episode in the lair of Polyphemus where Ulysses's men are eaten can be read as an author's self-reflective parody on the general theme, "Mas quando ya estuuimos alexados / De tierra, quan[d]o vn hombre se podria / Oyr llamando a bozes, yo hablaua / Palabras injuriosas al Cyclope, / Diziendo, Polyphemo, no deuias / Comer los infelices compañeros / Vsando de fuerza tan estraña" (201b).[74]

VI

A reader familiar with both works might connect other textual elements in the *Ulyxea*. The first is the importance of food.[75] In the *Ulyxea* the day ends, unlike in *Lazarillo*, with a celebration of food and drink, a feast of "carne en abundancia" ("abundant meat") and "vino dulce" ("sweet wine"), whereas Lázaro spends the first night in the service of the squire in relative hunger (156–57).

The figure of the squire as well as the avaricious priest of Maqueda easily come to mind when we read of Polyphemus' devouring of Ulysses' men, "Su cena tan cruel y lastimera. / Comía de los tristes, como suele / Comer vn león fiero montesino. / Cenóse en las entrañas lo primero, / Después no dexo cosa de la carne / Ni de los huessos duros, sin comerla" (194a).[76] Likewise, the squire, when he is able to cadge some crusts of bread from Lazarillo: "Y llevandolo a la boca, comenzó a dar en él tan fieros bocados como yo en lo otro" (154).[77]

Having succumbed to pity for the famished squire, Lázaro gives in and offers him some bread. The squire's reaction, inasmuch as it is compared to a possible canine reference ("fieros bocados"), is reminiscent of Homer's feline one, but the effect is the same: to depict hyperbolically the enormity of the appetite because of a similar enormity of hunger, "Póngolo en las uñas la otra y tres o cuatro raciones de pan de lo más blanco. Y asentóseme al lado y comienza a comer como aquel que lo había gana, royendo cada huesecillo de aquéllos mejor que un galgo suyo lo hiciera" (164).[78] Circe says to the "miserables hombres" ("wretched men"), "Vení, comed, y holgaos, estad alegres, / Y beued deste vino todo el día" (257a).[79] In *Lazarillo:* "Toma, come, triunfa, que para tí es el mundo" (133), and "Toma y vuélvela luego y no hagáis sino golosinar" (132).[80] The function is the same in both texts, and no reader of the *Lazarillo* would have overlooked or ignored such a detail, certainly in the Spanish translation of the *Odyssey.*

The festive hospitality, kinship, respite, and repose, the vivid enjoyment of food and drink of the *Ulyxea* become the emblem *against which* the author of *Lazarillo* creates his story of hunger, want, exploitation, and the moral decadence that accompanies such a situation.

Just as Amadis and Ulysses could fulfill certain prerogatives, and just as the classical world could envisage particular forms of life and mores, these viewed by the author of *Lazarillo* in an ideal light. His composition is crafted accordingly on a *rejection* of such ideal conduct and life, because morally, socially, politically, and economically, the life surrounding him could not warrant such idealism.

VII

Other connections between the two texts merit discussion. A characteristic of picaresque literature is the presence of mendicants. Traditionally, this carried with it a picture of the *pícaro* as unkempt, dirty, and disheveled.[81]

Numerous theories purport to account for the origin of the word *pícaro*, and one of these is associated with soldiers deserters who roamed the byways and had to live by their wits in order to survive.[82] The presentation of the major picaros of Spanish literature—Lazarillo, Guzmán, and Pablos el Buscón—and their experiences verify that the picture of a *Schelm* was intimately identified at some stage with a shabby, dirty appearance. When Ulysses reappears, he comes changed by the goddess into an old man, "Cubriole luego vn manto remendado / Encima de vna vil y ruin camisa / Muy rota y muy grossera, que hedía / A humo de que estaua teñida" (293b).[83]

Ulysses, in this guise, may easily have suggested one of the most obvious and most enduring physical characteristics of the *pícaro*: his dirty, unkempt appearance.

I have offered connections with particular characters of the Spanish novel and the *Ulyxea*. Ulysses' blinding of Polyphemus is premeditated (194b). Likewise Lazarillo, after receiving the punishment of the sausage/turnip episode, bides his time until the right moment, thereby sharpening the edge of his resentment and anger. When Ulysses puts the lance in Polyphemus's eye, the giant monster responds in pain, "Lloraua horrible y espantosamente, / La cueva de su llanto retinia" (198a).[84]

The ultimate aim in each case is to utilize cunning and ingenuity to carry out a fairly heinous act. Lazarillo tricks the blind man into thinking that he must cross a stream and watches him dash himself against a post. Ulysses gets Polyphemus drunk enough so he can pierce the cyclops's eye with the lance. The physical consequences are both grotesquely extreme, although not lethal for either.

Another feature of the picaresque is the concept of the rogue as an avenging medium for grievances. Lazarillo, Guzmán, and Pablos all develop the concept of vengeance as a fine art. Vengeance is a source of action also in the *Ulyxea*. As Athena says, "Como podras vengarte por tus manos / De aquellos importunos servidores / De tu muger" (291a).[85]

Ulysses' return will mean not only the restoration of the unit of kinship, but it will also mean a settling of moral debts. The boorish greed of the suitors will be rectified in blood.

Certain phases of Renaissance literature can be conveniently divided into Neoplatonic and Neostoic tendencies.[86] The picaresque was decidedly anti-Platonic in all its manifestations and it follows the Neostoic concern with this-worldliness in all its guises, especially in the less favorable aspects of human conduct. Homer presents the suitors as a vulgar and inconsiderate presence. When Telemachus takes his journey, he is running the risk of being killed, but his *hazienda*, as goods, objects, become the focus of attention. A person says to a suitor, "Pues desto ¿qu[é] trabajo nos vernia / De auer de andar partiendo su hazienda, / En partes, como a cada vno cupiesse?" (38a).[87] This particular pettiness and the suitors' opportunism in consuming Ulysses' estates are depicted in an effort to present less-than-admirable aspects of human behavior, a fundamental feature of picaresque literature.[88]

The task of confronting the Spanish version and the translation of the *Odyssey* with the earliest of picaresque tales, *Lazarillo de Tormes*, would have been easier had I possessed certain facts, such as the date of composition of the Spanish work. As it now stands, an asserted influence of the Spanish *Ulyxea* on *Lazarillo* is a very suggestive one, and one that has credibility to support it. (More than an influence, the coexploration of various themes, common to each text, justifies the juxtaposition of texts.)

The Spanish *pícaro* in the figure of Lázaro de Tormes could owe his existence in part to the trickster figure of Ulysses as well as to the general atmosphere of deceit and deception in the classical work—to the uses of the topoi of hunger and the satisfaction of hunger, to the motifs of fortune and adversity, to the resemblance either by adoption or by recoil of particular characters and events.

It is rare to find a great work that can boast only one textual incitement. For *Lazarillo de Tormes*, there are various and many, but I would count among them the figure of Ulysses, for which the Spanish translation by Gonzalo Pérez of the *Ulyxea* may have played a major role.

Notes

1. For the bibliography of this work consult Bartolomé José Gallardo, *Ensayo de una biblioteca española de libros raros y curiosos* (Madrid: Tello, 1888), 3:1163–64; M. Menéndez Pelayo, *Biblioteca de traductores españoles* (Santander: Aldus, 1953), 4:36; A. González Palencia, *Gonzalo Pérez, Secretario de Felipe Segundo* (Madrid: CSIC [Instituto Jerónimo Zurita], 1946), vol. 1.

2. Concerning the confused authorship question, see Menéndez Pelayo, *Biblioteca*, 36ff.; González Palencia, *Gonzalo Pérez*.

3. González Palencia, *Gonzalo Pérez*. M. Bataillon includes information on Pérez (*Erasmo y España*. [Mexico: Fondo de Cultura Económica, 1950], 233, 240, 264, 376, 414, 676).

4. For more imformation on Antonio Pérez, see Gregorio Marañón, *Antonio Pérez* (Madrid: Espasa-Calpe, 1947).

5. See Menéndez Pelayo, *Biblioteca*, 36ff. For a fundamental work regarding the translation of Greek, see Ezra Pound's "Translators of Greek: Early Translators of Homer," in *Literary Essays of Ezra Pound*, ed. T. S. Eliot (New York: New Directions, 1968), 249–75. Pérez's name must be added to the list of translators of Homer. See also T. S. Beardsley on "the increase in the number of translations of works of imaginative literature" as "a relaxation in the defense of fiction" in "The Classics and Their Spanish Translators in the Sixteenth Century," *Renaissance and Reformation* 8 (1971): 1–9. Classical works framed as Christian allegory would justify their use in the spiritually turbulent 1500s in Spain.

6. For this dating problem, see my *Bibliografía razonada y anotada de las obras maestras de la picaresca española* (Madrid: Castalia, 1980), 348.

7. Francisco Rico, *Vida de Lazarillo de Tormes y de sus fortunas y adversidades* (Madrid: Cátedra, 1987), 13–14. See also J. Ch. Brunet, *Manuel du libraire et de l'amateur des livres* (Paris: Didot, 1860–80), 2:270, and (Berlin: Fraenkel, 1921), 3:383–84.

8. See n. 6.

9. With regard to influence, I agree with Harold Bloom: "Like my earlier book [The Anxiety of Influence], A Map of Misreading studies poetic influence, by which I continue not to mean the passing on of images and ideas from earlier to later poets. Influence, as I conceive it, means that there are no texts, but only relationships between texts" (A Map of Misreading. [New York: Oxford University Press, 1975], 3). J. Kristeva, similarly, avoids intertextuality as mere source hunting. See her Revolution in Poetic Language, trans. M. Waller, introd. L. S. Roudiez (New York: Columbia University Press, 1984), 59–60. Earlier, M. J. Asensio urged caution in dealing with literary precedents. He said: "Nos interesa aquí consignar, no con el carácter de antecedente sino como prevención contra establecer relaciones, cuan lejos podemos remontarnos para estudiar el tratamiento artístico de lo ínfimo, de lo antiheróico y la aparición del mendigo profesional, holgazán y glotón, baldón de las ciudades" ("We are interested in earmarking, not with the character of antedecent but as a precaution against establishing false relations, how far we can go back to study the artistic treatment of the lowest, of the antiheroic and the appearance of the professional begger, lazy and gluttonous, a disgrace to his cities"). See "El Lazarillo de Tormes: problemas, crítica y valoración" (Ph.D. diss., University of Pennsylvania, 1955), 117–18.

10. See Lazarillo de Tormes: "no hay libro por malo que sea que no tenga alguna cosa buena" ("There is no book, no matter how bad that doesn't have something good"); "si muy detestable no fuese, sino que a todos se comunicase, mayormente siendo sin prejuicio y pudiendo sacar della algún fruto" ("if it were not very detestable, but could be communicated to all, especially being without prejudgment and a source of some usefulness") (92). Citations from Lazarillo de Tormes are taken from my edition (Madrid: Cátedra, 1976) with subsequent editions.

11. "And in that work, treating his peregrinations and voyages, he writes many things, in which, when the crust is removed, very great secrets are discovered, from which not only your Highness with your most excellent judgment, but even any other prince who was not as perceptive, could extract much advantage, I have wished to try to see how he [Homer] would speak in our romance Castilian." See A2. Citations from La Ulyxea are taken from a microfilm of the Juan Stelsio 1550 Antwerp edition at the Middleton Library of Louisiana State University at Baton Rouge. I have occasionally edited the original text for clarity. These corrections are placed in brackets.

12. For the Greek world, see Denys Page's Folk Tales in Homer's Odyssey (Cambridge: Harvard University Press, 1973).

13. Cf. zozobra: "Inquietud, aflicción, congoja." Another interesting definition is the following, which is so remindful of Ulysses' life: "oposición de los vientos que ponen al barco en riesgo de naufragar" ("contrary winds that put the ship in danger of shipwreck"). Both definitions are in the Diccionario general ilustrado de la lengua española, 2d ed. (Barcelona: Spes, 1953), 1757b.

14. "But Fortune wished me to go to see the Ethiopians." Other examples: "Mas hora el desdichado se ha perdido / Por su contrario hado: y no me queda / Ninguna confiança de su buelta" ("But now the unfortunate one has been lost by his contrary fate") (8b). Telemachus says: "Si permitiera Dios, o la fortuna/ Que mi padre ya a ella fuera buelto" ("If God should permit it, or fortune, that my father now were returned to it") (11b). Ulysses' wanderings are not completely ordained by his own will. Nausicaa says: "que Iove Olympio / Da, como

y quando quiere, las fortunas / A buenos y a los malos, a cada vno / Como es su voluntad larga y diuina" ("that Jove Olympus gives, how and when he wishes fortune to the good and to the bad, to each one according to his [Jove's] good and divine will") (134a). Even Pallas Athena emphasizes that Ulysses' life "el hado ... ha dispuesto y ordenado" (288a).

15. See *Lazarillo de Tormes*: "Quiso nuestra fortuna" ("Our fortune wished") (104); "Otro día, no paresciéndome estar allí seguro, fuime a un lugar que llaman Maqueda, adonde me toparon mis pecados con un clérigo" ("The next day, since it did not seem to me that I was safe there, I went to a place they call Maqueda where my sins made me come across a cleric") (131); "Vino el mísero de mi amo, y quiso Dios no miró en la oblada" ("My wretched master entered, and God wished that he did not see the bread") (137); "Mas el mismo Dios ... trajo a mi memoria" ("But God himself ... brought to my memory") (139). In the last two examples the word *Dios* is used ambivalently and synonymously with *fortuna* or *suerte*.

16. "He sailed the sea such a long time, suffering a thousand toils and misfortunes, in his prudent soul desiring to save his companions and his life."

17. "vexations and quarrels with his own friends and allies ..."

18. "Hearing, then, what Ulysses is suffering, how, o father, does your heart not soften and be moved?"

19. "Since then, [Poseidon] pursues him; and does not wish him to die, but to wander, absent, beset and exiled from his sweet fatherland."

20. "a thousand labors and difficulties ..."

21. "dangers and toils in war ..."

22. "Your fates do not wish, nor permit that you be able to see your sweet friends."

23. "What fate inevitably threatens you, and how many difficulties and misfortunes it befits you to conquer before you arrive home."

24. The relationship between the *Odyssey* and *Lazarillo* is very complex and consists of a series of similarities, differences, parodies, and ironies. An important connection is the parodic one, and Lazarillo's "buen puerto" (as shameful as it is) with all the attendent vicissitudes is not totally unrelated to Ulysses' wish to arrive home where final verification of his heroic role will take place.

25. "placing food and mellow wine before Ulysses who ate and drank rapidly, like one who had been so many days without food and wearied with toil ..."

26. "I am not like the gods, but like fragile, mortal men who, as you know, are subject to suffer difficulties and toils." W. B. Stanford notes a difference between the *Iliad* and the *Odyssey*: "Odysseus' personality in the *Iliad* is that of an Achaean hero"; see *The Ulysses Theme*, 2d ed. (New York: Barnes and Noble, 1964), 66. His literary depiction in the *Odyssey* contains more antiheroic characteristics.

27. "Because the great, immortal gods have made me suffer strange evils."

28. "But as I see you, your soul has been moved to desire that I tell you now my pains, so full of sighs, so that my great suffering be renewed, and with my weeping this suffering grows more. Where will I begin the narration of my toils? Which will be the first and which the last?" One senses through Odysseus Homer's own self-reflective role as poet: "The poet's self-awareness is thematically explicit in the *Odyssey*, since that epic presents not only bards, in the persons of Phemios and Demodokos, but also authoritative aestheticians, in

Alkinoös and Odysseus" (K. J. Achity, *Homer's Iliad: The Shield of Homer* [Carbondale: Southern Illinois University Press, 1978], 245).

29. For Homer's view of life as cyclical and repetitive see Telemachus's concern when he says "Murió [Ulysses] sin nombre y déjame en herencia / Angustias, y trabajos, y cuidados" ("[Ulysses] died without name and leaves me as inheritance anguish and toil and cares") (12a). Ulysses' travails as well as other characteristics are well noted by critics, and the bibliography of the classics and the picaresque genre is extensive; see my *Bibliografía razonada*, entries 183, 184, and listings under entry 109. Asensio quotes Karl Vossler who views the *Lazarillo* as an "odisea" (*El Lazarillo de Tormes*, p. 116). Asensio also observes Marasso who "relacionó las 'fortunas' y 'adversidades' de Lázaro con los trabajos, peligros y desastres del héroe homérico: ¿Quién es Lázaro sino una parodia del errante Ulises a quien acecha, Neptuno implacable, el hambre" ("related the fortunes and adversities of Lazaro with the labors, dangers and disasters of the Homeric hero. Who is Lazaro but a parody of the wandering Ulysses whose hunger implacable Neptune watches") (*El Lazarillo de Tormes*). Asensio avers that it is the adventurousness, the view of life as "ínfimo," as well as other characteristics of Ulysses that makes of him a subject for comparison (118). For Ulysses as an archetypal precursor, see Stanford, *Ulysses Theme*, 7. Stanford also points out the inherent ethical ambiguity of Ulysses' intelligence (7). This quality of intelligence has defined picaresque characters of all centuries, especially Lazarillo. Moreover, another trait that is associated with intelligence is cunning and wiliness: "The significant fact is that Odysseus's wiliness is admitted, though not illustrated as freely in the *Iliad* as in the *Odyssey*" (M. I. Finley, *The World of Odysseus*, rev. ed. [New York: Viking, 1978], 13). Also see C. M. Bowra, *Tradition and Design in the Iliad* (Oxford: Clarendon, 1930), 208.

30. The blind man says when he takes Lazarillo as a guide: "El respondió que así lo haría, y que me recibía no por mozo sino por hijo" ("He answered that he would do it in this way, and that he was receiving me not as a servant-boy but as a son") (107). One can see a number of father surrogates in Lazarillo's masters. All display some aspect of authority that could confer upon them the general label of *padre*.

31. "weeping bitterly from her eyes." Cf. the reaction of Lazarillo's mother when they depart (107): "ambos llorando me dió su bendición" (she gave me her blessing as we both wept") (107).

32. "wondering whether her son would escape from cruel death, or by chance whether his evil and pestering servants, lying in wait, would kill him."

33. "I found [Eolo] eating with his children and his most chaste wife, and on entering we were seated in a place where they saw us."

34. "and you who are here with me in my royal palace, and at my table, drinking strong wine joyfully and hearing this sweet and soft singing."

35. "that the greatest gift they can give is when two spouses in conformity, with one soul and will, live happily."

36. "of such a father are you to the son [so] that you only speak with great prudence and understanding."

37. Lazarillo's mother's phrase: "Procura de ser bueno" ("Endeavor to be good") (107) must be ironic, since Lazarillo has no one other than his thief-father and later his thief-stepfather as role models. The narrator in other instances says: "y que ella [his mother] confiaba en Dios no saldría peor hombre que mi padre" ("And that she trusted in God that I would not turn out a worse

man than my father") (107), which further accentuates the ironic and sarcastic note. For genealogy in the *Odyssey*, see Finley, *World of Odysseus*, 77, and Stanford, *Ulysses Theme*, 12. Another link with *Lazarillo de Tormes* is the fact that Ulysses' mother does not completely conform to the ideal paradigm (Stanford, *Ulysses Theme*, 11). Yet another feature of genealogy and how it affects Ulysses' life (and the development of the poem) is the genealogical root of deception (*Ulysses Theme*).

38. "You seem to be quite similar to him [in lineage], for I remember well how they were."

39. Cf. *Celestina*: "Pues seme tú, como ella, amigo verdadero, y trabaja por ser bueno, pues tienes a quien parezcas" ("You, be a true friend to me, like her, and work to be good, since you have someone to emulate") ([Madrid: Cátedra, 1974], 159).

40. "You, my son, since you are of such rare beauty, and at once so fit, endeavor to be strong and courageous, so that future men who speak of you will speak well and consider you fortunate."

41. "that few sons turn out like their fathers, and many are worse, and few, [and] very rare are the better."

42. "Rather it seems well, and it is known, that you are sons of valiant kings, born of the eternal gods, because vile people are never born as you are."

43. "Do not think that the gods have now lost memory of your illustrious lineage; rather from now on, your glory and name with eternal fame will continue to grow because such a mother had birthed you as you are." Lazarillo's blind man has been compared with Tiresias. See C. Guillén, *Anatomies of Roguery: A Comparative Study in the Origins and Nature of Picaresque Literature* (New York: Garland, 1987); for the blind seer, see 416–21; for beggars and vagabonds, 71–76; for beggars and vagabonds in England, 76; for Spain, 89–99.

44. "There is no man in the world whose name when he is born is not [either] considered good or star-crossed."

45. "those who by blood or lineage should . . . be loved."

46. "as befit his illustrious and noble person."

47. "with an appearance apparently divine more than human."

48. "And you, son, since you are comely and so fit, take care to be valiant in your deeds, so that future men praise you and never stop blessing you." Nausicaa: "Y agora me paresce semejante / A los eternos Dioses, que poseen / El Cielo" ("And now he seems to me like the eternal gods who possess heaven") (136b); "El ruuio Menelao en la boz recio, / Y fuerte en las peleas y animoso" ("Blond Menelaus vigorous in voice and strong in fight and brave-spirited") (79a). See *Ulyxea*, 173ff., for a description of an aristocratic, rich, and sumptuous situation. Homer's idealism as chronotope extends not only to character but to space and environment.

49. For this term, see Arturo Marasso, "La elaboración del *Lazarillo de Tormes*," in *Estudios de literatura castellana* (Buenos Aires: Kapelusz, 1955), 157–74. See also his "Aspectos del *Lazarillo de Tormes*," in *Estudios*, 175–86. In addition Asensio points to "everyday" ingredients of canto 20, especially "faenas domésticas," "El *Lazarillo de Tormes*," 118.

50. "the divine Ulysses who knew how to conquer them with astuteness and with his cleverness."

51. "By my astuteness and cleverness mortals prize me, and my fame has spread to the high heavens."

52. "But after you have sent Penelope's suitors packing, by deceit or with

your sharp sword taking a blade..." He is called "Astuto" and "mañoso" "Sabio... y discreto" (wise... and discreet) Ulysses (219b). Here *sabio* (wise) is closer to *sabedor* (informed) as in *ciencia* (knowledge) than the philosophical meaning. Guile is usually cast in semantics as a negative trait. What saves Ulysses is the use to which he puts this trait, the pursuit of heroic goals (Finley, *World of Odysseus*, 70). As Athena says of this characteristic "Crafty must he be and shifty who would outstrip you in all kinds of cunning, even though it be a god that encountered you, Headstrong man, full of wiles, of cunning insatiate, are you not to cease, even in your own land, from deceit and artful tales, so dear to you from the bottom of your heart? But come, let us speak no more of these things, being both practiced in craft; for you are by far the best of all mortals in counsel and speech, and I am celebrated among all the gods in craft and cunning" (Finley, *World of Odysseus*, 138).

53. "They employed against me this cruelty and false deceit."

54. "Very astute, deceitful and dissembling would have to be whoever thought of being able to better you in cleverness, even though he were some more than human man. Evil, false, keen-witted, Though now in your own land, you still have not wished to forget the false astuteness and tricks in which since childhood you were reared? But I wish to omit this, since both of us know what in deceit is sufficient."

55. "a thousand deceitful tricks." In defense, Alcinous says "Ulyxes, los que aquí te estamos viendo, / No te tenemos cierto en mala estima, / Ni por embaydor ni mentiroso, / como andan por el mundo muchos hombres" ("Ulysses, we who are seeing you here certainly do not consider you poorly, neither as trickster nor a liar, like many men in the world") (244b).

56. "lengthy cloth." Allusion to Penelope, a popular name in fifteenth-century Castile (Asensio, *El Lazarillo de Tormes*, 117), in the *Lazarillo* text is precise: "Finalmente parecíamos tener a destajo la tela de Penélope. Pues cuanto él tejía de día, rompía yo de noche" ("Finally, we seemed to unravel into pieces the cloth of Penelope. Since whatever she wove by day, I undid by night") (143). Stanford even points to Homer himself as a "deceiver" and cites Aristotle on Homer's lying "in the right way" (Stanford, *Ulysses Theme*, 20).

57. "in which God wished to free us of the deceit in which he placed us." "Ay de mi, como temo, que aun alguno / De los eternos Dioses me apareje / Algún engaño" ("Woe is me, I fear that still one of the eternal gods prepares some deceit against me") (118b).

58. "I am called No one, this is my name."

59. "Help me, friends, for No one has slain me with deceit, not with force."

60. "Now, a bad man (and so small) has blinded me with no force after he conquered me with sweet wine."

61. Marasso, "Aspectos de *Lazarillo de Tormes*," 175–86. See also my note 25.

62. While Greek life harbored fear and suspicion, at the same time there were great expressions of hospitality (Finley, *World of Odysseus*, 101). The concept of "guest-friendship" should be given special notice. Finley says: "In the world of Odysseus they were technical names for very concrete relationships, as formal and as evocative of rights and duties as marriage" (99). This "guest-friend" was "an effective substitute for kinsmen, a protector, representative and ally" (102). A related concept deals with gift giving. Much of the activity of both Ulysses and Telemachus, and other characters, involves the

interchange between friends and neighbors (120–21). Surely the concept is abused by the suitors who only take.

63. "tell those who pursue your mother, procuring her prized matrimony, and who eat her goods and her sheep and spend and destroy her estate, to go home at once."

64. For further and similar complaints, see *La Ulyxea* 6b, 12b, 25a, 26a, 29a,b, 32a, 291a, 293b.

65. For this "solidly patriarchal society," see Finley, *World of Odysseus*, 88.

66. Pérez's translation leaves no room for doubt as to what Homer's view of the suitors was. The suitors had beasts killed "Para *glotonear* como solían" ("to gobble up as they were accustomed to do"; emphasis mine) (36b).

67. B. Croce, "La storia dell'Escudero," in *Poesia antica e moderna: Interpretazioni*, 2d ed. rev. (Bari: Laterza, 1943), 223–31.

68. Bowra notes the following: "He has no illusions about the heroism of ascetic practices, and he thoroughly enjoys his food and drink. On the night of the Dolon adventure he eats three meals, and when Achilles refuses to eat before fighting Odysseus insists that at least he should allow his soldiers to eat" (in Finley, *World of Odysseus*, 208).

69. "manjares muy diversas," "carne de todas suertes," ("very varied foods," "every kind of meat") (68b). The following allusion to bountiful nature already points to Góngora's *Soledades* and *Polifemo*: "Llenas de quesos muchos canastillos" ("very small baskets full of cheese") (190b).

70. "All that entire day until after, when the sun was setting, we spent in eating and drinking mellow wine to surfeit in great pleasure and rejoicing."

71. "When it drew near, the good aroma of what was being roasted hit me in the nose."

72. "They ate the haunches that had been roasted in a huge fire, and still happy as they were, prepared a sumptuous meal."

73. "Let me dine, because there is nothing worse than a hungry and fatigued stomach."

74. "But when we had drawn away from the land, to where a man could be heard if he shouted, I spoke insulting words to the Cyclops, saying: 'Polyphemus, you shouldn't have eaten my unfortunate companions, using such outlandish force.'" Not totally unrelated to this ironic and parodic note is also the episode of Ulysses' men who were converted to pigs (book 10).

75. Cf. *Ulyxea* (188b) and *Lazarillo*, 167.

76. "His meal [was] so cruel and pitiful. He ate the unhappy ones, as a fierce mountain lion is accustomed to eat. He ate their innard first, and after left no meat at all uneaten, not even on the hard bones." Cf. the description of the priest of Maqueda eating the sheep's head: "Aquélla le cocía y comía los ojos y la lengua y el cogote y sesos y la carne que en las quijadas tenía, y dábame todos los huesos roídos" ("He cooked [the sheep's head] and ate the eyes and tongue and neck and brains and the meat on the jaws, and gave me all the gnawed bones") (133).

77. "And carrying it to his mouth, he began to bite it off as fiercely as I did in the other [piece of bread]." While the figure of the squire may easily be studied within the concept of the *miles gloriosus*, I find in the text of *Ulyxea* a detail that readily calls to mind similar details of the squire's demeanor: "Se fue por la çiudad passo a passo, / Y a algunos que topaua les dezia / Que a la tarde se hallen en las naues" ("He went through the city step by step and some

people he ran across he told to be at the ships in the afternoon") (40a). Cf. *Lazarillo*'s encounter with the squire (150–51, 166).

78. "I put in his hands the other [hoof] and three or four pieces of the whitest bread. And he sat down next to my side and be begins to eat like someone with an appetite, knowing each little bone better than a greyhound of his would have done it."

79. "Come, eat, take pleasure, be joyous, and drink this wine all day long."

80. "Take, eat, triumph, the world is yours; Take it [the key] and bring it back immediately; you only think of your stomach."

81. See Covarrubias's definition of *pícaro:* (*Tesoro de la lengua castellana o española*, ed. de M. de Riquer [Barcelona: Horta, 1943], 869a). Asensio points to Arneo in canto 18 as an example of the beggar and glutton type as well as noting that begging was looked upon as a social epidemic in Homeric times (*El Lazarillo de Tormes*, 118). Within the social purview of sixteenth-century life, mendicants and generally the poor were outsiders to that life. Ulysses, for the various reasons we have offered, should also be seen as an outsider. Stanford sums this point up cogently (*Ulysses Theme*, 14). Indeed, individuality is one of the most fundamental features of picaresque existence. It emerges from the characters' exertion of the will to survive, and its origins, at least in part, can be traced to a similar impulse in classical literature. In this regard, see Achity, *Homer's Iliad*, 246.

82. See Ricapito, *Bibliografía razonada*, entries 79 (de Haan), 88 (Nykl).

83. "An old patched cloak covered him then over a vile and worn shirt—very torn and rough—that reeked of the smoke it was stained with."

84. "He wept horribly and terrifyingly. The cave retained his weeping."

85. "since you will be able to avenge yourself with your own hands on those importune suitors of your wife."

86. I find Luis Murillo's "El estoicismo de la novela picaresca española" (M.A. thesis, University of Southern California, 1949) very valuable in this regard.

87. "Well, of this, what work could we have dividing his estate in shares, according to what each one is entitled to?"

88. See J. Ortega y Gasset, "La picardía original de la novela picaresca," in *Obras completas*, 6th ed. (Madrid: Revista de Occidente, 1957–62), 121–25. Some of the same ideas are also to be found by Amado Alonso, "Lo picaresco de la picaresca," *Verbum* 22 (1929): 321–38; and J. F. Montesinos, "Gracián o la picaresca pura," *Cruz y Raya* 4 (1933): 37–63 (also in J. H. Silverman, ed., *Ensayos y estudios de literatura española* [Mexico: De Andrea, 1959], 132–45).

La Lozana andaluza as Precursor to the Spanish Picaresque

BRUNO M. DAMIANI

In the literary tradition of Spain, *El retrato de la lozana andaluza*, written by Francisco Delicado and published in Venice in 1528, is one of the most notable antecedents of the picaresque novel.[1] *Lozana* has been considered an important work of transition between *La Celestina* and the picaresque novel.[2] It has also been seen by some scholars as a literary creation that is close to being a picaresque novel[3] and by others as actually being the first picaresque novel.[4] Indeed, if we accept Gilman's assertion that "historically the *Lazarillo* lies in the immediate tradition of *Celestina*,[5] of which *Lozana* is an obvious imitation, the relation of Delicado's work to the picaresque novel becomes very plausible.[6]

Background, Attributes, and Philosophy of the Protagonist

Like the "prehistory"[7] of the later picaresque novel, Delicado begins his work with a description of the lowly origins and disreputable social environment of the protagonist. Lozana's father is a gambler and a pimp and her mother is a woman of dubious conduct. Like the *pícaro*, Lozana is seen as the product of her dishonorable background and sordid upbringing. From her parents she acquires a worldly education and licentious skills. Upon their death, she goes to live with an aunt, a woman of questionable character who, seeing the girl's beauty and promiscuous inclinations, tells her: "Your physical attributes and your knowledge will be your dowry" (II, 39). Lozana's education in the sensual arts continues under the guidance of the aunt. With her shrewd advice, Lozana succeeds in captivating the wealthy merchant Diomedes, thereby securing, at least temporarily, a happy and carefree life.

The course of Lozana's life is also very similar to that of the *pícaro*. The essence of both is the description of how a youth, born or plunged into a dishonorable environment, leaves home, struggles in a life of vagabondage, and reaches maturity with some degree of social success. Lozana, like Lazarillo, is confident that she will succeed in life. Her aunt's words, "My child, be good, that fortune will be with you" (I, 38), are echoed in the edifying advice that Lazarillo's mother gives him as he embarks on the service of his first master. After leaving the aunt's house with Diomedes, Lozana begins a long journey that takes her to several parts of Europe, including northern Italy. The journey is itself a requirement of picaresque narrative, as Penzol and Bélic have shown.[8] The happy interlude with the merchant ends when his father, scornful of the Andalusian girl's relationship with Diomedes, has her stripped of all her possessions, and arranges to have her taken to sea by a boatman in order to drown her. Impressed by her beauty and moved by pity, however, the boatman does not carry out his assigned mission, but takes Lozana to the safe port of Leghorn, and even gives her clothing. With a ring that Diomedes had given her, and which she had wisely hidden in her mouth, Lozana is able to buy a passage to the vicinity of Rome, thereby further removing herself from the danger of the wrathful father.

The episode with Diomedes' father is an eye-opener for Lozana. She comes to realize the harshness and deception of life and the need for ingenuity. As a result of that and subsequent episodes, Lozana, in the true spirit of the picaresque character, acquires a view of life as an adventure, an experience from which she learns the key to survival and success. "He is praised who looks, notes, and learns in time," says Lozana, and she adds, "In my youth I wandered through the East, I went to Nigroponte, I saw and heard many things; at that time I observed, and now I benefit from what I watched then" (XLVI, 185).

Lozana's ingenuity and sagacity, described by Delicado at the beginning of the work, are revealed in all that she does and says. Note, for example, her words as she ponders the state of her new life in Rome: "I know a great deal; if I now don't see to it that everyone becomes aware of my knowledge, it will all be for nothing" (V, 45–46). This philosophy and her self-esteem incite Lozana to make her natural talents known and to enter into a variety of social circles. Like the *pícaros*, Lozana begins her vicissitudes by skillfully performing various services, first as an expert in the art of cosmetics, then as a courtesan, and later as a go-between.

With each change of profession, Lozana rises in fame and in social stature, exemplifying in her ascent Claudio Guillén's view of the *pícaro* who "moves horizontally through space and vertically through society."[9]

Lozana, like the female rogue of the seventeenth century, uses her physical assets and practical knowledge to obtain food and clothing and to improve her lot in general. Realizing that her attainment of these material things is dependent on the proper use of her attributes, she remarks: "If I should fail to use them I would die, since I have always heard that only the food which is eaten is beneficial" (V, 46). For Lozana, astuteness is an indispensable quality that permits survival and even luxury at the expense of others. When Trigo, the Jewish vendor, asks her to visit a wealthy courtesan, Lozana responds: "Yes, I will go; it will give me a chance to observe and to experiment and also to eat at other people's expense" (XXII, 107). After all, Lozana asks, "Is there a wiser man than he who knows how to get money from other people's pocket without hard work?" (XV, 82).[10]

Egoism, materialism, and a perversion of moral values are traits easily discernible in Delicado's protagonist as well as in the *pícaro*. Lozana is an adventuress who acts without scruples because, she tells us, "To need there is no law" (XXIX, 134). What is important to her and to the later *pícaros* is to survive and to succeed in life, to arrive "a buen puerto," as Lazarillo will say,[11] without any consideration of what is right or fitting. Lozana's positive traits, her beauty, intelligence, and fecund imagination, permit her to survive in an adverse world. Her tasks as a courtesan and as a procuress should be seen in the same light as any service performed by the *pícaros* in their search for shelter, clothing, and food. As in the picaresque tradition, need, ambition, and pleasure are the primary moving forces in Lozana's life. The use of sexual attraction and contrived situations to deceive, fleece, and ridicule lustful and gullible men is a central motif in most of the picaresque novels with female protagonists, a point well studied by Ian Bagby.[12]

It is interesting to note that many of the corrupt individuals who surround Lozana and those who use her services as a procuress praise her for her audacity and astuteness, not for her being a harlot.[13] The ambassador, for example, recalling an earlier encounter with Lozana, tells his friend the knight: "I saw her in the Bancos district; she talked so pleasantly and with such audacity that she seemed a Seneca!" (XXXVI, 154). In fact, Lozana herself resents being compared with a prostitute (XXXVII, 161).

In her eyes and in the eyes of others, she is to be distinguished from the mass of courtesans by virtue of her superior physical endowments, her intellect, and her social aspirations. Lozana's goal is not merely to earn a living by using her body and mind to please and deceive others, but to seek fame by ensuring the integrity of her *honra*. At the beginning of the third part of Delicado's novel, Lozana affirms: "I want to look after my reputation, for, as they say, 'fortune helps the audacious'" (XLI, 172). The association Lozana makes between her reputation and audacity reveals her picaresque inclination to interpret success by one's boldness, venturesome spirit, and seductive abilities. Everywhere in Delicado's work we find references to Lozana's ingenuity and audacity, qualities she repeatedly relates to her ambition to gain the best possible life, to create, in essence, a success story.

From these observations we may deduce that Lozana is a proud, greedy, and lustful woman. As such, she shares yet another similarity with the *pícaro* who has been considered a compendium of capital sins.[14] Lozana's morality, like that of the Spanish female rogues, is shaped by the need to use her physical and intellectual attributes; only by doing so can she surmount the hardships of life, fulfill her basic needs, and satisfy her desire to improve her position in society.

Presumption and social ambition are intimately linked with Lozana's pride. Although a daughter of disreputable parents, Lozana strives to ascend the social ladder by changing professions and by attracting a variety of suitors including a cleric, a majordomo, and an ambassador. Her inordinate self-esteem leads her to assert that, in spite of her lack of formal education, she knows more than the erudite jurists (LX, 228). She takes delight in her achievements, prides herself on her skills as courtesan and go-between, and ostentatiously claims to be the most celebrated woman in Rome (XX, 101). Lozana's sense of fame and her presumed refinement find a parallel in the aspirations of Elena, the protagonist of Salas Barbadillo's *La hija de la Celestina* (1612).[15] Throughout the work, Lozana exhibits a preoccupation with her economic well-being and realizes her ambition by employing astute tricks analogous to those used by other well-known female rogues such as Teresa de Manzanares and Dorotea in the novels of Castillo Solórzano.[16]

The eagerness to be free and to enjoy life nourishes Lozana's lustful inclinations, as it does in the case of at least six other female protagonists of picaresque novels.[17] Her natural instincts find a propitious ground for development in the erotic world of

Rome.[18] The intensity of her passion is clearly perceived in the bedroom scene with Rampín (XIV, 73–76) and in references to aspects of love: "that kiss is worth more than the medal you are wearing on your cap," Lozana tells an infatuated mace-bearer (XIX, 98). After a night of "ecstasy" with the mail carrier, Lozana pleads with him to stay because she does not want to part with "such bliss" (XXII, 105). Lozana's passionate ardor is also manifested by other female rogues. Justina, for example, after an amorous encounter with a man of arms, sees herself burning with passion.[19]

A final point on Lozana as a picaresque character. At the end of the indefinite conclusion of the novel, Lozana becomes skeptical of and disillusioned with the world around her. Consequently, she seeks a change of environment on the island of Lipari, hoping that this will bring her peace and a new life. Her action is analogous to that of the best *pícaros*, who in the final stage of their lives no longer react against life's chaotic events but decide, in the words of Stuart Miller, "to leave the chaos altogether and become a hermit."[20]

The impudent Rampín can also be seen as a precursor of the literary *pícaro*. Lozana, in her early efforts to earn a living with her knowledge of cosmetics, seeks the help of Rampín's mother, a shopkeeper. Lozana's apparent familiarity with the beautifying arts impresses the Neapolitan woman, who swiftly grants the Andalusian lady's request that Rampín go with her to serve as guide.

One of the basic characteristics of several picaresque novels is that the rogue serves a number of masters and that, in his wandering, he is exposed to individuals of different occupations. For his part, Rampín is not a novice at serving masters. In the three months prior to the encounter with Lozana, he had served two masters, a cleric and a squire. The latter, an avaricious and corrupt individual, dismisses Rampín on the mere suspicion that he ate some leftover food (XV, 83). This episode recalls an analogous experience of Lazarillo, whose pilfering of his master's wine brings him a memorable punishment. Rampín, like Lazarillo, is the victim of his master's avarice, and the account of his past service is presented with that same satirical spirit that fills the pages of *Lazarillo*.

Rampín, like the *pícaros* after him, grows in a corrupt and cynical world that profoundly shapes his character, and contributes to the development of his astuteness and ingenuity. With these attributes he performs successfully a variety of roguish tricks and services, which include stealing some shoes as payment for his services (XV, 83), delivering messages, and buying cosmetics for the courtesans (XXXI, 138). His precocious experience with the world of the courtesans teaches him to exploit their needs and desires for his own well-being.

Worth noting, too, is the grotesquely humorous treatment of Rampín. In memorandum XXXIII Rampín runs away from a big rat and falls into a latrine (143). In memorandum XXIV, he is invited to eat some ham and vomits "even his intestines" at the sight and smell of the meat (XXXIV, 149). A variation of this incident occurs in the episode of *Lazarillo,* in which the young rogue regurgitates a piece of sausage.[21] In the *Guzmán de Alfarache,* too, the rogue, after eating an omelet of nearly hatched eggs and a piece of black bread, vomits everything.[22]

Realism and the Milieu of Delinquency

From the point of view of novelistic art and ideological intention, the picaresque novel represents a reaction against courtly literature, principally the chivalric romances and the pastoral and sentimental writings in which idealistic, magic, and supernatural elements abound. Contrary to the idealized nature and elegant models for love in courtly literature, the picaresque novel depicts a wicked and hostile world and the struggle of an individual to survive in it.

In the artistic representation of roguish life, some authors, particularly Quevedo, prompted by the aesthetic values of the time and his violent reaction against the idealism of courtly literature, exaggerate this anti-idealistic materialism, and produce a grotesque deformation of characters and situations.[23] In most picaresque novels, however, the *pícaro,* the other protagonists, and the world around them are related to a specific reality in time and space, and the protagonists' actions characterize them as being concrete and real persons.[24]

In this realism, *Lozana* can be considered an antecedent to the picaresque novel. Situations in both *Lozana* and the picaresque novel, in general, can be traced to the history of their epoch, and present social and ethical problems of great significance in the Spanish Golden Age, the European wars, the expulsion of the Jews and Moslems, the corruption of officials of the law and of the church.[25]

Realism in *Lozana* and in the picaresque novel is characterized also by the sketches of manners and of individuals of various social classes and professions encountered by the protagonist.[26] *Lozana* offers us a true "observatory" of life as it pertains to the libertine Roman society, and we can properly repeat what Erich Auerbach has noted in connection with the banquet scene in the *Satyricon:* "nothing is left mysteriously in the background, everything is expressed."[27] This artistic concern must have also been in the mind of Mateo Alemán whose *Guzmán de Alfarache* carries the subtitle of *Watchtower of Human Life.*

An integral part of *Lozana* and of the novel of roguery is the gallery of delinquency: rogues, vagabonds, charlatans, pretentious nobles, and corrupted clerics (VI, 50; XVI, 77; XXII, 107; XXXIII, 140).[28] The stage of *Lozana*, decadent Renaissance Rome, is analogous to the degenerate scenario in which the picaresque novel comes to life. It has been said that the most important example of the picaresque genre, *Guzmán de Alfarache*, reflects a society in progressive decadence and on the verge of collapse.[29] We can make a similar observation about *Lozana*, where social corruption and libertinism are seen as the cause not only of much physical suffering but also of the destruction that befell Rome in 1527.

Humor

"The classical rule of the separation of styles, which became influential in the sixteenth century, stipulated in practice that everything pertaining to everyday life—social classes and occupations, the common events of life in real places actually named and described—had to be written in the 'low style,' which meant that in theory it could not be treated on any level except the comic."[30] Alexander Parker reminds us that in theory this view "presupposed narrow boundaries for realism, since the comic excluded any serious treatment of a serious problem."[31] In fact, however, some of the best Spanish picaresque novelists succeeded in showing that literature can be "both truthful and morally responsible."[32] Delicado, a precursor of the picaresque novelists, shares with such writers as Quevedo and Cervantes the literary triumph of treating realistic subjects with a serious interest in the problems of everyday life. Delicado's ostensible intention of creating a faithful portrait of Roman life is linked to his morally didactic purpose of showing the foibles of human existence. His opulent use of comic scenes taken from life are entertaining, to be sure, but they are also thought-provoking for they reflect the magnitude of man's blindness to his destiny. The reader wishes to be entertained, and Delicado, like the picaresque novelists, gives him a chance to laugh away his sadness and suffering.[33] We will recall Delicado's view of *Lozana* as a work intended to alleviate the affliction of those who, like himself, had fled Rome under the fear of death and had now settled in Venice. The entertaining picture of the carefree life and jovial days of Rome will bring back happy memories to his Venetian readers but it will also make them aware of the futility of those delightful times.

In addition to reproducing comic scenes from contemporary life, Delicado frequently manipulates language for humorous purposes. Alliterations and puns as well as ironic and metaphorical expressions abound in *Lozana*, as for example, *cocho* ("cooked," "expert in love"); *asado* ("roasted," "tight," "virgin") (IV, 42); *trintín* (tin tin) *y botín* ("clink of metal and booty," "money") (XX, 102); *tercera* ("third on the guitar," "procuress") (XXI, 104); *alcuza de santera* ("bottomless well," "insatiable woman") (XXIV, 119).

Humor in *Lozana* goes beyond verbal effects; it is also used as an instrument of satire, burlesque, caricature, and parody.[34] Delicado's use of comic satire to denounce the social abuses of his times is a technique that was widely adapted by the writers of picaresque novels.[35] Stories and anecdotes in *Lozana* and in the picaresque novel capture the attention of the reader to expose him gradually to the negative aspects of its society, and learn something from it. Despite Delicado's contention that his work is devoid of things pertaining to clerics and the church, *Lozana* contains several humorously ironic and satirical references to religious figures.

The social satire of *Lozana* is mainly directed at the nobility. The protagonist's instruction of the young Coridon on ways to make himself acceptable to the beautiful Polidora is a good example of satire of the upper classes for their lofty and pretentious ideals. For Lozana, in the life of sixteenth-century Rome there is no room for courtly "suffering," there is only the reality of joyous and physical companionship. The world of the nobility is burlesqued by Rampín's aunt's reference to Rome as the *tierra de Cornualla* ("land of Cornwall") (XIV, 73), the celebrated land of knightly heroes. The reference is a pun, since in roguish jargon the *Cornualla* actually means "cuckold." Humor as an instrument for satirizing the nobility is also seen in a dialogue between

Lozana and the vagabond Sagueso, who asserts that the courtesan Celidonia enjoys a greater reputation than she. Distressed by Sagueso's opinion, Lozana reacts: "They [Celidonia and the other courtesans] may surpass me in money and opulence but not in lineage or blood." With an obvious intent to ridicule the system of differentiating nobility from the other classes on the basis of blood lineage, Sagueso gives a humorously ironic reply: "I bet you are right; but just to be sure, it will be necessary to bleed both of you to see who has better blood" (LII, 200).[36] The dialogue between Lozana and Sagueso is not only humorously sarcastic toward the social system in general, but it is also related to a specific sociohistorical preoccupation of the *converso*. Lozana's selfishness and her skillful efforts to succeed in life and achieve supremacy among courtesans and to reaffirm her nobility of blood are clearly related to the *converso*'s frustrated idealism and to his desire for *hidalguía* as is manifested in the picaresque novels.

Américo Castro and Marcel Bataillon have presented convincing theories that the picaresque novel is intimately linked with the social problem of the Jew and the *converso* in Spain.[37] For almost two hundred years following the political unification of Spain in 1492 the only Spaniards to enjoy full social rights were the *cristianos viejos*, or "old Christians," a group untainted by Jewish or Moorish blood. Under this unreasoning prejudice, the *conversos* were repressed, and as a result of their inferior social condition many of them reflected a subconscious desire for nobility of blood. In the *Lazarillo*, for example, the protagonist's first act upon the attainment of economic security is to purchase a sword, symbol of respectability and of traditional nobility. Yet in the social history of the period, the *converso*'s inability to cope with social prejudices resulted in an attitude of frustration and general despair. The *converso* frequently acquired a negative view of life and a rancorous attitude toward its values. It is in this anguish of the religious convert of Spain that Américo Castro sees the origin of the picaresque novel.[38]

Bataillon's study of the relationship of the picaresque novel and *converso* has been enriched by his careful scrutiny of the satire motif in Francisco López de Ubeda's *La pícara Justina* (Medina del Campo, 1605). A significant part of Bataillon's analysis of *Justina* revolves around the protagonist's consistent attacks against those who display an obsessive preoccupation with honor, reputation, and genealogical background. Justina, the daughter of innkeepers, frequently ridicules impoverished and proud nobles or spurious nobles in high positions. Ultimately, however, when she finds herself at the peak of her picaresque success, she, too, begins to acquire a spirit of nobility,[39] thereby becoming herself the object of ridicule, as does Lozana, in Delicado's novel.

In conclusion, then, although *La Lozana andaluza* may not be properly called a picaresque novel, it does exhibit several traits characteristic of the later novel of roguery. In contrast to the ideal and fantastic world depicted in courtly literature, Delicado's work reflects a world of material needs and recognizable geographical places. In a form analogous to that of the picaresque novel, *Lozana*'s components are historical, urbane, erotic, and adventurous; the external frame is picturesque and descriptive;[40] the characters are numerous and representative of various social classes. The satire of corrupt individuals, customs, and manners is didactically oriented. Similarly, the author interjects amusing episodes with the ultimate purpose of moral censure. Furthermore, Lozana and the world around her are depicted in a succession of scenes reminiscent of the episodic plot of the picaresque novel. Each memorandum registers the events surrounding different individuals and situations. The fundamental unity of *Lozana*, as of the picaresque, derives from the presence of the main protagonist, who serves as the link between the episodes, a central theme, and a uniform interpretation of life.[41]

Notes

1. F. Courtney Tarr, "Literary and Artistic Unity in the *Lazarillo de Tormes*," *PMLA* 42 (1927): 404–21. See my *Francisco Delicado* (New York: Twayne, 1974), 92–102, the basis for this study. Textual citations of *Lozana* are from my edition (Madrid: Castalia, 1969). For the English version, see my *Portrait of Lozana: The Lusty Andalusian Woman* (Potomac, Md.: Scripta Humanistica, 1987).

2. *La Lozana andaluza*, ed. Antonio Vilanova (Madrid, 1952), XXXI.

3. *La novela picaresca española*, ed. Angel Valbuena Prat (Madrid: Aguilar, 1956), 12.

4. George Tyler Northrup, *An Introduction to Spanish Literature* (Chicago: University of Chicago Press, 1926), 173; Ian Bagby, "La primera novela picaresca española," *La Torre* 18 (1970): 83–100.

5. Stephen Gilman, "The Death of *Lazarillo de Tormes*," *PMLA* 81 (1966): 156.

6. It is interesting to note that the allegorical gondola depicted on the title page of the Venetian edition of *Lozana* appears to be the direct model for the allegorical "Ship of the Picaresque Life" found on the frontispiece of *La pícara Justina* (1605). See *La Lozana andaluza*, ed. Vilanova, lx, no. 37; Alexander

Parker, *Literature and the Delinquent: A Study of the Picaresque Novel in Spain* (Edinburgh: University Press, 1967), xii–xiii. With regard to the relationship of *Lozana* to *Justina*, see the introduction to my edition of *La pícara Justina* (Madrid: Porrúa, 1980).

7. Carlos Blanco Aguinaga, "Cervantes y la picaresca: Notas sobre dos tipos de realismo," *NRFH* 11 (1957): 316.

8. Pedro Penzol, *Algunos itinerarios en la literatura castellana* (Madrid, 1934), 16, 17, 23–24; Oldrich Bélic, *Análisis estructural de textos hispánicos* (Madrid: Trurus, 1969), 26.

9. Claudio Guillén, "Toward a Definition of the Picaresque," in *Actes du III Congrès de l'Association Internationale de Littérature Comparée* (The Hague, 1962), 259.

10. For a study of these and other characteristics of the pícaro and some interesting observations on the three major picaresque novels, see César Barja, *Libros y autores clásicos* (New York: Stechert, 1941), 215–32, 313–25, 439–45; also Pedro Salinas, "El héroe literario y la novela picaresca española," *Revista de la universidad de Buenos Aires* (January–March 1946): 82ff.

11. *La novela picaresca española*, ed. Valbuena Prat, 84.

12. Bagby, "Primera novela," 96. Cf. Peter Dunn, *Castillo Solórzano and the Decline of the Spanish Novel* (Oxford: Blackwell, 1952), 115: "After *La pícara Justina* the service of masters was eliminated from those stories in which the central character was a pícara. It is preserved to a limited extent in that the heroine, while still a girl, serves in an inn or does some kind of needlecraft. . . . Her main adventures, however, are amorous conquests and 'confidence tricks.'" On the topic of the female protagonist's motives for sexual promiscuity, see Rosa Pastalosky, *Henry Fielding y la tradición picaresca* (Buenos Aires: Solar, 1970), 79.

13. The interesting article of Bagby makes this point clear ("Primera novela," 98–99).

14. Francisco Javier Sánchez Díez, "La novela picaresca de protagonista femenino en España durante el siglo XVII" (Ph.D. diss., University of North Carolina at Chapel Hill, 1972), 125; Pablo Javier Ronquillo, "Hacia una definición de la pícara del siglo XVII en España" (Ph.D. diss., Louisiana State University, 1969), 125.

15. Alonso de Salas Barbadillo, *La hija de Celestina*, in *La novela picaresca española*, 890–942.

16. Alonso de Castillo Solórzano, *La niña de los embustes*, in *La novela picaresca española*, 1350, 1352–53, 1354, 1361, 1395; Alonso de Castillo Solóranzo, *Las harpías de Madrid*, in *Colección selecta de antiguas novelas españolas*, ed. Emilio Cotarelo y Mori (Madrid, 1907), 7:143, 145. These novels were published in 1631 and 1632.

17. Pablo Javier Ronquillo, "Definición," 157.

18. Jose Antonio Hernández Ortiz, *La génesis artística de "La lozana andaluza"* (Madrid: Aguilera, 1974), 107.

19. *La pícara Justina*, ed. Julio Puyol y Alonso (Madrid, 1912), *Sociedad de bibliófilos madrileños*, 2:282–83. The erotic sentiments of other female rogues are discussed by Pablo Javier Ronquillo, "Definición," 161–66.

20. Stuart Miller, *The Picaresque Novel* (Cleveland: Case Western Reserve University Press, 1967), 26.

21. *Lazarillo de Tormes*, in *La novela picaresca española*, ed. Valbuena Prat, 90.

22. *Guzmán de Alfarache*, in *La novel picaresca española*, 256–58.

23. Dámaso Alonso, "Escila y Caribdis de la literatura española," *Cruz y Raya* 7 (1933): 78–101.

24. On this point, see Oldrich Bélic, "La novela picaresca española y el realismo," *Romanistica Pragensia* (1961): 5–15.

25. The historical background of the picaresque novel is thoroughly discussed by Alberto del Monte, *Itinerario de romanzo picaresco spagnolo* (Firenze: Sansoni, 1957), and by Oscar Borgers, "Le roman picaresque: Réalisme et fiction," *Les Lettres Romanes* 14 (1960): 23–38, 135–48, 295–305.

26. See Gustave Reynier, *Le roman réaliste au dix-septième siècle* (Paris: Hachette, 1914), 1–37, 43–55.

27. Erich Auerbach, *Mimesis: The Representation of Reality in Western Literature*, trans. Willard Trask (New York: Anchor, 1957), 23.

28. See Benedetto Croce, *La Spagna nella vita italiana durante la rinascenza* (Bari: Laterza, 1920), 164, 172, 242–44.

29. Ludwig Pfandl, *Historia de la literatura nacional española en la Edad de Oro* (Barcelona: Gili, 1933), 291–320.

30. Parker, *Literature*, 25.

31. Ibid.

32. Ibid.

33. See Fonger De Haan, *An Outline of the History of the Novela Picaresca in Spain* (The Hague: Nijhoff, 1903), 80. This aspect of the picaresque novel is documented and discussed by Joseph Ricapito, "Toward a Definition of the Picaresque: A Study of the Evolution of the Genre Together with Critical and Annotated Bibliography of *La vida de Lazarillo de Tormes*, *Vida de Guzmán de Alfarache*, and *Vida del Buscón*" (Ph.D. diss., University of California, 1966), 525. Expanded and revised version published by Castalia in 1980.

34. See James Stamm, "The Uses and Types of Humor in the Picaresque Novel," *Hispania* 42 (1959): 482–87.

35. Manuel Asensio, "*El Lazarillo de Tormes*: Problemas, crítica y valoración" (Ph.D. diss., University of Pennsylvania, 1955), 174.

36. I was inspired to cite this dialogue by the perceptive discussion on humor that José Antonio Hernández presents in *Génesis artística*, 260.

37. Américo Castro, *España en su historia* (Buenos Aires: Losada, 1948), 581–97; see also "Un aspecto del pensar hispano-judío," *Hispania* 35 (1952): 161–72; Marcel Bataillon, "Les nouveaux chrétienes dans l'essor du roman picaresque," *Neophilologus* 4 (1964): 283–98; idem, *Pícaros y picaresca* (Madrid: Taurus, 1980), 203–43.

38. Castro, *España en su historia*, 581.

39. *La pícara Justina*, ed. Puyol y Alonso, 2:581.

40. José Giles y Rubio, *Origen y desarrollo de la novela picaresca* (Oviedo: Brid, 1890). This work has not been available to me; I have used a summary of it made by Joseph Ricapito, "Toward a Definition," 20.

41. See Michael Ramon, "Nueva interpretación del pícaro y de la novela picaresca española hecha a base de un estudio de las tres obras maestras del género" (Ph.D. diss., Northwestern University, 1956), 89–98.

The Picaresque and Autobiography
RANDOLPH D. POPE

> After all, I was once like
> you are, but being the right
> sort I got where I am ...
> first a frog, now a king.
>
> —Trimalchio in the *Satyricon*

I

The first novel of a *pícaro*, the *Guzmán de Alfarache* by Mateo Alemán, was published in two parts. The first one appeared in 1599, yet not alone: the *Guzmán* generated a new edition of the *Lazarillo de Tormes* (1554), as if to show there was a Spanish precedent to this type of narration. At a time in which lineage was all, it was not honorable to come into the world alone, with no antecedents. Alemán was clearly concerned about ancestry, both in his family and in his intellectual activities. He portrays himself in the frontispiece of his work with his left hand resting on a book by Tacitus, to reinforce his credentials as a historian and classicist. In fact, Alemán's first publication was the translation of two odes of Horace (Carmina 2, 10 and 14), one a dithyramb—a song to Bacchus—the other an invocation to enjoy life. Ode 10 finds Bacchus teaching his songs to nymphs and satyrs, and the poet's contemplation of this scene pervades his spirit with play and dance. Ode 14 is dedicated to Horace's friend Postumus, advising him to drive away care and enjoy life wisely.

Curiously, Alemán did not choose Horace as the author to identify with, but the grave Tacitus. If the portrait on the cover had been of the young Guzmán, the *pícaro*, would he not have preferred the festive odes, as the translator Alemán did? But the narrator of Alemán's novel, an aged Guzmán who has become wiser in his speech and cynical in his actions, prefers Tacitus. The substitution of Horace by Tacitus, of the Dionysiac abandon for the Apollonian restraint, is emblematic of the unhappiness of the *pícaro* with his own self. Therefore, what better choice than a narrative structure, autobiography, that establishes from the very beginning that there is a difference between who Guzmán is, the narrator, and who he was, the character? Consider also the fact that Mateo Alemán, born in Seville in 1547 of a family of Jewish origins, had reached a certain respectability as a judge and accountant, despite his origin, constant debts, and gambling. He must have felt threatened, with a flimsy front to sustain.

Alemán adds to his portrait a coat of arms with which he wishes to pass as a nobleman. The sham is revealing, because he chooses a double-headed eagle. Two heads in one body, just as the autobiography is of two minds: the past, experiencing mind, and the present, reflective mind, both joined in the body of the text. There is also an emblem next to Alemán's portrait: a spider descending on a serpent, the schemer ready to entangle prudence: *ab insidiis non est prudentia*. There can't be enough prudence for readers slithering from line to line of the picaresque novel, when the writer, the spinner of the text, is leading them into a plot, into an ambush. Consider the evidence: Horace substituted by Tacitus, an unjustified identification with a bicephalous eagle, a spider descending on the prudent serpent, a masterful portrait of a deceitful author.

Alemán was not convincing as a nobleman or a historian, but he managed to invent for himself the tradition of the picaresque by associating his text and the *Lazarillo*, published more than fifty years earlier. That *to compile* means etymologically "to loot" should not be overlooked, since it points out the disruption brought about by Alemán's plundering of the past. Since 1599, the *Lazarillo* has been considered an anomaly for its own period, waiting to find its time in Alemán's beginning of a tradition. This is a distortion of literary history since, as Lázaro Carreter has proved, there were many fictive letters written by humanists in which a case was treated with jocund seriousness.

Both the *Lazarillo* and the *Guzmán* are pseudoautobiographies, and most works that have imitated them have kept the autobiographical form: it is there in Quevedo's *Buscón* and in Estebanillo González's autobiography, two works I will refer to later. And here again Alemán has successfully hidden his traces, since no serious and sustained thought has been given to the fact that the autobiographical mode is found imbricated with the picaresque. Alemán's pseudo-origin of the picaresque was so convincing, that it has taken considerable effort by, among others, Bell, Jauss, and Lázaro Carreter,[1] to realize that, as humanists, the anonymous author of the *Lazarillo* as well as Alemán and Quevedo were well versed in the classical Latin and Greek tradition, where there were many models of the ribald adventures of a petty delinquent transversing the darker regions of a corrupt society. Two of the most famous, Petronius's *Satyricon* and Apuleius's *The Golden Ass*, happen to be pseudoautobiographies. There was also the model of confession in literature—the most famous that of Augustine—and in the depositions taken by justices and the Inquisition from criminals, not to discount the importance of oral confession in the Christian tradition.

How important is autobiography for the picaresque? Is it as the color red in traffic lights—a conventional sign—or as light in films or words in a novel, an element that cannot be left aside and that carries with it its own cluster of necessary strategies, meanings, and conventions? Américo Castro claimed, without elaborating, that autobiography was essential: "Esta clase de obras, además de tratar de pícaros, nos ofrece la visión del mundo que puede tener uno de esos sujetos mal logrados, bellacos y ganosos de decir mal. De ahí que sean esenciales tanto la forma autobiográfica como la técnica naturalista," and he repeats: "son esenciales la técnica naturalista, el carácter autobiográfico y gustar la vida con el mal sabor de boca."[2] On the other hand, Alexander Parker flatly asserts: "La forma autobiográfica no es, sin embargo, esencial, aunque fue adoptada por la mayoría de los novelistas picarescos. La característica distintiva del género la constituye el ambiente de delincuencia."[3] But it should be noted that the delinquent who writes makes light of his actions and sufferings, and what defines him is not only what he does, deceiving in order to live, but also and more important what he writes, creating his own image of his life. Is the autobiographical form only "adopted," as Parker claims, and therefore somewhat fraudulent, or is it a genuine and essential constituent of the picaresque, as seen by Américo Castro? Its pervasive presence would seem to indicate that Castro is right, but Alemán's spider descending on the snake shows that we should proceed with extreme prudence.

II

If the picaresque were only the adventures of a boy (or a girl) growing up in a situation where he has to use his wits in order to survive, serving many masters and resorting to petty crime, we should have also picaresque movies as a clearly delimited genre. Yet, if one remembers Buñuel's "Los olvidados," the Brazilian "Pixote," Mira Nair's "Saalam Bombay," and Bille August's "Pelle the Conqueror," it is easy to see that these adventures of Mexican, Brazilian, Indian, and Swedish children are heart-wrenching, with little of the humor we associate with the Spanish picaresque.

This appears to be the first and most immediate function of the autobiographical mode, to control the impact on the reader of the gruesome events the text narrates. And they are stark: child battering, double-crossing, abusive behavior, cheating, even murder. Francisco Rico reports that some readers do not consider the *Lazarillo* funny, but cruel.[4] That is not surprising, if one takes into account only the story line: a child sent away from home, beaten by a blind man; a blind man jumping and bumping his head against a stone pillar, left behind unconscious or dead in the street under pouring rain. In the *Buscón*, a young servant arrives with his master to the university and is covered by spit. In the *Estebanillo*, an apprentice barber cuts off half the ear of a child, and later that same fearless pretender paralyzes a patient's arm while clumsily trying to bleed him. On the screen, these would be frightful images. The gruesome events are shifted into humorous situations by the fact that the narrator, who lived them, has survived and considers them amusing. While readers perceive the pain, they also recognize the simultaneous defiance, sarcasm, irony, and indomitable courage of the narrators. After all, here they are, telling the story.

The *pícaro* has frequently been blamed for a heartless tendency to reduce everything to laughable material. But, would the narrator need the sharp wit and clever language if there were not a pain to bridge over, a heart to hide? He has not lost this heart, but sheltered it from undiluted pain in the otherness of language. Iffland, commenting on Pablos's report on the death of his brother, writes that "while there is nothing amusing in the event itself, the way it is narrated turns it into a prime example of black humor."[5] Later, in reference to Pablos's suffering at Cabra's table, Iffland notes again "Pablos's wit lightens the description of what otherwise might tend entirely toward the negative.... As it stands, we are forced into the problematical situation of having to laugh at something which is cruel and inhuman" (II, 90–91). Yet human it is, very human, to be cruel, stingy, hungry, desperate, and still be able to make merry, to infuse with the spirit of Bacchus the sufferings of Tantalus or

Sisyphus. To call these events inhuman is to deny their frequency and our capacity to descend into those levels of abjection. Being human—as all readers are—would be enough to save a person from such degradation, from such unnatural depravation. Lazarillo, Guzmán, Pablos, Estebanillo affirm in their autobiographies that they are the same person now and then, that they are human but have been treated as beasts and have behaved as beasts. The continuity between the innocent victim, the ruffian, and the narrator establishes the complexity of human behavior. The reader cannot just set them aside as marginal, monstrous examples of a decadent society. On the other hand, this is an uncomfortable identity, where a distancing and delimitation is desired to show that the gate to evil, pain, and debasement has been closed forever.

First, readers are enticed to read about actions and frames of mind that they would normally avoid. Humor is part of it, and another part is the assurance by the narrator that these events belong to the past, that they were endured and the narrator survived, with enough strength left to write the autobiography. Readers do not need to fear for the survival of Lazarillo or Pablos. While the negative is deflected to past behavior, it is not attributed to another person, nor is its seduction denied. There is pleasure in the open road, in outwitting the shrewd, in surviving the cruel, in fooling others, in seeing behind the masks of the respectable, the learned, the sacred, the pompous, and discovering the truth. Guzmán affirms: "No trocara esta vida de pícaro por la mejor que tuvieron mis pasados"[6] (I, 264–65), and he enjoys, clever and free, the "almíbar picaresco" ("picaresque syrup") (I, 265). And the pícaros also find pleasure in telling about their adventures, in finding an audience to believe their life stories, or the fabrication of their latest lies about themselves. Because it is clear to any attentive reader that Lazarillo has not reached the respectability and safe haven that he proclaims, since he is sharing his wife with his employer, and is forced to account for his actions to an unnamed superior. Nor has Guzmán reached the freedom he has bought at the price of sending other men to their death. And while the future of Pablos seems grim when he announces that he does not expect to change, he has taken drastic revenge against his enemies just by writing the book. And if Estebanillo appears to be prepared for early retirement as a court jester and expects to open a gambling house, he is clearly aiming still to show his superior wit and expects to become someone: a literary figure. Claudio Guillén has warned that the picaresque is the "confessions of a liar,"⁷ yet it would be more appropriate to call it "lies of a confessionalist," or a confidence game where everyone involved gets taken in.

What makes confession tolerable is the assurance that the person confessing his or her sins has repented, shied away from them, since he or she feels pain for the improper actions in the past. An example of this recoiling in pain into another version of the self is found in the *Lazarillo*, when the blind man discovers the trick Lázaro has used to steal his wine. The boy has made a small hole at the bottom of the jar and stopped it with wax that can easily be melted. Lying between the legs of the blind man, opening his mouth wide, and closing his eyes, he receives the heavenly trickle. When the blind man discovers this, he slams the jar on the face of the unsuspecting Lázaro, breaking jar, teeth, and the usual unity between narrator and character: "alzando con dos manos aquel dulce y amargo jarro, le dejó caer sobre mi boca, ayudándose, como digo, con todo su poder, de manera que el pobre Lázaro, que de nada desto se guardaba, antes, como otras veces, estaba descuidado y gozoso, verdaderamente me pareció que el cielo, con todo lo que en él hay, me había caído encima."⁸ This split of the narrator and the character that warps the syntax, rejecting pain into the third person, is exemplary of the more hidden split found in autobiography. Where there is total harmony and identity between character and narrator, the result is a portrait and memoirs. If narrators feel there has been no important change in themselves during their lifetime, they will speak about others. An autobiography needs a radical change that makes the distance between narrator and character puzzling and worth investigating.

Pablos has his face slashed, and this scar is the outward sign of the inner split between the innocent child and the skeptical grown up. On another level the scar is the text itself being generated from wounds and contradictions as a tissue of scars. Quevedo could have known of another exemplary break, since when he was writing the *Buscón* he was also writing his *Dreams*, modeled after the dreams written by Lucian of Samosata (c. 125–200), a superb satirist of the Greek late period. He has a piece called "The Vision," subtitled "A Chapter of Autobiography." Lucian tells about a decisive moment in his life, when his family decides it is time for him to start making a living. Although he was scarcely out of infancy, his family decided out of economic necessity to apprentice him to an uncle on his mother's side who was a sculptor. Lucian's memories belong in any picaresque novel:

> But the first thing to happen was what usually happens to beginners. My uncle handed me a chisel and told me to come down lightly on a slab that was lying between us, giving me at the same time the old saw about "well begun" being "half done." Since I had had no experience, I came down too hard and it broke. He flew into a rage, grabbed a stick lying nearby, and put me through an initiation ceremony that was neither gentle nor encouraging. As a result, the preface to my career was a flood of tears. I ran out the door and came home, bawling all the way, with the tears running down my cheeks. There I told the whole story of the whipping and showed my welts. Then I launched into a denunciation of my uncle as a monster of cruelty, adding that he had done this to me because he was jealous: he was afraid I'd turn out better at the craft than he. My mother got very angry and heaped abuse on her poor brother. Night came at last and I fell asleep, still in tears and with that stick very much on my mind.[9]

This broken plaque is replicated in a dream that offers the boy Lucian two possible paths: to become a sculptor or to devote himself to culture and literature. He chooses, without any hesitation, to become the apprentice of Lady Culture. Clearly Lucian portrays himself as having talent and imagination: he criticizes the remark of his uncle as not very original, and quite dramatically arrives at his house still howling and tearful, yet capable of telling the story of the stick—not of his own mistake—and of making a show of his bruises. He notices that he said "a great deal" about his uncle's brutality, and then *adds* that it was all envy. He is successful with his domestic public and moves on to conquer the world. How different are the stories of Lazarillo, Guzmán, Pablos, or Estebanillo? Have they not also tried unsuccessfully other crafts before devoting themselves to culture, to writing? Don't they also tell the story of the stick and make a show of their bruises? Don't they add explanations to avoid being considered guilty of the broken jar and the broken skull of the blind man in *Lazarillo*, the betrayed and hanged men in *Guzmán*, the scar and the murdered guards in *Buscón*, and the cut ear in *Estebanillo*? Are they not concerned with saving face? Guzmán writes:

> Común y general costumbre ha sido y es de los hombres, cuando les pedís reciten o refieran lo que oyeron o vieron, o que os digan la

verdad y sustancia de una cosa, enmaxcaralla y afeitalla, que se desconoce, como el rostro de la fea. Cada uno le da sus matices y sentidos, ya para exagerar, incitar, aniquilar o divertir, según su pasión le dita. (I, 104)

(A usual and widespread behavior of human beings has been and is that when you ask them to quote or tell you what they heard or saw, or to tell you the truth and essence of a certain matter, they mask it and beautify it until no one could recognize it, like an ugly face. Each one colors it differently and finds different meanings, be it to exaggerate, provoke, destroy or entertain, according to what passion dictates.)

The autobiographical form speaks of discontinuity and of continuity, of a break that becomes important enough to be remembered, or an original unity reconstructed in memory in order to be sundered again. No longer simple ruffians, now writers, their past is the material of their new existence, as if a clean start were impossible and there were no breaking away from the pain repented, repainted, reaped in words. Lazarillo writes: "Fue tal el golpecillo, que me desatinó y sacó de sentido, y el jarrazo tan grande, que los pedazos dél se me metieron por la cara, rompiéndomela por muchas partes, y me quebró los dientes, sin los cuales hasta hoy día me quedé" (101).[10] The diminutive "golpecillo" and the augmentative "jarrazo" are the subjective additions with which the narrator and/or the character wishes first to smile ironically but is then undercut by his fear and the missing teeth that join that moment in the past with the present of writing. He, as Pablos, must still show in his face the brutal punishment of his audacity, since the pieces of the broken jar pierced his skin and were stuck in his face.

When Pablos receives the news that his father has been hanged and quartered, he feels ashamed and stays at home "disimulando mi desventura" ("hiding my disgrace"), pretending not to be suffering. He burns the letter he has received from his uncle, the letter that is so deeply engraved in his psyche that he can easily reconstruct it for his autobiography. It appears that as the text moves forward, escaping from the past and adding to it a written version, it recreates the offense and reconstructs the pain. When his only friend, don Diego—himself of *converso* origin—to whom he has confessed without shame, turns out to be the undoing of his plans, Pablos is stunned: "Acostáronme, y quedé aquella noche confuso, viendo mi cara de dos pedazos" (233).[11] Seeing my face split into two pieces: what better definition of picaresque autobiography? Whereas Narcissus is fatally seduced by his reflected flawless face, the narrators of the picaresque novels expect to be saved by their broken objects and scarred faces.

The distancing of the autobiographical mode splices the self temporarily into two: the old and the new person, the acting and the narrating self. But they also are all conciliated in the text, a tissue of truth or lies where they are made whole. Without the autobiographical mode, this healing—described by Jung in his brief but brilliant article on the picaresque[12]—could not take place, this delicate balancing act between separation and compassion would be endangered, and the wound would remain open. The *pícaro* must become a writer to spin the web—spider webs were frequently used to heal wounds—to trap the snake that brought the first division, the knowledge of bad and good. Mateo Alemán's swindle turns out to have been, as most of the picaresque novel is, absurdly foolish and brilliantly insightful. He has gained his arms. The bicephalous eagle—picaresque and autobiographical—has had a long life.

Notes

1. Horst Baader, "Noch einmal zur Ich-Form im *Lazarillo de Tormes*," *Romanistisches Jahrbuch* 76 (1964): 437–46; Aubrey Bell, "The Rhetoric of Self-Defense of 'Lázaro de Tormes,'" *Modern Language Review* 68 (1973): 84–93; Hans R. Jauss, "Ursprung und Bedeutung der Ich-Form im *Lazarillo de Tormes*," *Romanistisches Jahrbuch* 8 (1957): 290–311; Fernando Lázaro Carreter, *Lazarillo de Tormes en la picaresca* (Barcelona: Ariel, 1972).

2. Américo Castro, *El pensamiento de Cervantes*, 2d ed. (Barcelona: Noguer, 1972), 230. "This type of work deals with rogues, but it also offers us the vision of the world that one of those characters can have, people who are unsuccessful, evil-minded and love to bad-mouth everything. Therefore, the autobiographical form and the naturalist technique are essential," and "naturalist technique, autobiographical traits, and the bad aftertaste of enjoying life are essential."

3. Alexander A. Parker, *Literature and the Delinquent: The Picaresque Novel in Spain and Europe 1599–1753* (Edinburgh: University Press, 1967). "The autobiographical form, although adopted by a majority of the picaresque novelists, is not essential; the distinguishing feature of the genre is the atmosphere of delinquency" (6).

4. Francisco Rico, *La novela picaresca y el punto de vista* (Barcelona: Seix Barral, 1970), 52.

5. James Iffland, *Quevedo and the Grotesque* (London: Tamesis Books, 1982), 2:80.

6. Mateo Alemán, *Guzmán de Alfarache*, ed. Benito Brancaforte (Madrid: Cátedra, 1979), 1:264–65. "I would not exchange this life as a *pícaro* for the best life that my ancestors had."

7. Claudio Guillén, *Literature as System: Essays toward the Theory of Literary History* (Princeton: Princeton University Press, 1971), 92.

8. *La vida de Lazarillo de Tormes y de sus fortunas y adversidades*, ed. Alberto Blecua (Madrid: Clásicos Castalia, 1972), 101. "Lifting with both his hands that sweet and bitter jar, he rammed it against my mouth, using, as I tell you, all his strength, so poor Lázaro, who was not expecting any of this, on the contrary, as other times, he was relaxed and happy, it truly seemed to me that sky and all that is in it had fallen on me."

9. Lucian of Samosata, *Selected Satires*, trans. and ed. Lionel Casson (Chicago: Aldine, 1962), 4.

10. "That little blow was such that I lost my senses and was unconscious, and the jar jolt was so big that its pieces got into my face, cutting/breaking it in many parts, and it broke my teeth, that I still miss today."

11. "They put me to bed and I was puzzled that night, seeing my face split into two pieces."

12. C. G. Jung, "Zur Psychologie der Schelmenfigur," in *Picarische Welt: Schriften zum europäischen Schelmenroman*, ed. Helmut Heidenreich (Darmstadt: Wissenschaftliche Buchgesellschaft, 1969), 245–54.

Richard Head and Origins of the Picaresque in England

CALHOUN WINTON

The picaresque novel in England is in some sense like a landscape by Claude or Poussin: the background is more interesting than the foreground. Or, to alter the literary topography somewhat, there is *more* background than foreground. In the background, that is to say, one descries the indispensable if apparently undefinable term "picaresque"; the existence of famous Spanish models or prototypes against which English examples are to be judged; the important literary motif of the rogue making his way in a hostile world. All these seem to be materials necessary to criticism of the novel, but when one focuses on the foreground, the English novel itself, one is hard put to find an example, other than translations of European originals such as *Gil Blas*, of which it can be said confidently, this is a picaresque novel.

English origins of the picaresque are very difficult to trace. If one may deconstruct briefly, the origins lie, in the dual sense of "lie: reside in" and "lie: falsify," in that murky swamp which is seventeenth-century London printing and publishing practice. Before one can follow Paul Julian Smith's recent article on Spanish literature[1] and discuss the "rhetoric of representation" in English picaresque narrative, one must know what one is discussing, what the texts are. In seventeenth-century English literary history we have no *Lazarillo*, no *Guzmán*, no *Buscón*, no establishing texts, as it were; or, more precisely, we have these in translation, in uneasy, problematic relationship with exemplars in English.

Translations are discussed by Professor Jerry Beasley in another essay of this collection, so I shall quit the subject except to observe that the existence of these great picaresque exemplars has led scholars of English literature to seek similar, substantial works—books, that is—with disappointing results. Thomas

Nashe's *The Unfortunate Traveler* (1594) is often cited, and Richard Head's *The English Rogue* (part 1, 1665) is almost always included, for obvious reasons. Scholars, I would argue, have been looking in the wrong place: origins of the picaresque narrative in English literature are to be found for the most part not in book-length narratives but in shorter works: in pamphlets, in chapbooks, and, especially during the early eighteenth century, in periodicals.[2] These narratives were often written anonymously, published by obscure or even unknown printers, and addressed to audiences whose very existence can only be surmised.

The approach of this essay will therefore be both modal—with emphasis on the picaresque *mode*, that is, rather than on generic examples—and by the route of what Professor Donald F. McKenzie has termed "the sociology of the text," the marriage of "verbal preoccupations ... material concerns ... and social dimensions."[3] By whom were these examples of the picaresque mode in English written, for what expectation of reward, and with what audience in mind? These are the questions; all the answers will not be provided in a brief essay. The sociology of this particular text, picaresque narrative in English, is especially challenging. Richard Bjornson has observed that the "history of the European picaresque has not yet been written. When it has, the complex interaction between Spanish literary models and seventeenth-century social realities in France, England, and Germany will perhaps finally receive the emphasis they deserve."[4] Two of these interactions, both most significant for the English picaresque, have to do with the picaresque as travel literature and with the moral character of the protagonist. Percy G. Adams includes Head's *English Rogue*, mentioned earlier, in his work on *Travel Literature and the Evolution of the Novel*, pointing out that Head selects and rearranges the facts of "travel books for their exoticism, and ... their pornographic value." Michael McKeon, on the other hand, places the picaresque in his chapter on "Histories of the Individual," and traces an evolution from picaresque narratives to criminal biographies.[5]

Both are correct; this is not a paradox. Spanish picaresque narratives, in translation, were of course ipso facto travel books for English readers. James Mabbe, who translated *Guzmán* into English as *The Rogue* (1622), called attention in the shoulder notes of the translation to interesting Spanish places, and social and religious practices, almost as if writing a travel guide.[6] But English picaresque narratives themselves were also typically "on the road"; anything beyond the next county town was likely to seem exotic to an Englishwoman or Englishman in the seventeenth century.[7] The narratives were also, as McKeon argues, histories of the individual, usually rapacious or criminal individuals. Almost without exception in English picaresque, the protagonist operates at or beyond the limits of criminality. This, I would argue, constitutes a delimiting characteristic; the English rogue is a genuine rogue. For these reasons Richard Head himself is significant both as a creator of picaresque narrative that contains or makes use of travel narrative and as an embodiment of the mode. He composed rogue narratives and he had, as we shall see, much of the rogue in him. The presence or absence of criminality, furthermore, may serve to identify the picaresque mode in a given novel; for example, as will be seen, *Tom Jones* may be differentiated from *Joseph Andrews*[8] in this regard.

Richard Head merges with his creation in a manner disconcerting to formalist criticism, or to common sense for that matter. The narrator of *The English Rogue*, Meriton Latroon, professes to have been born in Ireland of English parents; so, too, was Head, whose father may have been an Oxonian (there was a John Head, B.A., of New Inn Hall in 1628). Head's father was, Head asserted, a clergyman in the Church of Ireland. Latroon describes his descent from English farmer stock who could not "speak above the reach of their Horses understanding."[9] The quotation is from the second paragraph of the first chapter; from this point on, all conjecture about the relationship between narrator and author is simply that: conjecture.

Within the context of the work, however, the character Latroon's sardonic rejection of family ties is significant: he comes to reject all relationships except the most transient. His father, who was intelligent and handsome enough to escape the barnyard for Oxford, was unfortunately sent down from there, as Latroon says, 'for his lewd carriage, inimitably wicked practices, and detestable behavior" (4). Like father, like son. In fact, the father's lewd carriage and detestable behavior are a come-on for Head/Latroon's audience, who might expect some additional inimitably wicked practices from the son and who would not be disappointed. The father somehow gets into (Anglican) holy orders in Ireland as a domestic chaplain, taking with him Latroon's mother whom he has impregnated and secretly married.

Latroon is a child of about three or four when the Irish rebellion of 1641 erupts, but he has, like Edgar Allan Poe, a mostknowing eye. He can and does describe some of the grotesque cruelties of that rebellion, professing to have the information from his mother. The rebels kill his father, and Latroon and his mother escape to the west of England, where he grows up, a "beautiful child," who discovers how to torture cats and steal from neighboring gardens.

"Being enricht with all the good properties of a good face" (14), he proceeds rapidly through puberty, debauches the servant maid, and is sent off to boarding school. After a flogging, Latroon runs away and joins a gypsy band. At this point he introduces a long disquisition about the gypsies' criminal argot, which he calls "the canting language." John Aubrey the biographer, who knew Head, asserts flatly that he "had been amongst the gipsies."[10] To what extent is Richard Head drawing on his own experience in this episode? The point is not trivial; a "sociology of the text" is called for urgently here. For example, Latroon asserts that among the gypsies "nab" signifies to take or catch. Interestingly, the *Oxford English Dictionary* traces the usage back to Head, but notes its "Origin obscure." Apparently neither the *OED* nor we can make a judgment on the value of Head/Latroon's account of gypsy language and life.

This long series of episodes, each complete in itself (as a beggar in London, as a professional thief, as a London apprentice, and so on), ends with a voyage to the East Indies, where he takes to wife a rich native woman. Head closes the first part with a pious statement from Latroon that he hopes his account will serve as a "warning to another to avoid the danger" (397). And sell books, one might add.

And sell it did, *The English Rogue*: the first edition sold out in 1665; in the following year Francis Kirkman published three editions, and by 1667 it had gone to a fifth. The ending of the first part promised more to come, but when the continuing second part was published in 1668, Kirkman, in a preface to the reader reprinted in later editions, revealed that Head objected to being taken for his creation Latroon. Head, he says, tried to "possess the Reader with a belief, that what was written, was the life of a *Witty Extravagant*, the Authors Friend and Acquaintance. This was the intent of the Writer, but the Readers could not be drawn to his belief, but in general concurred in this Opinion, that it was the Life of the Authour."[11] The second, third, and fourth parts of the *Rogue*, which subsequently appeared, were presumably not written by Head but by, or at the direction of, Francis Kirkman. The readers had some reason to identify Head with Latroon: like his creation he had been born in Ireland; his father, an Anglican priest, had been killed in the rebellion; he, Richard Head, had been an apprentice in London. Where did the parallels end? they might have asked.

His friend William Winstanley does not take a position in this issue, but he does recall amusingly his recollection of the *Rogue's* first appearance.

> At the coming forth of this first part, I being with him at three Cup Tavern in *Holborn*, drinking over a glass of *Rhenish*, I made these verses upon it.

> What *Gusman, Buscon, Francion, Rablais* writ,
> I once applauded for most excellent Wit;
> But reading thee, and thy rich Fancies stor
> I now condemn what I admir'd before.
> Henceforth Translations pack away, be gone,
> No Rogue so well-writ as the *English* one.[12]

Winstanley, called by William Riley Parker a "pioneer in biographical and bibliographical research,"[13] here identifies Head's work from its earliest appearance with the continental picaresque tradition. This obviously represents one of Bjornson's "complex interactions."

It is important to note that Latroon moves easily through all societies and that women are universally susceptible to his charms. During a period of prosperity, fraudulently obtained of course, in London he tots up accounts:

> In three years that I lived as a Mr. [i.e., master] I had nine illegitimates, which I knew, four whereof were begotten by my maids, which put me to vast expence. Two of the Mothers would have forced me to have married them, or allowed them competant maintenance (for they were subtil cunning baggages) had I not by a wile got them aboard a Vessel bound for *Virginia*, and never heard of them since. Besides two or three terrible claps, which cost me a considerable sum in their cure (174).

Latroon, thus, is not unlike the predatory heroes of Restoration comedies that were appearing on the London stage about this time; he is certainly a rogue, but like Horner in *The Country Wife* or Dorimant in *The Man of Mode*, he fancies himself an aristocratic rogue, grandly sending pregnant females to the plantations. He lards his account with Latin tags and poetry in English, displaying his learning, as in the address to his old cloak:

"Thou wert so thin, and light, that some have thought Thee made of that same web *Arachne* wrought" (138).

It is difficult to fit *The English Rogue* into a definition of popular literature, though that is its usual, allowed position. One scholar judges that it was "consciously aimed . . . at the sensation-seeking lower class reading public of the time."[14] But what would this sensation-seeking public have made of allusions to Arachne, or of the Latin tags? Even the first part alone is a thick book with two engraved plates, not cheap, and without the concessions (provided in chapbooks) for a reader of limited vocabulary. It was certainly popular, however, in the sense of being a best seller. Charles Mish has enumerated twelve editions by the end of the century.[15]

Head, an inveterate gambler, tried to make ends meet as a bookseller and writer of miscellaneous verse and prose. One of his later publications is significant for the purposes of this essay. It is entitled *The Complaisant Companion, or New Jests; Witty Reparties; Rhodomontado's and Pleasant Novels* (1674). This work enjoyed some popularity in Head's time, appearing in three later editions as *Nugae Venales*. It is essentially a joke book, divided into "Domestick Jests," "Foreign Jests," and other handy categories for the would-be jester. "Rhodomontados," for example, collects boasts, and provides the reader a boast for every occasion. The elaborated boast, or "brag," became a popular feature of American picaresque narrative in the humor of the Old Southwest, and was employed by Mark Twain in *Life on the Mississippi* in the famous rafters' episode.

For the present essay the most interesting section of Head's collection is the "Cluster of Choice Novels." In an epistle to the reader, Head avers that "the Novels I have affixed to the Jests . . . are not only true, but will be found I doubt not indifferently Pleasant." These prove to be short, crude trickster tales, a page or two long. Though not picaresque as such, they are like many of the episodes in *The English Rogue*.

No satisfactory critical term exists to describe these short fictions masquerading as fact. Head's and his era's use of "novel" is, of course, hopelessly confusing now. I have termed these pieces "nugget fictions." When they appear later in the English novel, as the story of Leonore the Fair Jilt in *Joseph Andrews*, for example, or the Man on the Hill's story in *Tom Jones*, they have been called "interpolated narratives," but they were originally freestanding, as it were, not interpolated into anything.

Nugget fiction was especially well suited for use in periodicals, when periodical publications began to proliferate in the English-speaking world after the turn of the eighteenth century. Very little bibliographical work has been done on this topic, but one volume that has appeared provides some indication of nugget fiction's scope: Evans and Wall's *A Guide to Prose Fiction in the Tatler and the Spectator*[16] identifies hundreds of examples in the original runs of Steele and Addison's two papers. These papers, which began in 1709 and 1712 respectively, were reprinted and collected many times. They circulated throughout the English-speaking world in the eighteenth century. Their imitators and competitors flourished, in London, in the provinces, in the colonies. The possibility existed in a periodical published at regular intervals for serialized fiction, and this began to appear,[17] but for a long time the typical fiction was a single episode, like Richard Head's "novels," almost always represented as being true. This was where, I would argue, the overwhelming majority of English-speaking readers on both sides of the Atlantic first encountered fiction—not in what we would call novels or books, but in short fiction, in periodicals, pamphlets, or chapbooks. Many of these episodes, or nugget fiction, were in the picaresque mode. A good short example (presented here in its entirety), used by Head in the *Rogue* but which could equally well have been included as a "Novel" in *The Complaisant Companion*, describes how Latroon "puts a notable cheat upon a gentleman concerning his house." Within the context of the *Rogue* there is no transition from a previous episode nor to the one which follows.

> Walking one time in the Fields with an Attendant or two, who could be constantly bare before me, if in company with any persons of quality, but otherwise, "hail fellow well met," I was got as far as *Hackney*, ere I thought where I was; for my thoughts were busied about designs, and my wit was shaping them into a form. Casting my eye on the one side of me, I saw the prettiest built and well situated House that ever my eyes beheld. I had a covetous desire to be Master thereof: I was then, as Fortune would have it, in very [genteel] garb; I walkt but a little way further and I soon found out a Plot to accomplish my desires. And thus it was. I returned and knockt at the gate, and demanded of the servant whether his Master was within. I understood he was, and thereupon desired to speak with him. The Gentleman came out to me himself, desiring me to walk in. After I had made a general Apology, I told him my business, which was only to request the favour of him, that I might have the priviledge to bring a workman to Supervise his house, and to take the dimensions thereof, because I was so well pleased with the build-

ing, that I eagerly desired to have another built exactly after that pattern. The Gentleman could do no less than to grant me so small a civility. Coming home, I went to a Carpenter, telling him I was about buying an House in *Hackney*, and that I would have him accompany me to give me (in private) the estimate. Accordingly we went, and found the Gentleman at home, who entertained me kindly as a stranger. In the meantime the Carpenter took an exact account of the Butts and Bounds of the House on paper; which was as much as I desired for that time.

Paying the carpenter well, I dismist him, and by that Paper had a Lease drawn with a very great fine (mentioned to have been paid) at a small Rent; witnesses thereunto I could not want. Shortly after I demanded Possession. The gentleman thinking me out of my wits, only laught at me: I commenced my suit against him, and brought my own Creatures to swear the sealing and delivering of the Lease, the Carpenters evidence, with many other probable Circumstances to strengthen my cause; whereupon I had a Verdict. The Gentleman understanding what I was, thought it safer to compound with me, and lose something rather than lose all. (266–68)

With respect to intended audience, this bit of nugget fiction, a trickster tale, appears to be directed at readers of considerable sophistication, who will appreciate the finer points of real-estate law.

The chapbook was another form of short fiction directed at the less-educated reader. Estimating the form's influence is problematical because information is difficult to obtain on the circumstances of publication, authorship, or readership. Margaret Spufford has made judicious use of what evidence survives, and her account does not indicate that the picaresque played any important part in chapbook publishing.[18] The ubiquitous Richard Head, however, made at least one foray into chapbook publishing with his *The Wonderful Life, Prophecies, and Death of Mother Shipton, the Female Merlin*, apparently first published in 1667.[19] This account of the famous witch and prophet has much of interest, particularly in Head's detailed description of the circumstances. Satan, who begets Mother Shipton on an orphan girl, is a rogue on a grand or cosmic scale, most reminiscent of Jack Nicholson in *The Witches of Eastwick*. Did John Updike know the chapbook?

One suspects that Head learned his roguery from men—and women—not books. His biographer William Winstanley reported that he had "a good Proficiency" in the trade of bookselling, to which he had been apprenticed, but that when he set up his own shop he almost gambled his business away. When he made money at bookselling (which often included publishing at the time), he was so "bewitched to that accursed vice of Play, it went out by handfuls, as it came in piece by piece." Aubrey confirms Head's fondness for gaming and adds that he "looked like a knave with his gogling eies." *The English Rogue* he undertook in order to repair his fortune but in its original version it could not pass the censor: Winstanley reports that the *Rogue* "being too much smutty, would not be Licensed, so that he was fain to refine it, and then it passed stamp."[20] If what appeared in print is the refined version, then Head had a formidable acquaintance with life's seamy side.

On the other hand, the picaresque could be adapted to a family audience. Joseph Addison and Richard Steele were concerned in their pioneering periodicals to attract an audience wider than the literate aristocracy. Omitting the pornographic circumstances which Head included in the *Rogue*, Steele adapted the picaresque mode for one of his better-known issues of the *Spectator*, no. 11 of 13 March 1711. This paper shows clearly the picaresque influence, I would argue, in its exoticism, in its guise of "truthfulness" for what is essentially a piece of fiction, and in its aggressive central figure, here the businessman as rogue. As Steele puts it together, it is also an instrument of social criticism as *The English Rogue* was not. At this point the "rhetoric of representation" mentioned earlier might be employed. The story of Inkle and Yarico was enormously popular in Enlightened Europe. It was reprinted constantly, made into a most successful "opera" (more properly, a musical comedy) by George Colman the younger, and so on.[21]

Steele's narrator, the learned lady Arietta, informs her male visitor, who has been telling disparaging stories about women to her and to Mr. Spectator, that she has been "amusing my self with *Ligon's* Account of *Barbadoes*, and, in Answer to your well-wrought Tale, I will give you (as it dwells upon my Memory) out of that honest Traveller, in his fifty fifth Page, the History of *Inkle* and *Yarico*." The fact that Arietta (just recovered, according to Mr. Spectator, from "the serious Anger she was in,") is narrating this should alert the reader to expect Wayne Booth's "ironic reconstruction."[22] Notice also Arietta's emphasis on the truthfulness of this account; she even furnishes a page citation. Inkle, however, is entirely Steele's invention, as are almost all the details of plot.

> Mr. *Thomas Inkle*, of *London*, aged 20 Years, embarked in the *Downs* on the good Ship called the *Achilles*, bound for the *West-Indies*, on the 16th of *June*, 1647, in order to improve his Fortune by Trade and Merchandize. Our Adventurer was the third Son of an eminent Citizen, who had taken particular Care to instill into his Mind an early Love of Gain, by making him a perfect Master of Numbers, and consequently giving him a quick [i.e., lively] View of Loss and Advantage, and preventing the natural Impulses of his Passions, by Prepossession towards his [financial] Interests. With a Mind thus turned, young *Inkle* had a Person every way agreeable, a ruddy Vigour in his Countenance, Strength in his Limbs, with Ringlets of fair Hair loosely flowing on his Shoulders. It happened, in the Course of the Voyage, that the *Achilles*, in some Distress, put into a Creek on the Main[land] of *America*, in Search of Provisions: The Youth, who is the Hero of my Story, among others, went ashore in this Occasion.
>
> From their first Landing they were observed by a Party of *Indians*, who hid themselves in the Woods for that Purpose. The *English* unadvisedly marched a great distance from the Shore into the Country, and were intercepted by the Natives, who slew the greatest Number of them. Our Adventurer escaped among others, by flying into a Forest. Upon his coming into a remote and pathless Part of the Wood, he threw himself, tired and breathless, on a little Hillock, when an *Indian* Maid rushed from a Thicket behind him.

At the mention of an Indian maid American readers will immediately be reminded of the Pocahontas–John Smith story, which Steele might well have known. Ligon's *History* lacks the dramatic touch entirely. His protagonist is simply an English seaman, uncharacterized with respect either to beliefs or appearance.

> After the first Surprize, they appeared mutually agreeable to each other. If the *European* was highly Charmed with the Limbs, Features, and wild Graces of the Naked *American*; the *American* was no less taken with the Dress, Complexion, and Shape of an *European*, covered from Head to Foot. The *Indian* grew immediately enamoured of him, and consequently sollicitous for his Preservation: She therefore conveyed him to a Cave, where she gave him a delicious Repast of Fruits, and led him to a Stream to slake his Thirst. In the midst of these good Offices, she would sometimes play with his Hair, and delight in the Opposition of its Colour to that of her Fingers: Then open his Bosom, then laugh at him for covering it. She was, it seems a Person of Distinction, for she every Day came to him in a different Dress, of the most beautiful Shells, Bugles, and Bredes. She likewise brought him a great many Spoils, which her other Lovers had pre-

sented to her; so that his Cave was richly adorned with all the spotted Skins of Beasts, and most Party-coloured Feathers of Fowls, which that World afforded.

To make his Confinement more tolerable, she would carry him in the Dusk of the Evening, or by the favour of Moon-light, to unfrequented Groves and Solitudes, and shew him where to lye down in Safety, and sleep amidst the Falls of Waters, and Melody of Nightingales. Her Part was to watch and hold him awake in her Arms, for fear of her Country-men, and wake him on Occasions to consult his Safety. In this manner did the Lovers pass away their Time, till they had learned a Language of their own, in which the Voyager communicated to his Mistress, how happy he should be to have her in his Country, where she should be Cloathed in such Silks as his Wastecoat was made of, and be carried in Houses drawn by Horses, without being exposed to Wind or Weather. All this he promised her the Enjoyment of, without such Fears and Alarms as they were there Tormented with. In this tender Correspondence these Lovers lived for several Months, when *Yarico*, instructed by her Lover, discovered a Vessel on the Coast, to which she made Signals, and in the Night, with the utmost Joy and Satisfaction, accompanied him to a Ships-Crew of his Country-men, bound for *Barbadoes*. When a Vessel from the Main arrives in that Island, it seems the Planters come down to the Shoar, where there is an immediate Market of the *Indians* and other Slaves, as with us of Horses and Oxen.

To be short, Mr. *Thomas Inkle*, now coming into *English* Territories, began seriously to reflect upon his loss of Time, and to weigh with himself how many Days Interest of his Mony he had lost during his Stay with *Yarico*. This Thought made the young Man very pensive, and careful what Account he should be able to give his Friends of his Voyage. Upon which Considerations, the prudent and frugal young Man sold *Yarico* to a *Barbadian* merchant; notwithstanding that the poor Girl, to incline him to commiserate her Condition, told him that she was with Child by him: But he only made use of that Information, to rise in his Demands upon the Purchaser.[23]

This short narrative, picaresque in many of its aspects, becomes in Steele's hands a vehicle for satire of male arrogance, and an attack on a slaveholding society that treats humans as commodities, a market of blacks and Indians "as with us of Horses and Oxen." In the Schole–Wicks modal approach, picaresque is next to satire on the "spectrum of fictional possibilities."[24] In this case, the satire extends to *English* attitudes as well: on any conceivable human scale except that of power the rogue Inkle would be ranked below the "savage" Yarico. This is an example of what Charles A. Knight, in a recent essay, has termed "simple satiric nationalism," the satirist's use of supposed national characteristics to attack his own nation's shortcomings.[25]

At this point, with Steele and the *Spectator* in 1711, a "rhetoric of representation" becomes possible: enough is known about author, audience, printer, and publisher to flesh out the "sociology of the text" in a way quite impossible with Head's *Complaisant Companion*. By 1711 the picaresque was familiar to English readers of every capacity, by way of translations, periodicals, chapbooks, "novels"—that is, nugget fiction—and of course Head's and Kirkman's *The English Rogue*. The flood of criminal biographies, published separately and also in the periodicals, reinforced the association in the English tradition of rogue and criminality. Novelists could pick and choose: Defoe's *Moll Flanders* fits well into the picaresque mode.[26] Gay's *The Beggar's Opera* represents a, perhaps better *the*, use of the picaresque in drama.

Henry Fielding, an experienced hand in the drama and in periodicals before he turned to the novel, employed the genre of the criminal biography in *Jonathan Wild*, which is of course in the picaresque mode. Joseph Andrews, in the novel bearing his name, however, may best be seen as an exemplary character; Martin Battestin has argued that he is an exemplum of the virtue of chastity, like his biblical namesake.[27] Tom Jones, on the other hand, is cleverly cast by his creator as a rogue; the narrator finds himself obliged early on "to declare honestly, even at his [Tom's] first Appearance, that it was the universal Opinion of all Mr. *Allworthy's* Family, that he was certainly born to be hanged."[28] Although there is never any doubt in the reader's mind that Tom is a heroic character, he does suffer three lapses from chastity, each very much on his own initiative, and in the final sequence he finds himself in a London prison, apparently guilty of both incest and murder. The narrator affects to give up on the case of "poor Jones": "so destitute is he now of Friends, and so persecuted by Enemies, that we almost despair of bringing him to any good; and if our Reader delights in seeing Executions, I think he ought not to lose any Time in taking a first Row at *Tyburn*" (II, 875).

Our hero of course escapes a public execution on Tyburn tree and wins Sophia (Greek for "wisdom"). For the purposes of this essay, however, the important point is that Fielding was able by the 1740s easily to assimilate the traditions of criminal biography and the English picaresque, with its aura of criminality, into the comic novel. The picaresque mode had been domesticated. Samuel Richardson, in *Clarissa*, could draw on it as well, in very different but recognizable ways. Richard Head's rogue, in the guise of Tom Jones or Lovelace, had been thoroughly Anglicized.

Notes

1. Paul Julian Smith, "The Rhetoric of Representation in Writers and Critics of Picaresque Narrative: *Lazarillo de Tormes, Guzmán de Alfarache, El Buscón*," *Modern Language Review* 82 (1987): 88–108. Scholarship on the picaresque is of course vast. Dr. Smith's article and its footnotes conveniently summarize research on the Spanish picaresque, although from his somewhat polemical point of view.

2. Charles C. Mish has called attention to the importance and variety of these sources in the introduction to his *Short Fiction of the Seventeenth Century* (New York: New York University Press, 1963). See also John J. Richetti, *Popular Fiction before Richardson: Narrative Patterns, 1700–1739* (Oxford: Clarendon Press, 1969), who, obviously, begins his valuable study after Head's time, at the turn of the eighteenth century.

3. Donald F. McKenzie, *Buch und Buchhandel in Europa im achtzehnten Jahrhundert*, ed. Giles Barber and Bernhard Fabian (Hamburg: Ernst Hauswedell, 1981), 82. A modal rather than a generic approach seems better adapted to the heterogenous nature of the primary materials. I accept generally the argument of Ulrich Wicks in "The Nature of Picaresque Narrative," *PMLA* 89 (1974): 240–49, though I differ with him on some of his defining attributes. He and I are indebted, as he acknowledges, to Robert A. Scholes, "Towards a Poetics of Fiction: An Approach through Genre," *Novel* 2 (1969): 101–11.

4. Richard Bjornson, "The Picaresque Novel in France, England, and Germany," *Comparative Literature* 29 (1977): 124. See also Bjornson's *The Picaresque Hero in European Fiction* (Madison: University of Wisconsin Press, 1977).

5. Percy G. Adams, *Travel Literature and the Evolution of the Novel* (Lexington: University Press of Kentucky, 1983), 118; Michael McKeon, *The Origins of the English Novel 1600–1740* (Baltimore: Johns Hopkins University Press, 1987), 86–100.

6. *The Rogue; or The Life of Guzman de Alfarache*, trans. James Mabbe (London: Edward Blount, 1622). This sumptuous edition includes a commendatory poem to Mabbe by Ben Jonson.

7. See Peter Laslett, *The World We Have Lost Further Explored* (New York: Charles Scribner's Sons, 1984), 53–70.

8. The availability of criminal biography, in startling quantity, has recently been demonstrated by Lincoln B. Faller in *Turned to Account: The Forms and Functions of Criminal Biography in Late Seventeenth- and Early Eighteenth-Century England* (Cambridge: Cambridge University Press, 1987). It may be that the existence of this voluminous material influenced the English picaresque more in the direction of criminality than was the case with, say, the Spanish.

9. The bibliography of *The English Rogue* is very complex. A starting point is Strickland Gibson, *A Bibliography of Francis Kirkman*, Oxford Bibliographi-

cal Society Publications, New Series, vol. 1, fasc. 2 (Oxford: Oxford University Press, 1949). Text used is Folger Library copy, shelf mark 137325 which is London: for Francis Kirkman, 1668 [i.e., 1680], 2. Head's biography depends on a scattering of remarks made about him by Kirkman and John Aubrey (see n. 10), and on the account of his contemporary William Winstanley in *The Lives of the Most Famous English Poets* (London: H. Clark, 1687).

10. John Aubrey, *'Brief Lives' chiefly of Contemporaries, set down by John Aubrey, between the Years 1669 & 1696*, ed. Andrew Clark (Oxford: Clarendon Press, 1898), 305.

11. *English Rogue*, sig. π 3r.

12. Winstanley, *Lives*, 209–9.

13. W. R. Parker, introduction to reprint of *The Lives of the Most Famous English Poets* by William Winstanley (Gainesville, Fl.: Scholars' Facsimiles & Reprints, 1963), v.

14. Michael Shinagel, introduction to *The English Rogue* (Boston: New Frontiers Press, 1961), iii.

15. Charles C. Mish, *English Prose Fiction, 1600–1700: A Chronological Checklist* (Charlottesville: Bibliographical Society of the University of Virginia, 1967).

16. James E. Evans and John N. Wall, Jr., *A Guide to Prose Fiction in the Tatler and the Spectator* (New York: Garland, 1977).

17. See Roy M. Wiles, *Serial Publication in England before 1750* (Cambridge: Cambridge University Press, 1957). Lennard Davis, writing of a somewhat later period, says serialized fiction "was the predominant reading material for a good deal of the literate public": *Factual Fictions* (New York: Columbia University Press, 1983), 102.

18. Margaret Spufford, *Small Books and Pleasant Histories: Popular Fiction and Its Readership in Seventeenth-Century England* (London: Methuen, 1981).

19. Mish reports the first edition of that date, which he had not seen nor have I. I used an 1870 London facsimile by Edwin Pearson of the 1687 edition in the Folger Library.

20. Winstanley, *Lives*, 208; Aubrey, *Brief Lives*, 305.

21. See *The London Stage 1660–1800*, part 5, *1776–1800*, ed. Charles Beecher Hogan (Carbondale: Southern Illinois University Press, 1968), 2:910: "most popular musical comedy of the late 18th century."

22. I refer, of course, to Wayne Booth, *A Rhetoric of Irony* (Chicago: University of Chicago Press, 1974), 33–40. The honest traveler is Richard Ligon, *A True & Exact History of the Island of Barbados* (London: for Humphrey Moseley, 1657). In a somewhat unromantic detail not hitherto noted by scholars, Ligon relates (65) that the unfortunate Yarico removed "chegoes" [i.e., chiggers] out of his foot with a fine needle. Ligon's usage also antedates the earliest reference to those infamous insects in the *OED*.

23. *The Spectator*, ed. Donald F. Bond (Oxford: Clarendon press, 1965), 1:49–51. My paragraphing.

24. See n. 3.

25. Charles A. Knight, "The Images of Nations in Eighteenth-Century Satire," *Eighteenth-Century Studies* 22 (1989): 489–511. Martin Wechselblatt's recent essay, which sees the story as "an apology for mercantilism," seems mistaken from the outset, making as it does the familiar error of identifying Steele with his narrator; see Leslie E. Brown and Patricia Craddock, eds., "Gender and

Race in Yarico's Epistles to Inkle: Voicing the Feminine/Slave," *Studies in Eighteenth-Century Culture* 19 (1989): 197–223.

26. See Edward H. Friedman, *The Antiheroine's Voice: Narrative Discourse and the Transformation of the Picaresque* (Columbia: University of Missouri Press, 1987), 121–47. See also J. A. Michie, "The Unity of *Moll Flanders*," in *Knaves and Swindlers: Essays on the Picaresque Novel in Europe*, ed. Christine J. Whitbourn (London: Oxford University Press for University of Hull Publications, 1974), 75–92.

27. *The Moral Basis of Fielding's Art: A Study of Joseph Andrews* (Middletown, Conn.: Wesleyan University Press, 1959), 34–43.

28. References are to the standard edition of *The History of Tom Jones: A Foundling*, ed. Martin C. Battestin and Fredson Bowers (Oxford and New York: Oxford University Press and Wesleyan University Press, 1975), 1:118.

Translation and Cultural *Translatio*
JERRY C. BEASLEY

I want to confess at the very outset of this essay that I am no expert on the subject of translation. I know little about translation theory or practice—less, in fact, than some of those seventeenth- and eighteenth-century writers who so busied themselves with rendering works (including the Spanish picaresque novels discussed with such frequency in this collection) from a foreign language into their own. And those writers did not know much, or so it would seem if we measure their translations by the most sophisticated modern standards. Very often—and this seems to have been especially true of popular fiction of all kinds—they indulged their own taste or judgment or sense of the marketplace with great abandon, hesitating not in the least to rewrite and restyle, to condense originals by eliminating material perceived to be offensive or irrelevant to the experience or values of their readers, or to recast narrative shapes and re-create characters, using the mold of their own cultural beliefs or obsessions.

Such practices, I want to emphasize, were by no means limited to translators of fiction; one thinks immediately of Dryden's *Aeneid* and Pope's Homer. But it is nonetheless true that early European prose fiction, freely written as it was in the first place—without the powerful restraints imposed upon poetry and drama by long critical tradition—was frequently subject to the whims or revisionist impulses of translators. These whims and impulses ran to surprising extremes, as may be illustrated by reference to a pair of interesting examples, both from eighteenth-century England. In 1742 the prolific and versatile Eliza Haywood published her version of the Chevalier de Mouhy's imitation of Marivaux, *La paysanne parvenue* (1735–37), transforming the original story of an orphaned country girl's metamorphosis into a genteel lady by rewriting it in an English idiom and by injecting conspicuously English middle-class values and bourgeois morality, more in imitation of Samuel Richardson's celebrated *Pamela, or Virtue Rewarded* (published just two years earlier, in

1740) than in fidelity to Mouhy. Haywood's title, *The Virtuous Villager, or Virgin's Victory*, deliberately echoes Richardson's and thus much more than hints at her real allegiances, which were English rather than French. It also clarifies her writerly purposes, which were obviously more commercial than literary: What will sell after *Pamela*? Why, of course, tales of poor, innocent maidens catapulted into high station. Interestingly, Haywood's adapted version of Mouhy's narrative answered a more literal (but still loose) translation published anonymously in 1740, whose title (*The Fortunate Country Maid*) rather nearly approximates that of the original.

More than a decade later, at another extreme, Tobias Smollett published (in 1755) his long-delayed translation of *Don Quixote*. While remaining scrupulously faithful to the details of plotting and indeed to all other important features of the original narrative, Smollett departed deliberately from the sometimes strict literalness of recent translations by Peter Motteux, John Ozell, and Charles Jarvis. His aim, obviously, was to replicate as fully and as lovingly as possible the Cervantean comic spirit by giving it expression in a distinctively *English* but still reverential novelistic language—transcending lexicographical accuracy, as it were, so as to get even closer to the original than literalness could do. Many readers over the years have judged Smollett's translation the best ever completed. Carlos Fuentes, for example, in the foreword to a recent paperback reprint, describes it as an instance of that rare "clash between one great writer and another in which a foreign, a *strange* language becomes the authentic vernacular version." For Fuentes, Smollett's *Don Quixote* is most emphatically "the homage of a novelist to a novelist. It is a novelist's translation."[1]

I have paused over the two examples from Haywood and Smollett because they provide the outline of a general context within which we may understand some of the specific issues raised by translations of the picaresque. These issues I shall discuss briefly, and then go on to a second topic, closely related but (I think) more important, the impact of the picaresque on broader novelistic discourse throughout Europe but most especially in England—the "*Translatio*" of my title. Smollett is relevant again. In 1748, just seven years before the appearance of his *Don Quixote*, he published a similarly faithful and loving translation of Alain-René Lesage's *Gil Blas* (1715–35), surely the most celebrated of all works of French picaresque fiction and perhaps—simply because it is still so well known—the supreme example of the simultaneously imitative and transformative habit so common among writers of picaresque narrative. Smollett, as he acknowledged in the preface to his first novel, Roderick Random (also published in 1748), felt the influence of Lesage very deeply; and he understood very clearly the significance of Gil Blas as a purposeful re-creation of earlier picaresque tradition in response to new cultural conditions and changed literary, social, and moral values. He attempted a re-creation of his own in Roderick Random, which he actually wrote while the translation of Gil Blas was either being planned or was already underway.

But more of this later. Let us return for a moment to the subject of translation itself. The almost immediate popularity of the picaresque throughout western Europe may be measured in part by the great activity of translators beginning in 1561, when Lazarillo (1554) was first rendered into French; an English version followed in 1569, and a Dutch version a decade later. Part 1 of Guzmán de Alfarache, by Mateo Alemán, was translated into French in 1600, only a year after the appearance of its original Spanish edition. The first English version of both parts of Alemán's novel was published in 1622 by James Mabbe, who called it The Rogue. Mabbe, a flabby stylist, was nonetheless more faithful to his original than was common among translators at the time, and his care was rewarded by the continued popularity of The Rogue throughout the remainder of his century. His translation was, in fact, the primary source for Richard Head and Francis Kirkman, who paid it direct tribute by calling their own very popular work of 1665–71 The English Rogue. The honor of this homage was small, as Head and Kirkman reduced the model of Mabbe and Alemán to coarse vulgarity in their sensational, morally ambivalent story of Meriton Latroon, a common criminal. A second source for Head and Kirkman was Francisco de Quevedo's El Buscón of 1626—again a superior work, whose tightly controlled style and sardonic wit, sharply defined portrait of an aberrant character, and darkly earnest vision of a decaying society The English Rogue in no way approaches. The point here is that imitations—perhaps adaptations is a better word—like the one by Head and Kirkman register the enduring appeal of picaresque narrative. That, of course, is a commonplace, and does not need further elaboration here except by mention of a few extremely important titles: Sorel's Polyandre (1648), Scarron's Roman comique (1651), Grimmelshausen's Simplicissimus (1669), Defoe's Moll Flanders (1722), and, of course, Gil Blas and Roderick Random.

Translations, as opposed to imitations or adaptations, provide the most direct evidence—but, I believe, no more revealing or reliable for that—of the same appeal. Three Spanish works (*Lazarillo*, *Guzmán*, and *El Buscón*), together with Ubeda's *La pícara Justina* (1603), were variously rendered into Italian and German as well as French and English; the translations multiplied over the years, well into the eighteenth century. I should here repeat that it was the habit of early translators not merely to render but to "improve" the texts upon which they worked—much as Dryden and Nahum Tate (among others) engaged in another arena of literary activity during the latter years of the seventeenth century, "improved" Shakespeare. Everyone knows Dryden's *All for Love*, which rewrites *Anthony and Cleopatra* by forcing upon it the neo-Aristotelian unities of time, place, and action. Tate's *King Lear*, which imposes the doctrine of poetic justice and gives the tragedy a happy ending, is less familiar now but eclipsed Shakespeare's original for some 150 years after its initial production and publication in the early 1680s.

The widespread assumption that "improvement" upon originals was an acceptable—even highly appropriate—literary practice gave particular license to translators. Their work with picaresque narratives reflects dramatically an important part of the process by which the Spanish tradition was both continued and assimilated, re-created and finally absorbed into other literatures. Let me illustrate this point by reference to two works only: Alemán's *Guzmán* and Quevedo's *El Buscón*. Alexander A. Parker and others have observed that Jean Chapelain's rendering of *Guzmán* (1619) and Sieur de la Beneste's version of *El Buscón* (1633) significantly revise the style of Alemán and Quevedo, stripping both writers of their idiomatic elegance and digressive richness—qualities thought inappropriate to the story of a low-life character; and in any case, digressiveness violated the principle of unity, no less in a work of mere entertainment (the category into which *Guzmán* and *El Buscón* seem to have been placed by their translators) than in one of the highest seriousness.[2] The revisionist impulse extended greatly beyond style to enforcement of the just-emerging neoclassical literary values later articulated so emphatically by Rapin in France and Thomas Rymer in England, and adopted with such conviction by writers like Dryden and Tate.

The translations of Chapelain and La Geneste also blur the intense moral vision of their originals. Chapelain, like later translators of *Guzmán* (including Brémond and Lesage), so minimizes the religious feeling and the exercises of conscience of Alemán's protagonist as to undermine the context within which the fractured events of the roguish story accumulate to take on their most significant meaning as an indictment of an impious, decadent society. Lesage's version of the work (1732) follows Brémond's (1696) in suppressing nearly all evidence of Guzmán's moral agency, simplifying his character to that of an unregenerate outlaw whose escapades nevertheless end in the expectation of happiness, and leaving Alemán's original conception entirely altered. La Geneste reverses this process and re-creates Quevedo's Pablos, represented satirically in the original as a shamed and suffering example of unrelieved and unresolved criminality, into a merry adventurer married at last to the daughter of a rich merchant. Long passages—even whole chapters—are omitted so as to permit this redefinition of character. The ending—opening into dark nothingness as Quevedo wrote it—is revised to supply closure for what has become, in the hands of La Geneste, a conventional comic narrative.

These translations were regularly read in France and England, apparently without any awareness of the indignities inflicted upon the originals, which they obscured; they sometimes became the sources for subsequent translations. They may even have helped to generate the old commonplace eventually promoted so influentially by Frank W. Chandler early in the present century: namely, that "pure" picaresque fiction, defined by the great Spanish originals, is principally to be identified by its unrestrainedly episodic narrative pattern and its focus on low-life characters—rogues, vagabonds, and criminals; that the typical picaresque novel ends "happily," but lacks a moral vision and rejects idealism along with the kinds of *a priori* assumptions about human nature and the world necessary to it; that for these reasons the picaresque must be understood restrictively as a type of writing significant primarily for its incipient "realism" and for its appeal (eventually shared with a larger body of rogue narrative and criminal biography) to curiosity about that underside of existence generally neglected in polite literature.[3] This commonplace, accepted uncritically by Robert Alter in his widely read *Rogue's Progress* of a quarter-century ago, has since been reexamined but still not altogether repudiated by such critics as Alexander Parker, Stuart Miller, and Richard Bjornson.[4] My own earlier writings on the picaresque in *Roderick Random* have too easily accepted the critical cliché that in this novel Smollett set out to revise the entire tradition, to adapt it to his own times and his own satiric and didactic purposes, by "moralizing" it—when in fact he was responding very directly to *Gil Blas*, itself an adaptation.[5] I like to think that what I have had to say about *Roderick Random* remains worthwhile on the whole, and I know that the contributions of the other critics I have mentioned are certainly worthwhile, but I believe we have all helped to obscure crucial issues and prevent proper understanding—either by confining the picaresque within too narrow definitions of it as a genre (Alter, Bjornson—and Beasley); or by limiting its subject matter (Parker); or by isolating its devices taxonomically, but then being mystified by the way in which those devices sprawl out all over our narrative literature, right into the twentieth century (Miller).

A decade ago, in *The Myth of the Picaro*, Alexander Blackburn provided the beginnings of a way through the obscurity of critical contradictions and toward better understanding.[6] The way is announced in the very title of Blackburn's surprisingly neglected book, which elaborates Claudio Guillén's suggestion (in *Literature as System*, 1971) that the picaresque in fiction is no mere matter of place, or time, or devices of plotting, or character type, or language; that, rather, it is best apprehended through the mythology it articulates and structures—a modern mythology of the rebel outcast, the resourceful alien, the paradoxically isolated but brave individual who, buffeted by crazy circumstances, either yearns (or, significantly, sometimes does *not* yearn) for order to be wrought from chaos, who sometimes finds that order and sometimes does not. I will not speculate upon the seemliness of Blackburn's ease in discovering this mythology in nineteenth- and twentieth-century novels by such writers as Melville and Twain, Gogol, Conrad, Joyce, and Mann. Sometimes he leaves me doubting; he may go too far. In his treatment of eighteenth-century fiction he does not go far enough. The myth of the *pícaro* is submerged during this period in France and especially in England, he says, because it was overwhelmed and rendered unnecessary by the power of traditional systems of belief.[7] This is a provocative point, but it is also (I believe) wrong. I shall take it up again presently.

It will be useful first, however, to pause once more over *Gil Blas* and *Roderick Random*, with very brief glances at some other novels of their period, so as further to illustrate the cultural *translatio* by which the adaptable picaresque simultaneously helped to shape and was absorbed by the larger developmental movement of early modern fiction. Both *Gil Blas* and *Roderick*

Random reflect their times, their cultures. We should note in passing that these two novels appeared during the period in European intellectual history when Cartesian rationalism and Lockean empiricism held sway, provoking the skepticism of Berkeley and Hume along with the sentimentalism of Mme. de Lafayette, the benevolism of Shaftesbury, and, gradually, the individualist cult of sensibility anticipated by Wesley and Richardson and then alternately celebrated and scorned in the writings of Goldsmith, Sterne, Mackenzie, Goethe, and Laclos. Lesage and Smollett were extremely sensitive to all these conditions, though they responded to them quite differently.

Gil Blas, it may be said, is a sentimentalized version of the picaresque, unmediated by skepticism. Lesage, in his translation of *Guzmán*, reduced Alemán's original to an entertaining story of roguish adventure, and in conceiving his own picaresque hero he seems to have had the same reductive principle in mind. Gil Blas is a rascally, clever fellow who possesses a goodness of heart and soul that keeps him safe from the moral corruptions he encounters during his mercurial risings and fallings in a society that is ostensibly Spanish but really French. Richard Bjornson has remarked that Lesage was intent on appealing to the bourgeois tastes of a growing audience of middle-class readers hungry for tales of the familiar and for the vicarious pleasures of roguery, while he also meant to preserve aristocratic ideological assumptions.[8] The result is a division of sensibilities that, not surprisingly, reflects a similar division in contemporary French culture—a new social and political order was emerging in confusing challenge to the old. Gil Blas is a naturally endowed rationalist and a skillful narrator of his own tale, able to describe in great detail the characters he meets (noblemen, bishops, virginal maidens, shopkeepers, thieves) and the settings through which he passes (cities, villages, country estates, taverns, prisons). Here is his author's answer to the empiricist curiosity about specific time and place and about the means for authenticating records of experience. Questing for definition of his own identity, Gil Blas is resilient in the extreme but self-contradictory—he is, like society itself, full of ambivalence: alternately villainous and heroic, cruel and kind, morally corrupt and morally superior, supremely self-indulgent and effusively sympathetic. In the end, having many times narrowly (but inevitably) avoided the complete undermining of his own good nature, he marries a noble and beautiful woman, retreats to his recently acquired estate at

Lirias, and looks forward to a life of peaceful domesticity and quiet, philosophical reflection.

Gil Blas echoes the Spanish delight in roguery for its own sake and, more distantly, the satiric spirit of moral criticism found in *Lazarillo*, *Guzmán*, and *El Buscón*. But finally, great novel that it is, it trivializes the tradition from which it derives—by which I mean that it turns the picaresque into something like a romance of low life. The division of sensibilities by which Lesage mirrored (but without really seeking to interpret or to reconcile) the ideological, class, and moral tensions of early eighteenth-century French society runs very deep. His novel lacks a center of urgency, lacks the toughness of authorial conviction and the clarity of moral purpose that distinguish (especially) the works by Alemán and Quevedo. Smollett's *Roderick Random* is liable to some of these same charges. Like *Gil Blas*, it presents the autobiographical narrative of a good-natured young fellow thrown upon the world, where he is beaten, robbed, swindled, and abused, and where he often yields to and becomes complicit in the violence and corruption of a sordid environment. In the end, like Lesage's hero, Roderick marries a lovely girl (hers is a nobility of nature, not of birth) and settles happily on a country estate—in Roderick's case, it is his ancestral estate in Scotland. There is a similar division of sensibilities; Smollett was as attuned as Lesage to the fracturing of traditional order in the society reflected by the story his hero tells. Roderick is thrust roughly out of the genteel class into which he is born; exiled and outcast, he is a constant reminder of the debasement of that class and its aristocratic ideology. The rest of the world—its bureaucrats, professional men, shopkeepers, sailors, sharps, and fortune-hunters—is rarely any better or kinder; until the end when, after reaching his *nadir* in the Marshalsea Prison (an echo of Gil Blas's similar experience in the Tower of Segovia), Roderick is rescued providentially by his author and his inherent goodness is rewarded.

The resemblances between *Gil Blas* and *Roderick Random* are certainly obvious enough, but at last (I think) more superficial than real. Smollett's imagined world is insistently dark, much darker than that of Lesage, occasionally approaching the qualities and texture of modern absurdist narrative. It incorporates the grotesqueries of a nightmare existence—its people are often more animal than human, its streets and ships and prisons are foul and violent and dim and malodorous. Roderick's suffering as the victim of a society gone mad in all its chaotically dehumanizing confusion of moral and social values is genuine, and it is relentless; and the language of deep indignation and outrage in which he renders his suffering is so intensive (Damian Grant has called it "language as projectile"[9]) as to leave the reader off-balance: what does this world mean? just who is Roderick? and how is he to be understood? Such loss of balance never occurs for the reader of *Gil Blas*. Smollett clearly understood the difference between his novel and its model. In his preface, after affectionately acknowledging the influence of Lesage, he remarks provocatively that the

> disgraces of Gil Blas, are for the most part, such as rather excite mirth than compassion; he himself laughs at them; and his transitions from distress to happiness, or at least ease, are so sudden, that neither the reader has time to pity him, nor himself to be acquainted with affliction.—This conduct, in my opinion, not only deviates from probability, but prevents that generous indignation, which ought to animate the reader, against the sordid and vicious disposition of the world.[10]

This statement clearly signals Smollett's fiercely didactic intention, a departure from Lesage; and it further indicates his desire, worked out in the story that follows, to be more faithful to the examples of *Lazarillo*, *Guzmán*, and *El Buscón*, works he knew and mentioned several times elsewhere in his writings.

Roderick Random, like *Gil Blas* and like the two other novels by Smollett bearing close—if varied—resemblances to the early Spanish picaresque tales (*Peregrine Pickle*, 1751, and *Ferdinand Count Fathom*, 1753), adds an overlay of sentimentalism in developing its story of roguery and reward. The hero gets the beautiful girl, though it might be (and has been) argued that he does not deserve her. In Smollett's case there is the further overlay of providential vision—Christian, redemptive, transforming. This is more than a matter of mere literary convention. Smollett shared with Defoe and Fielding, both of them authors of works familiarly associated with the picaresque tradition in particular and with rogue biography in general (*Moll Flanders*, 1722; *Jonathan Wild*, 1743; and *Tom Jones*, 1749—Tom, we are told ironically, was "certainly born to be hanged"), a conviction that reality was harsh, cruel, and violently destructive to the individual moral life. He fantasized—in his novels, at the level of metaphor—about the possibility of a meaningful order imposed through the restoration of traditional moral and religious values, broadly conceived. Smollett represented reality with a particular ferocity born of an almost Humean skepticism—but empirically, in great detail and with remarkable precision; and he redeemed it at last by resorting to an expression of faith, not (as has sometimes been charged) to a shoddy exercise in self-delusion or to cheap manipulations of romance conventions. In other words, he did exactly what Defoe had done in *Moll Flanders*, what Fielding had done in *Joseph Andrews* and *Jonathan Wild* and would soon do again in *Tom Jones*.

Roderick Random is the most vigorously dramatic, most excruciatingly painful story of the outcast, isolated character to be found in mid-eighteenth-century British fiction. In this lies its most important relation to picaresque tradition. Smollett, a Scot, was extremely sensitive to his own status as stranger in a strange land. The echo of the *converso* issue as it appears to have affected Mateo Alemán is unmistakable. Smollett made his young hero a Scot, too, thus intensifying his identity as alien and, certainly not by accident, giving new focus and definition to the most pressing human issue of his time and the most familiar theme in the narrative literature of his period: the solitude of the dislocated individual caught in the midst of an indifferent and hostile world changing so rapidly that its center cannot hold. The lesson of so many eighteenth-century novels (English and French alike) is that every person is an exile. No easy comfort is to be taken from a traditional system of beliefs, however much one may yearn for such comfort, as that system may not survive—except, of course, in the grand Christian conception of human history. Late in the century, some writers and thinkers—Thomas Holcroft, William Godwin, Mary Wollstonecraft, Pierre Laclos (not to mention the French revolutionaries)—tried to ensure that certain social and political traditions *would* not survive.

It is a moot point whether *Roderick Random*, or Fielding's *Tom Jones*, or Defoe's *Moll Flanders* and *Colonel Jacque* and *Roxana* are truly picaresque fictions. In the strictest generic sense—if we must resort to that sense, so limiting—none of them is. More to the point is the fact that they are all stories of the outcast, and their deliberately episodic structures reflect a way of seeing the world that is very close to picaresque. Here I pause to emphasize (belatedly) what I suppose must always get emphasized in any discussion of the picaresque: that episodic plotting is one of its most important distinguishing features. I have written elsewhere of purposeful episodic design as an early fictional metaphor for life in a changing and chaotic world,[11] and I will not belabor the same point here—except to say that many of the novels mentioned in the present essay figure prominently in the other. Rather, I should like to return to Blackburn's argument concerning the myth of the *pícaro*.

I do not subscribe to Blackburn's notion that the picaresque virtually disappeared in eighteenth-century England, that it was submerged beneath the overwhelming weight of traditional cultural values, widely and confidently shared. If those values had been truly dominant, would Pope—who certainly believed in them—have had any reason to write the *Dunciad*? Would Swift have written *Gulliver's Travels*, or anything else? The tension between the traditional and the modern in these writers, as in so many others (including the novelists I have mentioned), is powerful, unmistakable, energizing, arguably *the* primary determinant of both form and meaning in their works. But Blackburn is, I believe, absolutely right about the picaresque as a mythology. We know that he was not the first to advance this argument. Guillén anticipated him, as I remarked earlier, and so did Bjornson, who characterized the *pícaro* as an embodiment of the myth of the "outsider."[12] What is original about Blackburn's conception is his greatest insistence that the myth, once it emerged fully articulated in sixteenth-century Spain, generated not a genre, but a mode, like satire, or comedy, or tragedy; not a strict form about which literary taxonomists might argue, but a vision and a sensibility leading to certain common structures—fragmented, inorganic, apparently disordered, episodic (to use the key word again)—serving to authenticate fictional records of real experience in the modern world.

In eighteenth-century Europe, and especially in England, the picaresque mode became important far beyond its capacity to inspire the occasional narrative still recognizable as a more or less faithful replication of its earliest articulations. The myth from which the mode was generated paralleled, sharpened, and in fact joined with other powerful myths as they defined themselves—the fable of beleaguered virtue, for example, or the myth of the pilgrimage: think of *Robinson Crusoe*, *Clarissa*, *Tom Jones*, and, of course, *Roderick Random*, all stories of virtuous characters exiled from their homes and in quest of redemption and restoration. The autobiographical impulse and the inherent individualism typical of the picaresque both as mode and as myth was consistent with, surely even reciprocal with, a continually growing interest in the writing and reading of memoirs, travels, and "lives" or "histories" (the eighteenth century's familiar words for biography).

Just when the picaresque lost whatever specific formal identity it once had and expanded to myth and mode is impossible to say—after the popularity of the three seminal Spanish originals was established, certainly, when the translators and imitators and adaptors got seriously to work. But it is not necessary to fix the date of this transformation. It is much more important to emphasize and to clarify anew what we already know and indeed have known for a very long time: that the picaresque, understood now as myth and mode rather than as genre, was almost infinitely adaptable throughout all the cultural shifts in the history of early modern Europe—as adaptable, really, as any of its chameleon protagonists; that in this period, very largely through the efforts (fair or foul) of translators and imitators *and* precisely because of such adaptability, it was absorbed, assimilated (but *not* submerged), and did not disappear—still has not disappeared; that it was therefore formative in an essential way to generations of European writers practicing a dizzying variety of narrative types, and that its example was in the end pervasive instead of merely distinctive and separate. To say all this, of course, is simply to acknowledge once again—as so many others have done before—that the picaresque helped to make the modern novel first a possibility, and then a reality.

Notes

1. Carlos Fuentes, "Foreword," in *The Adventures of Don Quixote*, by Miguel de Cervantes Saavedra, trans. by Tobias Smollett (New York: Farrar, Straus and Giroux, 1986), xiii.

2. Alexander Parker discusses these revisionist translations at length in *Literature and the Delinquent: The Picaresque Novel in Spain and Europe 1599–1753* (Edinburgh: University Press, 1967), chap. 5.

3. Frank W. Chandler, *The Literature of Roguery*, 2 vols. (Boston: Houghton Mifflin, 1907).

4. Robert Alter, *Rogue's Progress: Studies in the Picaresque Novel* (Cambridge: Harvard University Press, 1964); Parker, *Literature and the Delinquent*; Stuart Miller, *The Picaresque Novel* (Cleveland: Case Western Reserve University Press, 1967); Richard Bjornson, *The Picaresque Hero in European Fiction* (Madison: University of Wisconsin Press, 1977).

5. See my essay, "*Roderick Random*: The Picaresque Transformed," *College Literature* 6 (1979): 211–20; and my *Novels of the 1740s* (Athens: University of Georgia Press, 1982), chap. 4.

6. Alexander Blackburn, *The Myth of the Picaro: Continuity and Transformation of the Picaresque Novel 1554–1954* (Chapel Hill: University of North Carolina Press, 1979).

7. Ibid., 95–97.

8. *The Picaresque Hero in European Fiction*, 207, 209–12.
9. See Grant, "*Roderick Random*: Language as Projectile," in *Smollett: Author of the First Distinction*, ed. Alan Bold (London: Vision Press, 1982), 129–47.
10. *The Adventures of Roderick Random*, ed. Paul-Gabriel Boucé (Oxford: Oxford University Press, 1979), xliv–xlv.
11. See my essay, "Life's Episodes: Story and Its Form in the Eighteenth Century," in *The Idea of the Novel in the Eighteenth Century*, ed. Robert W. Uphaus (East Lansing, Mich.: Colleagues Press, 1988), 21–45.
12. *The Picaresque Hero in European Fiction*, 5–7.

From Duplicitous Delinquent to Superlative Simpleton: *Simplicissimus* and the German Baroque

GERALD GILLESPIE

Johann Jakob Christoffel von Grimmelshausen's quintessential Baroque novel *The Adventurous German Simplicissimus* now stands next to Sebastian Brant's *Ship of Fools* and the Renaissance chapbook *Faustus* as the best-known work of imaginative literature in German between the Middle Ages and the Enlightenment.[1] Since Grimmelshausen placed teasing clues to his own identity within the original five books of 1668 and wrapped these and the hastily appended "Continuatio" or book 6 of 1669 in layers of editorial and authorial masks, we might well suspect some Cervantine influence. Actually, although many picaresque works of Iberia—for example, the *Lazarillo, La Pícara Justina, Guzmán de Alfarache,* and *Rinconete y Cortadillo*—were available in German, there is scant evidence Grimmelshausen directly exploited the not yet fully translated *Quixote*, which his countrymen read mainly in French or the original Spanish. The connection resides in the enormous indebtedness of the French satiric and comic modes of the earlier seventeenth century to the Spanish disillusionistic and picaresque modes.[2] No less sagacious a reader than Isaac Newton's contemporary, the great polymath Gottfried Wilhelm Leibniz, a confirmed fiction addict, pointed out to his bluestocking friends that the then anonymous Grimmelshausen bore resemblance to the likewise still anonymous French author Charles Sorel.[3]

Translations of Spanish novels of roguery were so popular in France that the magician in Corneille's baroque comedy about life as theater, *L'illusion comique* (staged 1635), compared the transformations of the appealing artist–con man Clindor with those of Lazarillo, Guzmán, and El Buscón. The French direction for assimilating the picaresque was set by Sorel's *Histoire co-*

mique de Francion, published from 1623 to 1633. Influenced by Rabelais and by Cervantes, whom he admired and translated, Sorel countered the improbability of the romances with the commonplace, often vulgar, and scabrous realities of his own times. His antihero Francion, however, is endowed with inherent nobility of mind, and no ruling delusion about being a knight errant disconnects him from the normal world of France. It is in following his struggles to rise in society and find happiness despite his common origins that we witness the malice and hypocrisy of a corrupt world, where money-power is clearly a new, perverse, destabilizing force behind the scenes. Still fascinating for modern readers is the extent to which Sorel perceives the cities and courts to swarm with dubious and desperate pretenders, often fantastical intellectuals, who rub elbows with the aspirant Francion. At the same time, the novel remains primarily baroque in its generic concept and narrative principles.[4]

Sorel, who was of libertine persuasion and believed in natural worth and talent, fed the appetite of the ascendant bourgeois readership for success stories. Michael McKeon has shown a similar appeal of the Spanish patterns of picaresque narrative in the British seventeenth century, a time of widespread "status inconsistency."[5] The picaresque mode subserved both "conservative" and "progressive" responses, and well suited not just British authors attracted to creating fictions about upwardly mobile heroes, but also real-life British rogues desirous of shaping their own biographies for the public. Thus Grimmelshausen, reading Sorel in the German edition of 1662, found not only the techniques of satirical exposure preshaped in the contemporary novel, but also the sentimentalized rogue whose experiences connected all spheres of social life. Grimmelshausen may also have been influenced by the ground pattern in *Guzmán de Alfarache* when he decided to structure the original five books of *Simplicissimus* to conduct us to the revelation of the title figure's noble parentage, and thus underscore his falling away from and regaining of a higher nature.[6]

German readers of the baroque era, before paying heed to the first-person voice, were expected to puzzle over the frontispiece emblem, which Grimmelshausen himself probably designed. It has the standard tripartite structure so prized by seventeenth-century wit in its scrutiny of the world as book and theater. The *superscriptio* restates the curious title of the work we are about to fathom. The German term *abenteuerlich*, "adventurous," also connotes "quixotic, fantastic, wonderful," which with rich ironic potential the hero's name promises anything but what is "most simple." For in the *pictura*, it is a most unsimple composite monster who treads on the mask-strewn state of the world, itself a *theatrum emblematicum*, and points quizzically, with ambiguous gesture, at the plethora of emblems in the emblem book he holds in his hands. While we study the suggestive attributes of this beast who sports a cavalier's sword and a clown's grimace, we ponder the *subscriptio*. This epigrammatic poem is about wandering and erring through the world and its four elements, yet rising again as a phoenix and finally finding rest and peace of soul. French criticism would speak of a *mise en abime*, a dizzying, infinite self-reflection of the system of a work of art. This experience is familiar since the early sixteenth century when, for example, Il Parmigianino foregrounded his own hand, the instrument of artistic execution, in his *Self-portrait in a Convex Mirror*, or Giulio Romano, in building and decorating the Palazzo del Te, played upon the illusion of space in Renaissance painting and Renaissance assumptions about architectural functions. As an emblem about emblematic art, the novel's self-referential hieroglyphic frontispiece pushes beyond maneristic complication. It announces and ostentates baroque universality. Therefore we are missing the point if we look for some unity of character in the educational protagonist, according to Enlightenment or romantic organicist conceptions of personality. The vagaries of his journey and the sometimes grim naturalism of the disorders of the age he witnesses constitute materials for meditation and moral analysis.

Grimmelshausen's hero with a thousand faces, who will strip away masks and pretenses, appears to start life simply enough; and yet the novel's opening sentences, setting forth his peasant origins and his correspondingly rustic education, confirm an inevitable duplicity. The double consciousness of the matured Spanish genre inheres in the jesting first-person voice, which simultaneously conjures the picaresque malady at the heart of things and reenacts the rural idyll of boyhood innocence, disrupted when the Thirty Years' War intrudes its murderous fist. The speaker comes to life before our eyes with biographical immediacy in these opening paragraphs as the actor who will sin in the world theater, but his voice already resonates with the accrued wisdom of one who has graduated to the rank of a spectator and interpreter of temporality. Indeed, to judge by the elegant classical references so glaringly in contrast with his rude early circumstances, the speaker possesses impressive encyclopedic knowledge. The list of low-life types in paragraph one—straight from the urban squalor known to Lazarillo and El Buscón and effectively announcing a host of parvenu roles and encounters just over the horizon in the camps and cities—thus also functions unmistakably as literary quotation. Like López de Úbeda in the opening of *La pícara Justina*, the German author is inviting us to play mentally with the established motifs of picaresque literature.[7]

But the tone is inevitably different because Grimmelshausen conflates the story of delinquency with another powerful German tradition. His novel clearly opens with the thematics of the quester fool, popular since the printing of Wolfram's *Parzival* in 1477, the European vogue of Brant's *Ship of Fools* (1494), Erasmus's *Praise of Folly* (1505), and a host of other books. When ejected from the instable, representative paradise of country life into the turbulence of passion-wracked, strife-torn Europe, the very first refuge the boy seeks out is ambivalent. He flees from the disrupted garden cultivated by man into the wild forest, that dark place in the middle of human experience where Dante found himself, the labyrinth in which the exile must search for a pathway. In the woods, at the witching hour, terrified of the threat from the wolf of whom he has been warned, Simplex is saved, symbolically, by the hermit's pious hymn. At the close of the tale in book 5, this figure from medieval romance will prove to have been his father. As the boy has no known name, the elder dubs him Simplicius on account of his still intact "pure simplicity" toward the world (a genuine *sancta simplicitas*), instructs him in the fundamental catechism, and teaches him the mysterious code of letters for reading and writing. Both in the Bible and in Nature, Simplicius discovers the model Book. The hermit's woodland school, setting forth the primary order of spiritual truth, remains throughout the unimpeachable guide. So too does the earliest informed spiritual act, the work of art, the song as worship, a meaningful utterance that has been prefigured in Simplex's pipe playing as a shepherd lad, or Christ-figuration, in charge of the flock.

In *Simplicissimus* Grimmelshausen uses unspoiled nature to represent man's primeval innocence, and associates the distancing from nature through assimilation into human society with corruption, whereas in *Guzmán de Alfarache* Alemán lacks this pre-Rousseauian bias and is suspicious of nature as hostile to human purposes, as the source of our irrational passions, and as inherently deceptive in its appearances. On the one hand, Alemán seems closer to the principle of human self-definition in the world theater espoused by Baltasar Gracián in *El Criticón* (1619). For Gracián, the mission of art is to rival and outbid nature, and he champions the superiority of the achievements of civilization, the City over mere nature. On the other hand, Alemán's predominantly naturalistic, though satirical and disillusionistic, realism contrasts with Grimmelshausen's daring emblematic, visionary, and allegorical constructs. The German author seems to create an artifice closer in spirit to the principle of Baroque *ingenium*, the creative wit praised by Tesauro and Gracián. The elements of apparent hard reality or history in Grimmelshausen's work prove to be kaleidoscopic pieces of various puzzles, pieces subordinate to ingenious metaphors or conceits or unmaskings that establish a relationship of similarity between seemingly disparate phenomena.

On closer inspection, the original five books of *Simplicissimus* reveal a remarkable symmetry and circularity underneath the novel's superficially episodic character and rhythmic and generic shiftings. The main line of rising action from book 1 to book 3 takes Simplex from lowly, peripheral roles in society, by way of crime, cunning, and art, to the higher, prestigious spheres. The falling action sets in at the start of book 4 in Paris, the core of modern sophistication, and rapidly brings Simplex back to the lower depths and spiritual desperation, the need to choose, and actual conversion. The pilgrimage and discovery of his true origins and calling in book 5 balance the departure in book 1. Numerous features can be cited, in addition to the frontispiece, to support the contention that Grimmelshausen is aiming at a grand analogy to baroque theater with five acts, in which the spiritual nadir and worldly glory coincide as climax. Books 1, 3, and 5 are connected formally in that each contains a major visionary passage. This subgenre of the mirror exposing social ills derives mainly from the example of Quevedo's *Sueños* and makes its appearance in German around 1640 in Hans Michael Moscherosch's *Wondrous and Veracious Visions of Philander von Sittewald*, based on Sieur de la Geneste's French translation of Quevedo (1633). In book 1, the still innocent boy Simplex has a dream of the Tree of War, the antitree to that of life and salvation. In terms of the later European Bildungsroman, the social and imaginative complexity here is wholly out of keeping with the protagonist's stage of development. However, in baroque art, this terrifying vision represents both the truth of our access to spiritual insight and the lure of sin and the attraction to the power and violence exhibited by the pillaging soldiers.

In book 3, the daring self-made cavalier Simplex, who by this time is secretly both a published novelist and the masked bandit called the Green Huntsman, will meet the irenic fantast who thinks he is Jupiter. Some critics have suspected Cervantes' ingenious gentleman Quixote might have inspired the portrait of this would-be savior who is so entertainingly vexed over human folly. But more probably he is an avatar of the cracked intellects in the "théâtre du pédant" in book 4 of the *Francion*, where the crisis of intellect emerges as a nucleus of Sorel's work. In any case, Jupiter's brilliantly mad ideas on how to restore peace in Europe trigger Simplex's own dream of the Tree of Life, a sign of the deeper transformation running counter to his corruption. In book 5, in the Lake of Mummel chapters, we travel with the hero on a symbolic underwater journey to a kingdom that is a utopian antipode to the real one. Before retiring into hermitage, Simplex openly revels in satiric fantasy and universal exploration. In congruence with his arrival at anagnorisis, the converted *pícaro* has been lifted to a new status as a Christian humorist.

Books 2 and 4, mirrored as rising and falling action, similarly evidence Grimmelshausen's purpose in subordinating romanesque elements of plot to the larger symbolic pattern. In book 2, the simple fool Simplex grows into a clever fool and learns all about deception and appearances when, regarded as daft, he is literally thrust into the role of jester at Hanau. In cap and bells, like a Shakespearean fool, he must entertain a wayward society quite capable of making men mad. This is his early initiation into the social, religious, governmental, and military life of the Thirty Years' War seen from the rogue's perspective. The theme of the labyrinth comes to the fore, and Simplex hears dark prophetic hints from various quarters, most notably from the revered Heartbrother Senior. By observing with Simplex the drama of the conflict between the principled Heartbrother Junior and the unscrupulous Olivier, who ruins his rival, we are filled with cravings for further developments to resolve the oppression of the meek and the good so manifest in the society. These expectations are answered after the false triumph of Simplex who in book 3 gains the title of count, wealth, and a wife. Willy-nilly he has drifted into being a Duplicius. In book 4, Simplex-Duplex is still at a more elegant level as he travels to Paris as a tutor, finds out about contemporary intellectual passions such as alchemy, and rises meteorically to fame on the stage of the metropolis. His social triumph as an opera star in Paris is explicitly portrayed as threatened captivity in a dangerous labyrinth, specifically labeled the "Venus-Berg." Summoned to a love tryst by a masked lady of august rank, he flees the city with what he thinks is a dose of venereal disease. Ironically, it turns out to be chickenpox, disfigurement as a secret stroke of grace. Elsewhere I have argued that, when Simplex emerges from his many transformations as the Beau Aleman or handsome German in book 4, he is a Hermes figure and meant to be read hermetically—also that Thomas Mann came to appreciate him as such.[8] But Simplex is also a Christian Hermes. Book 4 reintroduces him to Olivier and Heartbrother Junior as his dark and luminous alter egos. The justifiable slaying of Olivier, who tries to indoctrinate him in hellish Machiavellianism, signifies the release of Simplex from the curse of crime.

It is not surprising that Simplex's innumerable roles give the novel the feeling of a masquerade. Because prudentialist philosophy regarded dissimulation as a necessary tool of wisdom in a world of deceit, the mask is also an expression of baroque aesthetics. Consequently, dissimulation means not only deception, which is morally problematic, but also irony. The discrepancy between the unknowing of the *dramatis personae* caught up in misunderstandings and the insights gained by the audience, once enlightened through ironic signals, constitutes one of the chief aesthetic stimuli of both the tragic and comic plays of this era. Simplex encounters and practices the intrigue and dissimulation we know from baroque high political drama, which flourished especially in Germany. In exploiting the ironic tension inherent in the split picaresque voice and in the self-exposed picaresque thematics of crime, Grimmelshausen's novel restates the principle of dissimulation. Negatively exhibited in Olivier as criminal hubris, it has its positive counterpart not only in the wisdom of sound guides like Heartbrother on the human level, but is manifested in the larger drama of history as the secret working of Providence. Providential impulses and opportunities bring about Simplex's ultimate reorientation to his true father. The clues and cues of Providence peek through the costumes and props of the world theater behind which God's plan is veiled. Simplex's salvation, as the hidden meaning that must be worked out, beckons to him through the sins and errors he commits.

There is no freedom in the sense of humanistic options; beyond the symbolic sanctuary in nature, the narrator's social world is not bound by an inherent morality or has ceased observing it. Society is suffering a drastic decades-long lapse, not unlike Simplex's own. The antihero's seeming lack of awareness of his own mortality as the threatened youth and wayward adult and the protean endlessness of his transformations as an actor in the world belong to a flood of phenomena of the Thirty Years' War that evidenced transitoriness. There is no consistent, overt, ethical-religious development as in the later Bildungsroman, because in baroque art the confrontation of the moment with eternity produces an instantaneous possibility that the infinite power can break through, once the soul makes its decision. Simplex also transcends the specificity of any one confession and becomes ambiguously an irenic participant in all forms of religion. Life is grasped in terms of metaphors (theater, chase, war, the Venusberg, etc.) because the experience of inconstancy, change, illusion, and life's emptiness is indeed the perception of being lost in the terms of some puzzle. Grimmelshausen builds into the texture of his novel several interlacing motivic systems, which, mainly by suggestion, reinforce the sense of the mysterious unfolding of a personal destiny within the unfolding of salvational history. These systems of reference blend as a kind of semitransparent jell binding together the disparate emblematic elements that, for today's reader certainly, often possess a convincing, naturalistic immediacy, even though the realist then roguishly takes us on symbolic special excursions of an obvious fairy-tale quality. Together, these esoteric trips constitute a game into which the reader is invited and by which the artist tries to link the humoristic-encyclopedic exploration of the human estate to higher cosmological and divine patterns.

In essence, the narrator's life is the story of the strange, new type of artist-intellectual produced by post-Reformation urban society. A dense network of numerological, cosmological, astrological, and mythological motifs connects this life to the religious and social crisis of the late Renaissance. As Aby Warburg showed in 1919 in his monograph on the role of ancient and pagan prophecy in art and literature at the time of Luther, there was widespread concern upon the outbreak of the Reformation over the possibility that a great and, for many, baleful conjunction of the planets, above all Jupiter and Saturn, had occurred in 1483 or 1484.[9] This was viewed as a turning point introducing a new epoch in Western religious development and/or an apocalyptic catastrophe. The fear of an Antichrist associated with the breakup of civilization was a prominent theme in Sebastian Brant's popular *Ship of Fools* in 1494. Although Luther himself rejected astrological thinking, other Protestants of note attempted to discern in their leader's horoscope—he was born at the time of the conjunction—the promise of revolutionary renewal because of his Jupiter-like qualities, whereas Catholic enemies interpreted Luther under the sign of Saturn as the incarnate monster of regression and disaster for civilization. Through humorous deprecation Luther tried to defend himself from the political harm of being identified as the emissary of Saturn, but the fear persisted. In 1524, for example, there was a significant new phase, the "Deluge panic," based on further projections from the earlier conjunction, and the rebels of the Peasants' War of 1525 were viewed as "children of Saturn" because of the symbolic connection of their class with the god. Limits of time exclude any detailed discussion of this important facet of late Renaissance culture, and it must suffice to note that Grimmelshausen's world was awash with learned and popular works on astrological and planetary signs. The twelve-part zodiacal correlations of ancient divinities and of the planets seem to be a less immediate source of references for Grimmelshausen than the seven-part treatments. In German Baroque literature, such predecessors as Johann Valentin Andreae had used the Chaldean series as the ground pattern of *The Chemical Wedding of Christian Rosenkreuz* (1616). In that narrative of mystical initiation, the soul ascends through seven levels during seven days, and the corresponding planets Saturn, Jupiter, Mars, Sun, Venus, Mercury, and Moon—with all their emblematic and figural connections—hold sway.

Günther Weydt, the pioneering investigator of Grimmelshausen's use of such planetary books as that by Georg Pencz, has suggested that the author of *Simplicissimus*, beginning with the disruption of the Saturnine country life in book 1, reordered the sequence of dominant orbs to bring the thematics of war to the fore.[10] Thus the waxing and waning planetary influences, overlaid upon the structure of a grandiose five-act drama, are those of Saturn, Mars, Sun, Jupiter, Venus, Mercury, and Moon in the original five parts of *Simplicissimus*, with the reassertion of Saturn in the *Continuatio*. The effect is, if we draw the structural implications from Weydt's thesis, that the climax of the narrative as drama is delayed and pitched somewhat past the middle, and therefore the rhythm of the novel better fits the recommendations in Lope de Vega's treatise on the *New Art of Making Plays* than a strict neoclassical arrangement. Such a rhythm also fits with the habit of German baroque playwrights, as Walter Benjamin has observed, to turn our attention to an absorbing new phase, personage, or subject in act 4 and to fashion act 5 into a virtually independent drama in its own right.[11]

According to Weydt's reading, the peaking of worldly entrancements, under the briefly reigning planetary influence of Venus, overlaps the end of book 3 and start of book 4 of *Simplicissimus*, and Mercury ascends to rule during most of the last two books of the novel. This shift into the mercurial is appropriate, since Simplex has clearly emerged by this time as a full-fledged Hermetic figure: thief, confidence man, actor, writer. Grimmelshausen demonstrably expands his first-person narrator's visionary function and capacity and sends him on totally magical journeys, including one beneath the surface of the waters, which ambivalently are those of the treacherous seas of fortune and of baptism. In an editorial closing remark to the *Continuatio*, the persona H. I. C. V. G. P. zu Cernheim notes that *Simplicissimus* is a work by Samuel Greifnson von Hirschfelt, as allegedly we can detect from mention of other works from his pen strewn as clues in the novel. Cernheim also deduces that the name German Schleifheim von Sulsfort, to whom the Dutch sea captain Ioan Cornelissen sends a memoire on the encounter with Simplex as well as the latter's manuscript, must be an acrostic for Samuel Greifnson von Hirschfelt. Because of a lucky archival find in the twentieth century, we now know that Grimmelshausen's name is behind all of these editorial personae. The many water signs and remarkable water episodes in the novel—at the Danube, Rhein, Sauerbrunnen in the Black Forest, Baden, the Lake of Mummel—also may hint at correspondences between the historical author and Simplex.[12]

What is all the more remarkable is that Grimmelshausen packs into his novel a myriad of details that function as a motivic network, usually invisibly, but sometimes are openly associated with the overarching planetary level. These motivic complexes of colors, things, occupations and classes, types of human activity, moments and states of nature and culture, ancient myths, and so forth, organize the baffling diversity of reality into manageable compartments. Grimmelshausen pilfers materials already organized in this way from sources such as the contemporary encyclopedias, and critics have identified certain major quarries like Thomas Garzoni's *Piazza Universale*. The baroque novelist's drive to attain universality unites the emblematic principle of the world grasped as the *mundus pictus*, the encyclopedic principle of inclusivity from the humoristic tradition, and the disillusionism of the baroque "world theater." If we apply the categories suggested by Herman Meyer and by Mikhail Bakhtin, we can legitimately claim Grimmelshausen exhibits the grand baroque climax of Renaissance forms. What Meyer describes as the "art of quotation" and Bakhtin as "polyphony" and "heteroglossia" is profusely evident.[13] Grimmelshausen's discourse admits the diverse particularity of actual speech, as heard by Simplex—various literary genres are tried out within the comprehensive comic framework and idio- and sociolects, regional dialects, the specialized vocabularies of religion, politics, warfare, the arts, and other realms jostle one another as elements incorporated in Simplex's own multilayered authorial voice. Although masked in anonymity for a couple of centuries, Grimmelshausen also conveys the sense of what Bakhtin calls "contemporaneity," because the author and the related events share the same time zone, and thus the reader, too, has immediate access to the discourse—in contrast to the epic in which events, whether real or imaginary, occur in an absolute past.

Closure has deep implications in *Simplicissimus*. As Frank Kermode, Northrop Frye, and many others have argued, the ground model for the problematics of closure and rebeginnings is the Bible with its succession of Testaments.[14] Squaring accounts as medieval culture founders and marking a rebeginning, Rabelais's five books of Gargantua and Pantagruel establish a new comic doctrine that redemptively opens into the future anywhere and whenever we imbibe the refreshing Pantagrueline sacrament. Sterne will attempt to reconstitute and modernize Rabelais's Pantagruelism, the ongoing, never finished discourse, as Shandyism. Midway between these comic geniuses, Grimmelshausen fashions out of the original novel *Simplicissimus* a never closing discourse he calls the "Simplician Scriptures"—a series of books that reexamine and expand from the core. The essentials of this act of reoverture can be grasped by looking at the *Continuatio* or attached book 6. How firm the resolution of book 5 sounds as a closing; Grimmelshausen literally intones in German the Spaniard Guevara's stern farewell to the vile world and nestles down in the woods with his heart and mind focused on his end, the necessary end of all things, and the end of the work, to which he sets the word *end* as the last word of the last sentence. Nonetheless, there soon follows the *Continuation of the Adventurous Simplicissimus or the Close of the Same*. To take this title literally, continuation necessitates reclosure, or closure is always tentative. Grimmelshausen underlines the salvational message of his novel by exploiting in book 6 the new story form of shipwreck on a paradisaic island in the midst of the dangerous remoteness of the farthest ocean, in the ambivalent watery element associated with Simplex.

Many later works of literature have so conditioned us that today we feel no surprise upon learning that the thief, con man, and self-styled author of fictions, Simplex, has left behind a spiritual biography and confession, inscribed on palm leaves, in the innermost retreat of the cave on his island from where the Dutch captain carries them back to Europe as a precious bequest. The primary story of erring and wayfaring is superseded on the island of book 6 by the announced form of the diary, the genre of interiorization.[15] This kind of mental exploration inevitably had to spring from the first-person voice of the high baroque, no matter how complex is its encyclopedic absorption of otherness. As the novel *Simplicissimus* unfolds, Grimmelshausen adroitly manages to transcend all sectarian boundaries with his ecumenical pilgrim. Simplex has been tutored by Protestant pastors of variant shading, has spoken favorably of the virtues of such extreme dissenters as the Anabaptists, has wandered with Heartbrother to the Catholic shrine of Einsiedeln where he undergoes conversion, explores the lands of heathen peoples, and reaffirms the image of his noble hermit father with Catholic aura, only to have his relics translated by Protestant seafarers. After the reaffirmation of hermitage in book 5, the newer universalism—despite all the entertaining episodes—will openly be that one associated with the acceptance of the immensity of the expanded world and cosmos and the interiorization of discourse.

In book 5, a major theme of the Lake of Mummel is man's ambivalent endowment with "curiosity." This itch to know begins to afflict Simplex in book 6 as he gazes at the world through his "Perspektive" or spy glass and listens to it through an ear horn. And these instruments of temporal perception, plus the efforts of the Devil, frantically increased, upon the disappointing news of the just concluded peace of 1648, lure the restless mind back into action. Of course, in chapter 5, Simplex directly reminds the reader: "What I'm presenting is a vision or dream . . . ; I mayn't rush so quickly to the end, but must bring in a few particularities and circumstances so that I may narrate more completely what I've in mind to communicate to people." After following a more familiar subject, the fortunes of some elegant travelers about France and England, and before entering into his own new and exotic adventures that carry us into just about every corner of the world of vicissitudes, Simplex also conducts us through the playful encounter with Soonother (Baldanders) in chapter 9. Through this key lesson on how to read the transformations of reality, the protean shifting that will last as long as the creation does, Grimmelshausen breaks any ordinary romanesque progression and teaches us to string the elements of narration on a thread of thoughts and visions and riddles.

Later chapters of book 6 are again replete with hermetic lore, and adventures of Oriental cast and location. The pilgrim Simplex wanders to the Near East, falls into Ottoman captivity, and is ransomed—all familiar subgeneric moments in contemporary literature of the Romance nations. But, homesick for Europe, he makes the symbolic wrong choice not to set out again for Jerusalem in thanks for this rescue and instead sails with a Portuguese ship bound around Africa for Lisbon. Here Grimmelshausen switches into the genre that we are to know centuries later as the Robinsonade. Shipwreck in the South Sea maroons Simplex with a sole companion, the Portuguese Simon Meron. After a dangerous trial by the Devil in the guise of a luscious Abyssinian woman, the two men set about the practical tasks of survival with great ingenuity. Their reconciliation after concupiscent rivalry exhibits the purest form of ecumenical community. Obtaining foods from nature, drinking palm wine, and devising clothing of animal, bird, and vegetable provenance, they eventually regress—as Simplex states—to the condition of the "first men in the Golden Age." Having outlived Meron, Simplex turns to intensive study of the island as part of the world book and transcribes the things of nature as spiritual memories and lessons. His mind is furthermore occupied with writing his own life story and confession. Fifteen years pass, and the sudden danger of outside reality intervenes with the landing of Europeans who may menace him. The wise Simplex traps this party in his immense cave, with its natural defense system, until he can assure himself they will pursue a peaceful course. Unafraid to remain and die alone in his garden, he eschews the opportunity of returning to Europe, as he believes this would again be a mistake, a rejection of grace. Simplex, who now prefers water and never gets sick, cures the sick. In return, the intruders give him European implements and supplies. The Dutch captain, amazed at the wonders in this natural kingdom of sanctity and the hermit's testimony, describes him thus:

> He was a tall, strong, well proportioned man with straight limbs, vivid fine color, coral-red lips, gentle black eyes, very bright voice,

and long black hair and beard peppered here and there with a few gray strands, the hair on his head hanging down over his waist and the beard down past his navel. He had covered his shame with an apron of palm leaves and upon his head was a broad hat woven of reeds and coated with rubber, which like a parasol could protect him both from rain and from sunshine. And for the rest he looked almost the way the Papists are used to portraying Saint Onofrium.

Right to the end, we hear in endless detail about the realia that are the marks of European existence, but the character of these realia somehow is altered and strangely profiled because they are now viewed against the backdrop of immense distances. Imaginatively, Grimmelshausen invokes the astonishing cosmographical spaces Europe has mapped, but at the same time he bears witness to the isolation of the soul, hearing itself speak far from the strife and cares of the homeland Europe. It reverberates from the world's periphery like a ghostly voice. These outer and inner dimensions of book 6 of *Simplicissimus* come to constitute a new orientation and genre in the novel, with prominent analogies in Britain. The tendency of Grimmelshausen's elaborate encyclopedic humor and conflation of genres at the end of *Simplicissimus* is toward the first-person tale told by a pseudopicaresque voice as in Defoe's *Robinson Crusoe*. This new species of voice will, in yet another sea change in the European novel, become that of Sterne's Tristram.

Notes

1. References to Grimmelshausen's novel will be by book and chapter following the edition of Alfred Kelletat, *Der abenteuerliche Simplicissimus* (Munich: Winkler-Verlag, 1956); the original edition of 1669, brought out by Johan Fillion in Mömpelgart, would read in English: *The Adventurous German Simplicissimus; that is, the Description of the Life of a Rare Vagrant, Called Melchior Sternfels von Fuchshaim, Where and in Which Guise Namely He Came into This World, What He Saw, Learned, Experienced and Endured in It, and Why He Quit the Same Again of His Free Will.*

2. On the reception of the Spanish picaresque in France and England, see especially Richard Bjornson, *The Picaresque Hero in European Fiction* (Madison: University of Wisconsin Press, 1977), chap. 7, "Translations and Transitions."

3. For a thorough treatment of this relationship consult Manfred Koschlig, *Das Ingenium Grimmelshausens und das Kollektiv: Studien zur Entstehungs- und Wirkungsgeschichte des Werkes* (Munich: Hanser, 1977), 45–89.

4. On the significance of *Francion* as a baroque antinovel that challenges literary tradition and probes its own fictionality, consult Martine Debaisieux,

Le procès du roman: Écriture et contrefaçon chez Charles Sorel, Stanford French and Italian Studies 63 (Saratoga, CA: Anma Libri, 1989). Debaisieux treats such major phenomena as textual monstrosity, masquerade, and doublings, but regrettably does not discuss the importance of Spanish fiction for the French baroque or mention Sorel's influence on Grimmelshausen.

5. See especially the section "Ideological Implications of Generic Models" in Michael McKeon's The Origins of the English Novel 1600–1700 (Baltimore: Johns Hopkins University Press, 1987), 238–55.

6. Cf. Hans Gerd Rötzer, Picaro—Landstötzer—Simplicius: Studien zum niederen Roman in Spanien und Deutschland (Darmstadt: Wissenschaftliche Buchgesellschaft, 1972), 96, 142–43.

7. Cf. my comments on La pícara Justina in Garden and Labyrinth of Time: Studies in Renaissance and Baroque Literature (New York: Peter Lang, 1988), 258–60 (in "Transformations of the Female Delinquent in Fiction").

8. See the chapter "Estebanillo and Simplex: Two Baroque Views of the Role-Playing Rogue in War, Crime, and Art (with an Excursus on Krull's Forebears)" in Garden and Labyrinth, 279–295. I agree with the view, argued in detail by Bruno M. Damiani in Francisco López de Úbeda (Boston: Twayne, 1977), that besides parodying the contemporary moralizing genre epitomized by Mateo Alemán's Guzmán de Alfarache, the Justina exhibits baroque complexity and introduces a witty literary referentiality that alters the more often somber, moralizing tone of the earlier Renaissance models out of which the baroque picaresque sprang, for example, Francisco Delicado's El retrato de la lozana andaluza. I also agree, as Damiani argues in Francisco Delicado (New York: Twayne, 1974), and Pamela S. Brakhage confirms in The Theology of "La lozana andaluza" (Potomac, MD: Scripta Humanistica, 1986), that the ironic, didactic, antiecclesiastical Lozana represents the Renaissance moment of the shaping of the picaresque narrative.

9. My comments on Saturn anxiety are indebted to Aby Warburg, Heidnisch-antike Weissagung in Wort und Bild zu Luthers Zeiten, Sitzungsberichte der Heidelberger Akademie der Wissenschaften, Philos.-hist. Klasse, Jg. 19, 26. Abh. (Heidelberg: Carl Winter, 1920); reprinted in Aby M. Warburg, Ausgewählte Schriften und Würdigungen, ed. Dieter Wuttke (Baden Baden: Valentin Koerner, 1979), 199–304.

10. On planetary symbolism, consult Günther Weydt, Nachahmung und Schöpfung im Barock: Studien um Grimmelshausen (Berne: Francke, 1968); and Klaus Haberkam, "Sensus Astrologicus": Zum Verhältnis von Literatur und Astrologie in Renaissance und Barock (Bonn: Bouvier, 1972).

11. Walter Benjamin, The Origin of German Tragic Drama, trans. John Osborne (London: NLB, 1977).

12. Weydt points to such details as the fact the great conjunction of 1524 was in the sign of Pisces, and argues the birth of Simplex or Melchior is datable by reference in the novel to the battle by Höchst to 22 June 1622 or shortly thereafter—in line with a great conjunction of Saturn, Jupiter, Mars, and the Sun in the house of the Moon and sign of Cancer. However, the title page of Grimmelshausen's Everlasting Calendar shows Pisces concealed in two places and an arrow locates the date about at St. Gertraud's Day or 17 March, a date mentioned by Simplex in connection with his year of testing in book 1, chapter 9. The Moon in the blazon of Baldanders, the protean comic monster who figures mutability in book 6, may transcribe the name "At the Silver Star," which Grimmelshausen's inn bore in real life. Through various other such

clues and numerological calculations in which the favorite number seventeen often plays a role, one can arrive at the hypothetical date of 17 March 1621 for Grimmelshausen's birth.

13. Herman Meyer, *The Poetics of Quotation in the European Novel*, trans. Theodore and Yetta Ziolkowski (Princeton: Princeton University Press, 1968); M. M. Bakhtin, *Rabelais and His World*, trans. Helena Iswolsky (Cambridge: MIT Press, 1968); idem *The Dialogic Imagination*, trans. Caryl Emerson and Michael Holquist (Austin: University of Texas Press, 1981).

14. Frank Kermode, *The Sense of an Ending: Studies in the Theory of Fiction* (London: Oxford University Press, 1968). Northrop Frye, *The Great Code: The Bible and Literature* (New York: Harcourt Brace Jovanovich, 1982).

15. I have touched on the connection between interiorization and ecumenical pilgrimage in Grimmelshausen's "pre-Robinsonade" in *Garden and Labyrinth*, 312–13, 318–20.

A Latin American Enlightenment Version of the Picaresque: Lizardi's *Don Catrín de la Fachenda*

NANCY VOGELEY

As I reflect on the transfer of a fictional form from imperial center to colony, from an authoritarian period to another historical moment beginning to tolerate questioning and diversity, I find A. A. Parker's work on the picaresque invaluable.[1] In Parker's translation of the term *pícaro* as "delinquent," he opens up an understanding of the mode's subject matter as transgressional behavior, as serious deviance rather than mischievous roguery. Parker's discussion of the eighteenth-century English and French novel directs critics interested in more modern versions of the picaresque to important changes in this literary rendering of delinquency.[2] In Parker's examination, for example, of Lesage's *Gil Blas*, the possibility of miscreance at the middle and upper levels of society is made apparent. And, although I do not agree with Parker's judgment that with works by Defoe and Lesage, "the picaresque tradition has moved away from a religious-moral preoccupation to humanitarianism and thus . . . it constitutes a literary world of lower intellectual and emotional significance,"[3] I believe Parker here rightly calls attention to fundamental changes in the genre as a result of Enlightenment thought.

The eighteenth century witnessed great changes in the language of vice and virtue. The Christian terms were being recast in several important ways. The *philosophes* in France, as Carol Blum has shown, helped in transferring the concept of virtue from the person of the monarch to the body politic by means of their advancement of republican values.[4] The "monkish virtues," as David Hume termed them, of celibacy, fasting, penance, mortification, self-denial, humility, silence, and solitude were being transformed by Hume into vices according to a category of social usefulness.[5] In the work of painters like Hogarth—or Greuze in France—such individual sins as alcoholism and profligacy were shown to have consequences for the social unit of the family.

Greuze's work, especially appealing to a growing bourgeoisie, demonstrates the way in which new communicative forms such as genre painting increasingly took over the function of the Church in spreading the message of morality. And the novel, which grew in popularity in France and England in the eighteenth century, was another communicative form whose images, through the story and the book illustrations, significantly extended the new standards of behavior.

Clearly, changing thought patterns and new art forms helped the cause of those Americans in the Spanish colonies taking up arms to declare independence from Spain in the first decades of the nineteenth century. The redefinition and politicization of the concepts of vice and virtue could serve to condemn Spain's actions during the period of colonial rule and thus justify the colonial revolt that many, even in the colonies, feared as their own crime against God and king. If Spain could be understood as evil, if the rights to the colonies could be shown to be the unjust claims of a tyrant who had gained control forcibly, then certain virtue attached to ending that evil. If a cultural product such as the picaresque novel, validated by tradition and accepted by the Spanish ruling classes, could be appropriated by a domestic elite, if the same literary structures utilized by powerful interests in the European context to represent and control their working classes could be adapted to express American interests, American writers and readers could begin to rethink the grounds for their oppression.

My aim in this essay is to sketch ways in which the picaresque mode with its Enlightenment complexities entered Latin America and affected literary production there. I draw my example of the Latin American picaresque from the first decades of the nineteenth century when a new social and political consciousness was beginning to develop in the American colonies of Spain, France, and Portugal as these pieces of empire in varying ways sought independence. European Enlightenment ideas transmitted through official and unofficial channels influenced American thought in this formative period,[6] so I believe it is useful to see how the new nations' first attempts at imaginative literature demonstrate imported topical debates at the same time they reveal original indigenous arguments. How the picaresque form, with its potential for describing negative behavior, came to colonial literature at a key moment in the region's history, and the way in which it authorized yet managed thought, suggest an ongoing dilemma in Latin America's decolonizing process. Both then and now, literary discussion of "vice" and "virtue," while it permits public discussion, nevertheless dictates the terms of that discussion. Implicit, not only in the text but also in the circumstances surrounding its publication and circulation, are the categories of thought and performance rules of the hegemonic culture.

In 1816, in the midst of Mexico's war of independence and at a moment of tight censorial control, José Joaquín Fernández de Lizardi published *El Periquillo Sarniento (The Itching Parrot)*, a work that most students of Spanish American literature recognize as the first Spanish American novel.[7] The novel had as its readership principally those *criollo* (European-blooded but American-born) citizens in Mexico City and outlying areas whose interests a new newspaper industry had begun to satisfy in the first decades of the nineteenth century;[8] in the *Periquillo*, Lizardi incorporated many of the elements of those early newspapers. Structurally, it is a picaresque tale of a *criollo* youth, educated according to the inferior colonial standards of the day and denied the real privileges of the Spanish elite, who recounts how, once his parents die and he spends his small inheritance, he experiences corruption and misfortune at all levels of the class structure. Interpolated along the story line are numerous moral and erudite discussions of seemingly nonessential subjects, which the colony's newspaper readers had come to expect in the newspaper format.[9] The voices of the repentant storyteller and Lizardi also break into the narrative line to explicate the moral meaning and correct any appeal the account of deviance might have. The *Periquillo* seems to have been a popular success when it was published, but it is also true that some contemporary critics found these digressions tedious and distracting.[10] The censors also must have found some political statement in this first novel of Lizardi's because they suppressed its last part on the grounds that its discussions of slavery and distinctions of birth were subversive.

Don Catrín de la Fachenda (roughly translated as *Sir Dandy from the Land of Vanity*), Lizardi's fourth novel and the one I shall discuss, tells essentially the same story as the *Periquillo*.[11] Both works at the moment of their publication seem to have been understood as conforming to a European picaresque tradition, and later criticism has generally agreed with that reading.[12] The *picardía* (delinquency or misbehavior) of the central characters has, without deeper study, largely been seen as a failure of education;[13] their story, a subterfuge for criticizing surrounding societal realities.¹⁴ My reason for singling out *Don Catrín*, a work that has lived for many years in the shadow of the *Periquillo*,¹⁵ is not to argue for a long-lost masterpiece but to uncover a powerful—and unresolved—historical dialectic in this superficially slight work. To a greater extent that the *Periquillo*'s, *Don Catrín*'s is a dark *picardía*, suggesting the thoughtful dimension of the disobedience of this generation of colonials; the book proves, I think, the wisdom of defining the picaresque according to its historically specific situation rather than as a generically immutable form transcending national boundaries and time periods.¹⁶

I

Don Catrín was probably written around 1819, but it was not published until the republican period in 1832. In his later novel, Lizardi is very consciously correcting mistakes he had been told he had made in the first novel; for example, he has his character begin the narrative with the following:

> No, no se gloriará en lo de adelante mi compañero y amigo el Periquillo Sarniento, de que su obra halló tan buena acogida en este reino; porque la mía, descargada de episodios inoportunos, de digresiones fastidiosas, de moralidades cansadas, y reducida a un solo tomito en octavo, se hará desde luego más apreciable y más legible; andará no sólo de mano de mano, de faltriquera en faltriquera, y de almohadilla en almohadilla, sino de ciudad en ciudad, de reino en reino, de nación en nación, y no parará sino después que se hayan hecho de ella mil y mil impresiones en los cuatro ángulos de la tierra.¹⁷

> (No, from now on my friend and companion *Periquillo Sarniento* won't gloat that his work found such a good reception in this kingdom; because mine, free of inopportune episodes, annoying digressions, tired moralities, and reduced to only a small little volume in octavo, will immediately become more appreciated and more legible; it will travel not only from one hand to another, but from city to city, from kingdom to kingdom, from nation to nation; and it won't stop until after thousands and thousands of copies have been made of it in the four corners of the earth.)

Thus, Lizardi relies on his readers' abilities to read the irony of Don Catrín's puffed-up sense of himself. By omitting the long, correcting passages of the *Periquillo*, Lizardi makes the readers' sense of how to read *Don Catrín* much more problematical. On the one hand, the character's exaggerated pride signals humor and suggests Lizardi is asking his readers to distance themselves from the ideas flowing from that point of view. But on the other hand, some of his speeches reproduce aspects of modern thought that colonial minds, in their increasing rejection of Spanish tyranny and awareness of specific internal needs, were beginning to take seriously. Therefore, I believe there is considerable ambiguity in the author's use of irony and that textual devices, such as allegorical names and the story's pious ending, are not to be trusted.

Masquerading behind the irony and the obvious colonial outrage over aristocratic privilege is an Enlightenment dialectic. Essentially, it is the struggle between Christian faith and ethics and traditional idealism, on the one hand, and materialist, utilitarian philosophies with secular underpinnings, on the other. Mexico, which had inherited a traditional religious belief structure from the colonial period, understood a cosmology in which a Christian God meted out justice in some afterlife. The doctrine of original sin was thought to curse men so that they needed discipline during their formative years. And charity, or love for one's fellow man, was thought to be the social ideal binding a society together.

Scholasticism had taught that truth, according to propositional logic, flowed from the working of the mind; it emerged as a result of the manipulation of words.[18] Theology was the queen of sciences, and colonial educational institutions, despite the occasional illustrious investigator,[19] throughout the eighteenth century generally insisted on the deductive method and obediently dispensed a curriculum laden with classical philosophy and orthodox theology. Indeed, colonial schools, distant from the centers of culture where scientific experiments and greater freedom of thought were altering intellectual discourse, characteristically emphasized memorization and mechanical recitation of standard arguments.[20] The circular language of these arguments usually failed completely to take into account the experiential realities of the colonies.

Yet eliminating that outmoded belief structure and epistemological faith threatened colonial thinkers uniquely. If they disallowed metaphysical presuppositions, they were left with the degraded realities of their colonial existence. If they called religious faith pious superstition and criticized the Catholic Church for backwardness in its teachings on revelation and the sanctity of tradition, they opened up a void that modern humanist, materialist philosophies had difficulty in filling. If, as one character argues to Don Catrín, the ideal of "honor" is only a word, what does a colony aspiring to independence base its civic life on? Most troubling of all would have been the question of justice because, if God's ultimate justice was not to be relied upon, if "eternity," too, is only a word, the evidence of colonial practice demonstrated that man-made legal systems were not to be trusted either. Therefore, Don Catrín, who held himself above the law of the land and who died unrepentant and denying God (even though a well-meaning Christian who witnessed his end says he did not), would have dramatized the dilemma of the modern colonial to those of Lizardi's readers sensitive to their historical situation.

Lizardi uses the language of fortune characteristic of the Golden Age picaresque to develop the story of Don Catrín. In a chapter heading, "En el que se verá cómo empezó a perseguirlo la fortuna y los arbitrios que se dio para burlarse de ella,"[21] he recalls earlier Peninsular forms of the novel; yet his message is clear that "fortune" for the nineteenth-century Mexican is not fate or providence; instead, it is a historical process that individuals set in motion.[22] Don Catrín is shown to bring about his own sorry end when he chooses to reject his elders' advice. Yet the "choices" of the Mexican *pícaro* are nevertheless demonstrably limited by colonial birth and opportunities for honorable work and success in the American field. If Don Catrín tries to live like the much-admired Mexican nobility and assumes the external signs of that class, such as rich dress and extravagant use of resources, as a *criollo* he does so without the economic base to sustain ostentation. If he seeks nobility in virtuous living, as traditional Christianity teaches, he must have recourse to the mental system, which colonial practice demonstrates yields no rewards, and new materialist philosophies tell him is only the false use of language.

There is nothing in Don Catrín's character to suggest that he is inherently bad; instead he appears as the product of his environment. His selfishness begins as the result of indulgent parents; his idleness originates in the attitudes toward work characteristic of his station in life; his blind pride also has its source in the *criollo*'s mistaken sense that title assures a person's worth. If, like Don Quixote, whose name and title the Mexican's ironically imitates, Don Catrín lacks *juicio* (judgment), this incapacity seems more a function of his colonial bewilderment as to what to believe than any inability to distinguish between reality and illusion. Indeed, at one point in the novel (chapter 8), Lizardi arranges a discussion between an old man, a clergyman (both creditable voices), and Don Catrín, to define the generic term *catrín*. The older men see *catrines* (dandies or fops) as responsible for the decadence and corruption of the period. Yet the exchange makes clear that those who dress according to the latest fashion are not all *catrines*, (ne'er-do-wells). Thus, Lizardi begins to question the scope and referential value of the term. However, at the most obvious level he makes this colonial imitation, this indiscriminate desire to keep up-to-date with foreign modes, symptomatic of the colonial problem.

Patterns in dress reflect patterns of thought; and whether one adopted a conservative or liberal stance at this moment of Mexico's development surely reflected allegiance to Spain and traditional values, in the first instance, or, in the second instance, espousal of modern ideas as propounded by France, England, the new American nation to the north, and related independence movements throughout Spanish America. Expressed negatively in the language of the period, faith meant fanaticism and the superstitious beliefs of women and the lower classes; modern thought connoted materialism, egoism, and the unconsidered approval of callow youths such as Don Catrín. Lizardi fictionalizes this historical equation of the *catrín* with the influence of European Enlightenment thought when he has Don Catrín describe (73) his picaresque education thus: "Me ilustré tanto"[23] And, in the midst of a group of traditional-thinking Catholics who are discussing the truth of the faith (73), Don Catrín enjoys his identity as an "espíritu fuerte" ("brave spirit") emboldened by "la ilustración de este siglo" ("the Enlightenment of this century").[24] In the following ironic defense of *catrines* (74), Lizardi invokes a truthful-sounding assertion that such behavior is to be found among the most noble, Christian, and enlightened members of society:

> ——Padrecito, modérese usted: los catrines son nobles, cristianos, caballeros y doctos; saben muy bien lo que hablan; muchos fanáticos los culpan sin motivo. ¿Qué mal hace un catrín en vestir con decencia, sea como fuere, en no trabajar como los plebeyos, en jugar lo suyo o lo ajeno, en enamorar a cuantas puede, en subsistir de cuenta de otros, en holgarse, divertirse y vivir en los cafés, tertulias y billares? ¿Acaso esto o mucho de esto no lo hacen otros mil, aunque no tengan el honor de ser catrines?
> Ahora ¿por qué se han de calificar de impíos e irreligiosos sólo

porque jamás se confiesan, porque no respetan a los sacerdotes ni los templos, porque no se arrodillan al Viático ni en el tiempo de la misa, porque no se tocan el sombrero al toque del Ave María, ni por otras frioleras semejantes?

(Dear Father, calm down: *catrines* are noble, Christian, gentlemanly and learned; they know very well what they are saying; many fanatics blame them without a motive. What harm does a *catrín* do in dressing decently, however that may be, in not working like plebeians, in gambling with his own money or his neighbor's; in wooing as many women as one can, in living off others, in relaxing, enjoying oneself and living in cafés, salons, and billiard parlors? Don't perhaps thousands more do this or much of this, although they don't have the honor of being *catrines*?

Now why are they to be called impious and irreligious only because they never go to confession, because they don't respect the priests or the churches, because they don't kneel before the viaticum or during Mass, because they don't tip their hat when the Ave Maria is sounded, or for other similar foolishnesses.)

Here Lizardi locates the *picardía* that most concerns him at the level of the upper and middle classes. In satirizing a ridiculous character such as the *catrín*, whose imitative behavior conveys the fascination of these classes with the latest foreign ways, Lizardi synecdochically—and indirectly—introduces the whole question of intellectual leadership and independent philosophical thought in the colony.

The picaresque narrative line in *Don Catrín*, therefore, develops the colonial ideological dilemma. The book proceeds according to a series of dialogues in which Don Catrín, at first, echoes the teachings of the Church on faith and morality because an inner voice constantly reminds him of what he learned from his uncle, an honest priest. However, his interlocutors, established *catrines*, argue the foolishness of such views. They hold up as civilized their amorous behavior with the ladies in polite society; they exult in their personal happiness as they realize their own ambitions at the expense of others; and they boast of the impunity they seemingly enjoy. Finally, Don Catrín silences his conscience and yields to their arguments. In his libertine existence he indulges in the behavior typically censured by a bourgeois society—drunkenness, idleness, gambling, and a common-law marriage. Unlike the Golden Age *pícaro* whose decision to steal food seems a spontaneous reaction to material deprivation, Lizardi's Mexican counterpart engages in semitheological/philosophical debate before abandoning himself to dissolution.

The mental process whereby Don Catrín becomes a *pícaro* traces the *criollo* predicament at this moment in Mexico's history. For example, Lizardi has one character indignantly describe a *pícaro* (45) as "sin ley y sin rey" ("without law and without king"). Once free of the restrictions Spanish colonial institutions imposed, Mexico was going to have to look elsewhere for standards of behavior; and an obvious source was the humanist philosophies being put forth in European capitals with a reputation for advancement in culture, such as London and Paris. Trying to convert Don Catrín to the new philosophies and playing on the colonial's sense of estrangement and inferiority (38),[25] a *catrín* argues: "tú tienes poco mundo y no conoces el siglo ilustrado en que vives" ("your world is small and you don't know the enlightened century you're living in").

By 1819 the retrograde policies of Ferdinand VII were causing many monarchists in the colony to consider republican concepts of government. And the institutional Church, even in the opinion of many faithful, had become so discredited that anticlericalism and secularism were rampant. A more acceptable movement many disaffected Mexicans turned to in order to satisfy their instinctual religious needs without sacrificing experimentation with foreign modernizing ideas was Freemasonry.[26]

Centrally placed in Lizardi's novel (70–72) is a list of ten rules for behavior, purporting to be the Decalogue of Machiavelli. A fellow *catrín* again is Don Catrín's instructor, and the special visual format of these ten commandments invites extra attention. At this point Lizardi partially guides his readers' reaction by having his character say that what many in fact do can be seen to be outrageous and offensive when spelled out. I cannot find this code in Machiavelli's major works; and in fact the rules are so baldly—and so badly—stated that I doubt Machiavelli formulated them as such. Lizardi says in a footnote that Machiavelli and then later "un falso político de Francia" ("a false politician from France") passed them on to the members of their sects, and that they were reproduced as the preface to a work by Albertus Magnus. Lizardi's scholarship here is clearly wrong; yet the attributions apparently rang true for contemporary readers. For them Machiavellianism was a key term in the discourse of the period, synonymous with political expedience and religious heterodoxy, if not atheism. Don Catrín's friend particularly calls attention to the precept that advises taking on the character of one's associates when it is useful. As he says (73): "dentro de pocos días era yo cristiano con los cristianos, calvinista, luterano, ariano, etc., con los de aquellas sectas; ladrón con el ladrón, ebrio con el borracho, jugador con el tahur, mentiroso con el embustero, impío con el inmoral, y mono con todos."[27] Machiavellianism, ironically formulated in Lizardi's book as a creed, meant an individual abandoned all creeds, a priori statements of truth and rules of conduct. A *catrín*, as Lizardi has his character argue at another point (64), would support heresy, "alegando la diferencia de opiniones que cada día se aplauden y desprecian."[28] Tolerance and sentimental love for one's fellow man would allow the *catrín* to excuse any manner of crime. It is clear, however, that behind Lizardi's parody were the very ideas of freedom of thought and mutual regard Mexico was entertaining for her independent future.

J. G. A. Pocock in *The Machiavellian Moment* has studied the way in which Machiavellian vocabulary affected political thought in the English-speaking world on both sides of the Atlantic in the eighteenth century. Particularly suggestive for my Enlightenment reading of Lizardi's picaresque novel is Pocock's discussion of the ways the terms *virtue* and *corruption* influenced republican concepts of individualism and capitalistic notions of self-interest. Machiavelli's political philosophy could be seen to have affected the development of the Florentine and Venetian republics in their respective periods of ascendancy; and these Italian republics, based on commercial values rather than on a religious organization of society and monarchical definitions of civic life, were historical models attractive to the nations in the Americas then in formation as the latter considered their own identity and plans for modernization. Eighteenth-century capitalism was rethinking Machiavelli's earthly philosophy of success and thereby interpreting aspects of it positively rather than negatively.

Some of the inversion of terms required by Machiavellianism or utilitarianism seems to have been acceptable to many Mexicans in the early nineteenth century. For example, newspapers of the period show that a spendthrift son who dispersed his father's fortune was commonly understood to be useful to society.[29] Actions that in themselves at one time had seemed sinful were now in the process of being reevaluated in terms of a larger good, a pragmatically justifiable end. The title of an 1810 loyalist pamphlet, *Males de la desunión, y utilidades que debe producir la confraternidad*,[30] also exemplifies how the anonymous writer at this revolutionary moment based his reasoning on the new philosophy rather than on traditional morality. Yet Mexicans appear to have had great difficulty incorporating Enlightenment notions of self-interest, which Machiavellianism put forward, into their national life. In the Mexican context, discussion of this concept generally employed the term *egoísmo* (egoism, selfishness) and attached negative connotations to it. In two newspaper articles of 1815, for instance, Lizardi identifies *egoísmo* as a philosophy whose many adherents believe in satisfying their individual passions at the expense of others.[31] In the first article, Lizardi's fictitious voices associate *egoísmo* with an uncaring monarch, a tyrant, or indeed any abusive authority: "Todo tirano es egoísta, y todo egoísta si tuviera autoridad y fuerza, fuera un tirano."[32] However, in the second article, the voices manifest a *criollo* sense that egoism is widespread in the population and that money, in various ways, is at the root of everyone's selfishness: "Casi siempre el dinero es el interés o el premio de las más de nuestras acciones buenas o malas."[33] The self-interest that Machiavellianism taught, then, is seen as a threat to the Mexican social fabric. Throughout the colonial period, despite an official Christianity, the colony had experienced much suffering as the result of social inequities. But if the common ideal to which men aspired, the commandment to love one's neighbor as oneself,[34] was replaced by a new lawlessness and matter-of-fact acceptance of greed, then many Mexicans foresaw an even worse situation.

The American intellectual predicament may be similar to that confronted by Europeans in the period. As previously religious societies became secular, a shift in the centers of power began to sow seeds of doubt and confusion among ordinary citizens. As feudal economic practices gave way to capitalism, the European peasantry began to feel the effects of seemingly impersonal market forces and the theoretical discussions of the intelligentsia. However, the American predicament, especially in the Spanish colonies, I shall argue, can be seen to be different. The religious character of the Spanish colonial enterprise had created an official loyalty based on the double notion of God and king. Consequently, any crime committed against the one automatically suggested an attack on the other; and, despite the declaredly religious language of the Mexican insurgency produced by such leaders as Hidalgo and Morelos, the concerns of faith complicated political action in the Spanish colonies in a manner that did not affect Britain's colonies.

Lizardi tells his readers that there are so many *catrines* in

Mexico because the problem is generational (50). Although Lizardi conceals any more explicit political statement, Don Catrín's religious and ethical dialogues bespeak the dilemma of the individual Mexican whose soul was in jeopardy if he participated in the collective crime of opposition to the Crown. Ecclesiastical authorities had made this clear in 1810 when they excommunicated for their treason Hidalgo and others who acted with him. Thinking colonials, however, could see the inappropriateness of religious punishment for a political crime; and they also were beginning to understand that the tyranny of religious beliefs depended on keeping the colonial childlike. As a friend of Don Catrín argues:

> El viejo rancio de tu tío te acosó a sermones, y por eso aún crees que te los echan después de muerto. Tú eres un tontonazo y te espantas como los niños con el coco; pero anímate, amigo, ensánchate; desprecia esas ilusiones del miedo; sábete que los muertos no hablan, y que en tu triste fantasía, agitada por tu miseria, se forman esos espectros de papel. . . . Gocemos de todos los placeres que están en nuestro poder. (69–79)

> (Your old uncle pestered you with sermons and that's why you still think he's throwing them at you after he's dead. You're a big fool and you get scared the way children do with the bogeyman; but get a move on, friend, broaden yourself, scorn those illusions of fear; learn that dead men don't talk, and that in your sorry fantasy, agitated in its misery, these paper specters are formed. . . . Let's enjoy all the pleasures that are in our grasp.)

Taught to be the *mono* (ape) of others—a phrase Lizardi uses here and elsewhere in his writings[35]—Don Catrín does not think for himself and learn from what he sees around him. He has no essential identity beyond that of an imitator. Deprived of any power to affect religious discourse, or indeed any other discourse emanating from European centers of control, the colonial historically had learned to gesture, to pay attention to symbols of obedience such as the correct use of language, and to invoke them in moments of crisis. Throughout his life, the individual colonial, who had internalized the voices of authority, heard their echo and suffered guilt when he transgressed; faced with death, the Mexican listened again to the words of the Catholic faith and was either comforted or horrified.

However, historical documents of the period show that Mexicans,[36] in attempting to end their dependent status and reach a collective maturity, increasingly were turning in their questioning of the instruments of imperial control to the *librepensamiento* (free thought) of the time as a prestigious alternative to Spanish Catholicism. In *Don Catrín*, however, Lizardi shows how accepting philosophical abstractions and linguistic concepts out of still another European experience is another manifestation of the *servilismo* (subservience) this generation of Mexicans was trying to combat. Lizardi dramatizes how Don Catrín, in listening to his friends and following their example (56), understands in a confused way the lessons of the European Enlightenment, perhaps because as a colonial he still only mimics its external signs. In seeking to acquire the veneer of civilization, he equates civility and gallantry with waste and debauchery. In *Don Catrín*, however, Lizardi also gives evidence of understanding the Enlightenment's profound challenge when he shows the logical extreme to which the decision to declare one's freedom leads. Once free, according to the thought of the period, an individual terminates all social obligations. He has no duty to a monarch—nor to his family and the poor around him. His only concern is to maximize his own earthly happiness. Clearly, this philosophical alternative, which Lizardi's picaresque story plays out, also presented problems for Mexicans dissatisfied with Spanish rule and anxious to create new definitions of social life.

II

Don Catrín can be understood as a fool. His disingenuousness, his gullibility are often the substance of comedy. In sophisticated metropolitan circles, the provincial who does not understand the concealed play of meaning among the instructed is often made the butt of jokes. In adapting the picaresque mode to the colonial condition, Lizardi shows that the colonial is vulnerable to such charges because of his intellectual indebtedness. The colonial's *picardía* is the result, not of naiveté or rebelliousness or willful disregard of authority, but of the conflict, felt personally and collectively, between opposing language constructs and inner needs, between sound and silence.

Roberto Fernández Retamar speaks of the American as Caliban, the brute slave who was robbed of his language by the Conquest and who uses the language of his master to curse him.[37] It is that perception of the American as a linguistic creature that I wish to extend to Lizardi's work. Fernández Retamar's linkage of colonial history and the psychosocial formation of the individual colonial opens up questions such as the degree to which the various classes in the American colonies were linguistically penetrated, or ideologically trained, and then the kind of language activity most cultivated by each class. Habituated by the colonial education system to the Spanish mind-set and professionalized in the legal, administrative, theological and educative work that made a business of words, the *criollo* class to which Don Catrín belongs would logically have been closer to the Spanish discourse system than those Mexicans of the lower classes who worked with their hands and who may have maintained their own Indian or African languages.[38] The *criollo* particularly would have had difficulty "cursing" Spanish usage—Fernández Retamar's term—because the character of his work prevented him from creating an original discourse with which to counter the dominant form.[39] Thus, although Lizardi's use of the picaresque mode must be seen to have provided an imaginative channel for dialogically exploring the Enlightenment set of terms, an alternative language of vice and virtue, at this key moment, it is clear that such borrowing was not a free choice. For various reasons the *criollo* still preferred a European system to one of his own making.

For years Europe had provided America with its own spiritual and intellectual vocabulary. The Mexican had learned to believe that any such level of thought required strict adherence to this European discourse, yet he increasingly was left with the conviction that what passed for knowledge usually failed to take into account the overwhelming materiality of his home existence. Surrounded by a natural world that challenged the European naming system and by social ills that demanded solutions—as well as by an oral world with which he was sometimes more familiar—the American in the first decades of the nineteenth century was beginning to learn through experience to distrust European knowledge and its working forms. Certainly the revolution in thought, which the Enlightenment particularly in France and England represented, introduced the American to an attitude of doubt and denial.

As if to illustrate this, at one important moment in *Don Catrín* (14ff.), Lizardi shows a nuanced understanding of knowledge ("las ciencias," the Spanish term suggesting an Enlightenment understanding of new scientific fields of inquiry). The priest/uncle is lecturing Don Catrín on the vanity of one man's aspiring to be completely wise in "teología, jurisprudencia, medicina, química, astronomía, ni en ninguna otra facultad de las que conocemos y entendemos."[40] In connection with his traditional-sounding lecture, he refers to Rousseau's *Discourse on the Arts and Sciences* in which the French philosopher demonstrates through logical proofs that knowledge is antithetical to the practice of virtue. The priest rejects this finding on the grounds that Rousseau, product of a superior education, misused his eloquence or skill with words; and the priest argues instead that knowledge and virtue are compatible. Lizardi's discussion, however, opens up in intriguing ways the question of knowledge for the colony. Was knowledge perceived there as the dazzling display of language, often regardless of false conclusions, by those who really knew the truth? Did the private thought of the Mexican intelligentsia, its special access to speculative activity, indeed affect lesser minds and harm the social order? If this was the case, then, did a concern for virtue—that is, a respect for certain fixed beliefs according to which the general population lived—override the publishing of any contradictory findings?

If an important aspect of the Conquest had been the despoliation of language, the struggle for independence meant fighting, not just militarily, but also linguistically against the preset usage that determined colonial thought. Lizardi gives evidence of this consciousness throughout *Don Catrín* as his character questions priests' sermons, the Gospel, legal strictures, and moral codes—words that signified the imposition of law and a loss of local and individual control. Colonial life had emphasized the need for law, yet the special privileges enjoyed by many were causing independence-minded Mexicans to examine the bases of these laws and the so-called reasons for exceptions. Significantly, Lizardi causes Don Catrín to pause in his exploration of a military career. The *catrines* momentarily convince Don Catrín (and those readers who are following Lizardi's argumentation) that a military officer who serves the king is not subject to the same laws as the civilian population (38–39). Taravilla (his name suggests vices of the town) then extends the exemption to the use of language: "diviértete al modo de los que llaman libertinos ... [así que] no haya virtud libre de tu fuerza, ni religión ni ley que no atropelle tu lengua."[41] And at another point (37), Lizardi emphasizes the soldier's freedom with language when he has Don Catrín say: "En pocos días me dediqué a ser marcial, a divertirme con las hembras y los naipes, a no dejarme sobajar de nadie, fuera quien fuera, a hablar con libertad sobre asuntos de estados y de religión, a hacerme de dinero a toda costa."[42]

In 1819, the date of the novel's supposed publication, the ongoing insurgency war would also have suggested to readers the ideological phraseology of alternative troops. These could not continue to be "unos serviles complacedores del gusto de los santuchos y moralistas rígidos," (39)[43] but instead they had to attack the language that perpetuated a corrupt system, as well as invent their own set of inspirational terms.[44] However, in the name of larger issues, intangibles that were being made known by their linguistic tags, both sides were terrorizing the Mexican population and destroying the country. Public opinion, the regard in which one was held, depended on the language usage of the particular set of friends one chose (Lizardi shows the polarization in Don Catrín's world by contrasting Precioso, Taravilla, and Tronera with Modesto, Prudencio, Constante, and Moderato).

The role of language in the colony's public discourse space, therefore, is a major concern in *Don Catrín*. As Lizardi makes clear in the following passage, Don Catrín's greatest sin is not his conduct but his blasphemous, impious use of language, his attack on sacred beliefs of the Catholic faith (24–25):

> Ninguna licencia le permite a usted el rey para ultrajar al paisano de paz, para atropellar su honor ni el de su familiar. . . . Sépase usted, amigo, que cuando comete estos delitos, sus cordones, sus charreteras, sus galones ni sus bordados le servirán de otra cosa sino de hacerlo más abominable a los ojos de los sabios, de los virtuosos, de sus jefes o de todo el mundo; porque todo el mundo se resiente de la conducta de un pícaro, por más que tenga la fortuna de pasar por un señor; en tal caso, sus superiores le desairan, sus iguales le abominan y sus inferiores le maldicen.
>
> Si cualquiera se hace aborrecible con estos vicios ¿qué será si a ellos añade el ser un blasfemo y un impío, que se produzca escandalosamente contra nuestra católica religión, religión la más santa, única verdadera y justificada? ¿No basta ser infractores de la ley? ¿Es menester destruir el dogma, burlarse de los misterios y hacer una descarada irrisión de lo más sagrado, a título de bufones, de necios y de libertinos?
>
> (The king permits you no license to offend the peaceful civilian, to ride roughshod over his honor or that of his family. . . . Be advised, friend, that when you commit these crimes, your aiguillettes, your epaulets, your military stripes, and your braid won't serve you for anything else but to make you more abominable in the eyes of the wise, the virtuous, your superiors, and everyone; because everyone resents the conduct of a *pícaro*, however fortunate he may be to pass

for a gentleman; in such a case, those above him will shun him, those who are equal to him will loathe him, and those beneath him will curse him.

If anyone becomes detestable because of these crimes, what will happen if to them are added being a blasphemer and an infidel, who emerges scandalously against our Catholic religion, the holiest of religions, the only one true and justified? Isn't it enough to be violators of the law? Is it necessary to destroy dogma, to laugh at the mysteries, and to make a shameless mockery of what is most sacred, under the guise of buffoons, fools, and libertines?)

Perhaps each age defines *picardía* according to what it most fears. In fictionalizing a world of competing language systems, where a discourse that is attacking a traditional one threatens anarchy and provides the individual with no consolation in the face of adversity or death, Lizardi expresses confusion, despair, and existential terror. In the preceding quote, the *pícaro*, whose rich and official clothes invite respect, is the Mexican who, in embracing the new thought, not only himself transgresses but also corrupts others. By acting out his philosophy, by verbalizing his personal belief in the public arena, the individual destroys the bases of society and sows unhappiness. The transformation of his private thoughts into deeds or words, which some might judge ridiculous and ultimately harmless, is indeed dangerous. Lizardi says that, although such a character may appear disguised as a buffoon, a fool, and a libertine (and thus he hints at his own fictional strategy), the *pícaro* may also be a person of high rank and/or profound thought (and here Lizardi only speaks through his invented story) whose deviance is serious.

Lizardi's novel textualizes the author's understanding of the importance of public opinion in an evolving nation, and of the public places and spaces where discourse is susceptible of change. Cafés, the *alameda* (promenade area), the theater, the Masonic Lodge were only some of the new secular areas where the members of the upper classes increasingly came in contact with one another; the lower classes might still continue to meet in the *pulquerías* (taverns where *pulque* was consumed), the jails, the streets (81, 87). Yet the military encounters—as well as the new popular literary forms such as the newspaper and the novel—also were bringing Mexicans together under circumstances that challenged the older order.

Lizardi as the first Latin American novelist, therefore, in intervening in this new public space was himself a kind of *pícaro* in giving voice to such a deviant persona and concretizing through his writing the possibility of oppositional thought.[45] If philosophical questions had been the prerogative of only a few philosophers and theologians in the past, the novel writer now introduced some of the same questions, albeit vulgarized, to a broader and more diverse section of the population. Earlier theoretical formulations were now subjected to the probings of colonial minds, increasingly aware not only of pragmatic concerns and material realities,[46] but of the language in which theoretical formulations were couched. Lizardi's use of the pen name "El Pensador Mexicano" ("The Mexican Thinker"), therefore, stands revealed as the declaration of his own thoughtful role—as well as that of his reader—in the new society.

III

Censors of Lizardi's day were apparently taken in by *Don Catrín*'s apparent adherence to orthodoxy, for they gave the following approbation on 20 February 1820: "La vida y hechos de D. Catrín de la Fachenda con las notas del Pensador americano es un jocoserio con que se ridiculiza a los viciosos merecedores de este epíteto por su vida libertina, deduciendo una sana moral con que arreglen sus sentimientos y deberes a los de la religión."[47] Yet, despite the approval, Lizardi did not publish the book during his lifetime.[48] Jefferson Rea Spell, who has written what must be the best of the slender accounts of Lizardi's life, suggests only that, because freedom of the press was reinstituted shortly thereafter, Lizardi no longer needed the indirection of novel writing but instead could devote himself almost entirely to the direct statement of political pamphlets and journalism.[49] It is only my conjecture that Lizardi postponed the book's publication because he judged the more philosophical and less conclusive ideological struggle, apparent in *Don Catrín*, inappropriate for public discussion in a nation that had just been born. It is also true that Lizardi was suffering considerable personal distress during those years as a result of the specific actions and policies he had advocated; in 1821 he was jailed several times and in February 1822 he was excommunicated, a ban that was not lifted until December 1823.

Notes

1. Alexander A. Parker, *Literature and the Delinquent: The Picaresque Novel in Spain and Europe (1599–1753)* (Edinburgh: University Press, 1967).

2. Ibid., chap.5; Jenaro Taléns in *Novela picaresca y práctica de la transgresión* (Madrid: Ediciones Júcar, 1975) takes issue with Parker's translation of *pícaro* as "delinquent" if it leads Parker to conclude that the *pícaro's* behavior is "dishonourable and anti-social" (quoted in Taléns, 21). Taléns concedes that this may be so, but that the *pícaro* is forced to be this way. However, Taléns's use of the term *transgression* throughout his discussion of the picaresque appears to indicate that he shares Parker's view of the individual and his troubled relation to society. Taléns also questions Parker's exclusion of the *Lazarillo de Tormes* from the category of the picaresque and Parker's inclusion of eighteenth-century French and English works (23). Taléns doubts that LeSage's *Gil Blas* belongs to the genre.

3. Parker, *Literature and the Delinquent*, 110.

4. Carol Blum, *Rousseau and the Republic of Virtue: The Language of Politics in the French Revolution* (Ithaca: Cornell University Press, 1986), 23–36.

5. *Enquiries Concerning the Human Understanding and Concerning the Principles of Morals*, ed. L. A. Selby-Bigge (Oxford: Oxford University Press, 1902), 268, 270, quoted in Parker, *Literature and the Delinquent*, 133–34.

6. Typical of studies of Enlightenment influence is Jefferson Rea Spell, *Rousseau in the Spanish World before 1833: A Study in Franco-Spanish Literary Relations* (Austin: University of Texas Press, 1938; repr., New York: Octagon Books, 1969), in which he traces the influence of specific authors such as Rousseau by means of Inquisition documents, book trade lists, and the visits of Americans abroad or foreigners in the colonies. Spell's focus on a doctrine like popular sovereignty particularly helps in understanding the impact of Enlightenment thought on the political leaders of American Independence. However, a work such as that by Bernabé Navarro, B. *Cultura mexicana moderna en el siglo XVIII* (México: UNAM, 1964), in its focus on Jesuit thought, tends to overlook any influence on them from French or British Enlightenment thinkers and instead makes their modernizing thought appear to be either a product of long-existing Renaissance humanism or their independent scientific interests. Also valuable are the collections by Arthur P. Whitaker, ed., *Latin America and the Enlightenment*, 2d ed. (Ithaca: Cornell University Press, 1961); and A. Owen Aldridge, ed., *The Ibero-American Enlightenment* (Urbana: University of Illinois Press, 1971).

7. E. Anderson Imbert, *Historia de la literatura hispanoamericana*, 3d ed., vol. 1 (México: Fondo de Cultura Económica, 1961), 185; Fernando Alegría, *Historia de la novela hispanoamericana*, 3d ed. (México: Ediciones de Andrea, 1966), 16; Luis Alberto Sánchez, *Proceso y contenido de la novela hispanoamericana*, 2d ed. (Madrid: Editorial Gredos, 1968), 108; Jean Franco, *An Introduction to Spanish American Literature* (London: Cambridge University Press, 1969), 34.

8. Nancy Vogeley, "Mexican Newspaper Culture on the Eve of Mexican Independence," *Ideologies and Literature* 4 (second cycle) (Sept.–Oct. 1982): 358–77. For *criollo* consciousness, see Francisco López Cámara, *La génesis de la conciencia liberal en México*, 2d ed. (México: UNAM, 1969), particularly the "Primera Parte." Although *criollos* were to be found at all class levels, they largely comprised the middle class. For an excellent description of the *criollos* who turned to intellectual activity because of their marginalized position, see Luis Villoro, *El proceso ideológico de la Revolución de Independencia*, 2d ed. (México: UNAM, 1977), 26–29.

9. Nancy Vogeley, "Defining the 'Colonial Reader': *El Periquillo Sarniento*," *PMLA* 102 (1987): 784–800.

10. Alfonso Reyes discusses early reactions to the *Periquillo* in "El Periquillo Sarniento y la crítica mexicana," in *Obras completas* (México: Fondo de Cultura Económica, 1956), 4:169–78.

11. See John Pawlowski, "'Periquillo' and 'Catrín': Comparison and Contrast," *Hispania* 58 (1975): 830–42.

12. José Mariano Beristain de Souza, censor in Mexico City, cataloged Lizardi thus in 1816, *Biblioteca hispano-americana septentrional*, vol. 2 (México: Instituto de Estudios y Documentos Históricos, 1816; repr., 1981), 191: "Ha escrito varios *Discursos* morales, satíricos, miscelaneos con los titulos de *Pensador megicano*, y de *Alacena de Frioleras*: y tiene entre los dedos la *Vida de Periquito Sarniento*, que según lo que he visto de ella, tiene semejanza con la del *Guzmán de Alfarache*." ("He has written various moral, satirical, and miscellaneous *Discourses* with the titles of *Mexican Thinker* and *Cupboard of Foolishness*: and he is presently working on the *Life of Periquito Sarniento*, which according to what I have seen of it, bears a resemblance to the *Guzmán de Alfarache*"). Luis González Obregón, *Don José Joaquín Fernández de Lizardi (El Pensador Mexicano). Apuntes biográficos y bibliográficos* (México: Oficina Tip. de la Secretaría de Fomento, 1888), 60, quotes Sr. Olaguibel (n.d.) with respect to *Don Catrín*: "Considerada bajo cierto aspecto esta novela, del género picaresco, pequeña pero bien escrita, ella sola sería bastante para hacer muy apreciable el nombre de su autor" ("Considered according to a certain aspect this novel, of the picaresque genre, short but well written, alone would be enough to make the name of its author very respectable"). Jefferson R. Spell in "The Intellectual Background of Lizardi as Reflected in *El Periquillo Sarniento*," *PMLA* 71 (1956): 414–32, is typical of the prevailing picaresque view of Lizardi's first novel: "From even a casual reading of the *Periquillo*, it is evident that the Spanish picaresque novel characterized in general by its marked contrast of roguery and ethics served Lizardi as a model. The organized band of beggars in the *Periquillo* (III, 160–59) recalls similar groups of rascals in *Rinconete y Cortadillo*, in *Guzmán de Alfarache*, and in *Día y noche de Madrid*.... The seed from which the *Periquillo* sprang was Spanish; the soil that gave it life and coloring was Mexican" (430).

13. See Jefferson R. Spell, "The Educational Views of Fernández de Lizardi," *Hispania* 9 (1926): 259–74.

14. See Spell, "The Historical and Social Background of *El Periquillo Sarniento*," *Hispanic American Historical Review* 36 (1956): 447–70.

15. I do not wish to become embroiled in the debate as to which is the better work since judgments depend on what artistic criteria one chooses. Robert L. Bancroft in "El 'Periquillo Sarniento' and 'Don Catrín de la Fachenda': Which Is the Masterpiece?" *Revista Hispánica Moderna* 34 (1968): 533–38, concludes that the shorter *Don Catrín* is formally the more artistic work. Pawlowski, "Comparison," also seems to prefer *Don Catrín*. Paul W. Borgeson, Jr., "Problemas de técnica narrativa en dos *novellas* de Lizardi," *Hispania* 69 (1986): 504–11, considers *Don Catrín* "lo mejor de Lizardi" ("the best of Lizardi"). For Anderson Imbert, *Historia*, 187–88, *Don Catrín* is "la obra maestra de Lizardi" ("the master work of Lizardi") primarily because of its excellent use of irony.

16. For an excellent review of picaresque scholarship, see Ulrich Wicks, "Picaro, Picaresque: The Picaresque in Literary Scholarship," *Genre* 5 (June 1972): 153–216. Wicks identifies two approaches, labeling them "historical"

and "ahistorical." Also see his recent book, *Picaresque Narrative, Picaresque Fictions: A Theory and Research Guide* (Westport, Conn.: Greenwood Press, 1989).

A historically or geographically specific concept of Spanish American picaresque is introduced by Luis Leal, "Picaresca hispano-americana: De Oquendo a Lizardi," in *Estudios de literatura hispanoamericana en honor a José Juan Arrom*, ed. Andrew P. Debicki and Enrique Pupo-Walker (Chapel Hill: University of North Carolina Press, 1974): 47–58. In arguing that the picaresque emerged in the New World at the same time as in Spain, Leal does not explore what the character of the Conquest may have been to cause both the oppressor and the oppressed cultures to produce this form. María Casas de Faunce, *La novela picaresca latino-americana* (Madrid: Cupsa, Planeta, Universidad de Puerto Rico, 1977), reviews the history of the genre in Latin America, helpfully updating it to 1962. She does not draw any conclusions about its special pertinence for the area and its development.

17. Jefferson R. Spell, ed., *Don Catrín de la Fachenda y Noches tristes y día alegre*, 2d ed. (México: Editorial Porrúa, S.A., 1959), 3. However, the edition Spell prepared for Editorial Cultura, México, 1944, is valuable for its textual notes, which are missing in the Porrúa edition. I have translated the text here and throughout my study.

18. See Pablo González Casanova, *El misoneísmo y la modernidad en el siglo XVIII* (México: Colegio de México, 1948); John Tate Lanning, *Academic Culture in the Spanish Colonies* (1940; repr., Port Washington, N.Y.: Kennikat Press, 1971), esp. chap. 3. For an overview of the primary system, see Dorothy Tanck Estrada, *La educación ilustrada (1786–1836): Educación primaria en la ciudad de México* (México: Colegio de México, 1977).

19. Typical is the generally excellent review by Rafael Moreno, "La filosofía moderna en la Nueva España," *Estudios de historia de la filosofía en México* (Mexico: UNAM, 1963), 145–202. Moreno tends to focus on figures like Sor Juana Inés de la Cruz, Carlos de Sigüenza y Góngora, and the circle of Jesuit scholars.

20. Perhaps the best record of the effect of this colonial education on the average university student is that to be found in the pages of Lizardi's *Periquillo*.

21. "In which it will be seen how fortune began to pursue him and the means he employed to fool her."

22. In an article "Discútese sobre lo que se llama fortuna de pícaros y en qué consiste ésta, entre Claudio y Benito" ("What one calls the fortune of *pícaros*, what it consists of, is discussed between Claudio and Benito"), published in his newspaper *Cajoncitos de la Alacena*, 16 September 1815, Lizardi raises the same question. "Fortune," or the apparently favorable visitation of luck, is shown to be the result of the lucky person's craftiness *(maña)*. Claudio, who is honest and poor, bemoans the fact that many in Mexico unjustly enjoy wealth and noble privilege; Benito offers the alternative Christian term *providence* to explain the distribution of differences and finds his solution in the traditional argument that virtue is rewarded and one should not envy a *pícaro*'s ill-gotten "fortune."

23. "I became so enlightened."

24. Julio Caillet-Bois discusses Lizardi's use of this French term in the introduction to his edition of *Don Catrín* (Buenos Aires: Editorial Universitaria, 1967).

25. The question of the psychological makeup of the colonial is complex. Albert Memmi studies the phenomenon in *The Colonizer and the Colonized*, trans. Howard Greenfeld (Boston: Beacon Press, 1965) and in *Dominated Man* (Boston: Beacon Press, 1968). See also O. Mannoni, *Prospero and Caliban: The Psychology of Colonization*, trans. Pamela Powesland, 2d ed. (New York: Frederick Praeger, 1964). For the identity of the *criollo* in Mexico, see Elsa Cecilia Frost, *Las categorías de la cultura mexicana* (México: UNAM, 1972). Particularly in chapter 2 she discusses the question of the imitativeness of Mexican culture in terms of "dependency" or "reflection."

26. Stanley Green, in *The Mexican Republic: The First Decade 1823–1832* (Pittsburgh: University of Pittsburgh Press, 1987), chaps. 4 and 6, discusses the important role of the Masonic Lodge in Mexican politics and popular thought of the period; he gives the date of the Lodge's appearance in Mexico as 1806.

27. "in a short space of time I was Christian among Christians; Calvinist, Lutheran, or Arian with those of those sects; a thief with thieves; a drunkard with a drunk; a gambler with a cardshark; a liar with a deceiver; irreligious with the immoral; and an ape of them all."

28. "alleging the difference of opinions, which each day are applauded as well as scorned."

29. See the unsigned article in the *Diario de México*, 6 November 1806.

30. *The Wrongs of Disunion and the Useful Returns That Confraternity Must Produce*.

31. "Las sombras de Heráclito y Demócrito," "Refútase el egoísmo, y trátase sobre las obligaciones del hombre" ("The Ghosts of Heraclitus and Democritus," "Egoism is refuted, and the obligations of man are dealt with"), in *Obras, Periódicos*, ed. María Rosa Palazón M. (México: UNAM, 1970), 4:229–47.

32. Ibid., 244. "Every tyrant is an egoist, and every egoist if he possessed authority and force, would be a tyrant."

33. James C. McKegney found a copy of the second number of "Las sombras de Heráclito y Demócrito" in the British Library, and it is published in his "Dos obras recién descubiertas de Lizardi," *Historiografía y bibliografía americanistas* 16, no. 2 (1972): 193–200.

34. *Don Catrín*, 21.

35. Ibid., 73; see also "Sobre una manera interesante" ("On an interesting subject"), *El Pensador Mexicano* (16, 30 December 1813), published in *Obras*, ed. María Rosa Palazón and Jacobo Chencinsky (México: UNAM, 1968), 3:253–75, where Lizardi writes: "España es el mono de la Francia, y la América el mono de la España" ("Spain is the ape of France, and America the ape of Spain"). However, in the same article Lizardi finds value in the American's capacity for imitating without having been formally instructed.

36. Typical is the language of the "Acta solemne de la Independencia de la America Septentrional," in which the Congreso de Anáhuac (6 November 1813, Chilpancingo) declares Mexican independence: "El Congreso de Anáhuac ... declara solemnemente ... que por las presentes circunstancias de la Europa ha recobrado el ejercicio de su soberanía, usurpado; que en tal concepto, queda rota para siempre jamás y disuelta la dependencia del trono español" ("The Congress of Anáhuac ... solemnly declares ... that on account of the present circumstances in Europe it has recovered the exercise of its sovereignty [which had been] usurped, and that accordingly, dependence on the Spanish throne has been broken and is dissolved forever"), in *Morelos, Antología documental*, ed. Carlos Herrejón (México: SEP, 1985), 140.

37. *Calibán, Apuntes sobre la cultura en nuestra América* (México: Diógenes, 1971).
38. See Shirley Brice Health, *Telling Tongues: Language Policy in Mexico, Colony to Nation* (New York: Teachers College Press, Columbia University, 1972). In Heath's generally excellent study, she shows (esp. in chap. 3) that, despite decrees from the court that Indians be taught Spanish, in fact most still spoke their native tongues until well into the eighteenth century and later.
39. I owe much of my thinking here to Diane Macdonell who in *Theories of Discourse: An Introduction* (Oxford: Basil Blackwell, 1986) discusses three notions developed by Michel Pêcheux (39-40). According to "identification" the docile subject accepts the dominant discourse; "counteridentification" describes the process whereby an antagonist refuses the terms of the discourse, yet bases his refusal on those terms; "disidentification," which is most difficult, requires that the individual disengage his identity completely from the dominant discourse and work actively to combat the ideology implicit in it. Many Mexican *criollos* in the early nineteenth century appear to have been struggling with this process.
40. "theology, jurisprudence, medicine, chemistry, astronomy, or in any other field that we have knowledge of and that we understand."
41. "Enjoy yourself in the style of those who are called libertines [so that] ... there may not be a virtue exempt from your force, nor a religion or law that your tongue doesn't revile."
42. "In a few days I devoted myself to being military, to enjoying myself with the ladies and at cards, to not letting myself be put down by anyone, no matter whom, to speaking freely about matters of state and religion, to making money at all costs."
43. "servile pleasers of the whims of the sanctimonious and rigid moralists ..."
44. However, Villoro, in discussing the direction provided the insurgency by members of the local clergy, shows their motivation to defend their downtrodden Indian parishioners to be anything but Enlightenment thought (85). Villoro thus demonstrates the ideological complexity of the insurgency movement.
45. Here I am mindful of Harry Sieber's important study, *Language and Society in Lazarillo de Tormes* (Baltimore: Johns Hopkins Press, 1978), in which he argues that the story plays out the *pícaro*'s discoveries about language and the book's writing confers status on the basically oral narrator. I find some of the same structure in *Don Catrín* that Sieber discovers in the *Lazarillo*; but whereas Sieber considers the sixteenth-century work as a "semiotic project" and understand historical and sociological concerns to be secondary, I judge the latter paramount in explaining the importance of language in both the making of the text and the book.
46. Today's liberation theology in Latin America shows this same need to incorporate material considerations and a desire for praxis into a religious belief structure. See Samuel Silva Gotay, "El pensamiento religioso," *América Latina en sus ideas,* coord. Leopoldo Zea (México: Siglo XXI and UNESCO, 1986), 118-54.
47. "The Life and Deeds of Sir Dandy from the Land of Vanity with notes by the American Thinker is a tragicomic tale with which the depraved persons who deserve this epithet are ridiculed. A healthy moral is deduced by which to arrange their sentiments and duties to those of religion." Quoted in Jefferson

R. Spell, "The Life and Works of José Joaquín Fernández de Lizardi" (Ph.D. diss., University of Pennsylvania, 1931; repr. University Microfilms), 33.

48. In 1822, at the end of one of his political pamphlets, ("Hemos dado en ser borricos y nos saldremos con ello," México: Imprenta del Autor), Lizardi announced his intention to publish *Don Catrín*; in fact, he said he had enough subscribers for an *imprentita* (small private run).

49. Ibid., 33.

Don Picaro: Lord Byron and the Reclassification of the Picaresque

JEROME CHRISTENSEN

I

Critics disagree on the vitality of the picaresque after 1800. Some say that the genre died out with Smollett's *Roderick Random*, which, according to Harry Sieber, is an "already disintegrated picaresque novel." Some say that the picaresque survived into the modern era as theme or myth.[1] According to both historical and thematic accounts, the picaresque gives way to the novel, which succeeded the picaresque temporally and comprehends it generically. For Mikhail Bakhtin the novel displays many of the traits that have traditionally characterized the picaresque, but in the novel a disintegrative form has been somewhat magically transformed into a progressive one.[2] So complete is that transformation that the novel can be said to have forgotten the picaresque; it defines itself instead against the epic and by means of a series of sweeping oppositions. For Bakhtin the novel is to the epic as the present is to the past, as the open to the closed, as the vulgar to the heroic, as the relative to the absolute, as the voice to the image, as the living to the dead. The epic stands in a space absolutely removed from the world in which the novel lives and speaks; it remains useful primarily as a kind of stereotype against which the conceptual and existential autonomy of the novel can be confirmed. At the same time, however, the novel—no respector of protocol—continually crosses the conceptual gap that the epic has instituted between it and the living world in order to touch and degrade the epic image, that is, to novelize it. The novel is simultaneously committed to the preservation of the ideal type (here called epic) and to its continual degradation. The novel wants both to ruin ancient monuments and yet to retain what Byron in *Childe Harold* 4 calls their "immaculate charm."[3]

The historical and thematic definitions of the picaresque ally with Bakhtin's version of the novel in their shared failure to take seriously the process of disintegration that each posits as central. The sociohistorical perspective regards the disintegration of the picaresque as concluded, whereas the thematic perspective classifies disintegration on a continuum of categories that runs from romance to satire.[4] Both approaches put disintegration under glass, regard it as something safely distanced by the passage of time or by the hygiene of formalization. Novelization, although ostensibly more dynamic, is in fact equally limited, for the novel is imagined as that genre which can degrade but which cannot be degraded. The novel can touch the epic, but by definition the epic cannot touch the novel. If we render this relation in terms of Frank Chandler's characterization of the "main business" of the rogue, which is "to obliterate distinctions of *meum* or *tuum*," we can see that the novel's development reflects the aggrandizement of *tuum* by a universalizing *meum*, which, in Bakhtin goes by the name of the present, of the "contemporary as such," and of "plasticity itself."[5] "Life belongs to me," states the novel. "Disintegration and ruin belong to what was once you"—whether that "you" is named "epic," "picaresque," or "Madame Bovary."

One name for that ruined *tuum* in Byron's corpus is "Childe Harold," whose career as a character in the series of poems that bears his name exemplifies the dynamics of novelization. From the second edition of *Childe Harold's Pilgrimage*, Byron complained of the public's refusal to credit his distinction between poet and character. Readers melded the two and identified with the product. The distinction between poet and character is only one of many failed boundary lines in *Childe Harold* 1: there is the territorial line between Spain and Portugal, the moral line between the British and the French, the gender line between Spanish men and women, and, most dramatically, the historical line between the wars of the chivalric past and those of the contemporary era. The obliteration of distinctions makes impossible the kind of war that the touring poet would like to see as well as the kind of poem he would like to make. When Byron returns to Spanish themes in *Don Juan*, he places the blame for this bad modernity where Bakhtin would agree it belongs, on that great novelizer Cervantes, who "smiled Spain's Chivalry away," thereby negating the conditions for heroic performance on the Iberian peninsula and on the British page (canto 13, stanza 11).

The development of the *Harold* series can be gauged precisely by Byron's prefatory remark to the last canto that "there will be found less of the pilgrim than in any of the preceding, and that little slightly, if at all, separated from the author speaking in his own person." The fact is, the poet adds, 'that I had become weary of drawing a line which every one seemed determined not to perceive" (2:122). The obliteration of the distinction between poet and character identifies a synthetic *meum*, the cultural figure named "Byron," to which the writer, under the pressure of his public, surrenders. Capitulation though it be, the collapse of distinction wonderfully produces the "surplus"[6] sufficient after Waterloo to aggrandize the ruins of Rome to the imperial *meum* of a system of representation called British literature.

The novel's aggression against the epic is, in part, an aggression against the classical sense of genre—that is to say, against the ancient mode of identifying a literature with a people. *Gens*, as Jacques Le Goff reminds us, is a Latin word, identifying the Roman kind. In his *Medieval Civilization*, he begins by describing Rome as a profoundly defensive civilization, a vast compound dedicated to preserving itself against barbaric threat. Consequently, according to Le Goff, Rome produced no innovations in any art but the conservative art of warfare. Roman civilization, with its defensive fantasy of an eternal and therefore universal *imperium*, best exemplifies the spirit and historical mission of the genre of the epic: the establishment of a walled genre—genre as walled city. Threatening, barbaric, the novel clamors outside the walls.[7] Novelization progresses in Byron's career apace with the development of his understanding of Napoleon Bonaparte's fall as a consequence of his mistake in modeling his regime on the pattern of the Roman Empire and of Byron's conviction that the destiny of an ever-greater Britain (not a people but a market system) was to expand as an empire without walls. The key document in this evolution is *Childe Harold* 4 where Lord Byron endorses the repeopling of the depopulated globe by the ideal characters of Shakespeare, Radcliffe, Otway, and, of course, Byron. There Byron meditates most searchingly the process of historical decay and the limits of degradation. Byron's sentimental naturalization of decay has the effect of removing decline and fall from the political sphere and the global advantage that Britain takes (which is not appropriative but commercial, transactional, elaborative, filling). Because it operates at the level of representation, Britain's empire is immune to the corruption that spoiled the dominion of Rome and, more recently, France. From its shakily experimental beginning in the episodic narrative of a down-and-out lord traipsing through landscapes of violated majesty, *Childe Harold* develops as a speculative vehicle to the point that, itself novelized, the poem can confidently predict the novelization of the world.

Another name for this *meum* that I have called life, the contemporary, and now Great Britain is, of course, the "bourgeoisie"; and it is conventional to associate the decline of the picaresque with the emergence of the bourgeoisie as a universal class able to imagine all possible subject positions as optional identifications within a plastic vastness. In this picture we can perceive the picaresque dying out at that historical moment when the appearance of an urban proletariat as a recognizable class with antagonistic interests vitiates the social basis for the personification of the *pícaro*[8]—just as the gentrification of the aristocracy had earlier tainted the enamelled naivetés of romance. The narrative of the *pícaro*'s movement from one master to another is generically tied to—that is, in the service of—the aristocratic genre of romance: both mystify social privilege as presupposing the right to master. Moreover, the decline of one involves the other: the conditions for mastery and the conditions for servitude underwent radical change during the eighteenth century, as *Pamela*, novel on the rise, attests. The end of both picaresque and romance announces the arrival of the novel: like the bourgeoisie, which profits from the disintegration of all kinds and which understands itself as immune to degradation, the novel serves no masters.

The distance of the English bourgeoisie from the English working class can be measured by its new-found ability to posit the aristocracy and the aristocratic genres of epic and romance as ideal types—that is, as kinds that pose no threat. Byron's rendering of an encounter with a contemporary Greece occupied and enslaved by the Turks is emblematic:

'Tis Greece, but living Greece no more!
So coldly sweet, so deadly fair,
We start, for soul is wanting there.
Hers is the loveliness in death,
That parts not quite with parting breath;
But beauty with that fearful bloom,
That hue which haunts it to the tomb,
Expression's last receding ray,
A gilded halo hovering round decay,
The farewell beam of Feeling past away!

(*The Giaour* 11.91–100)

Recent political and social historians have persuasively challenged the presuppositions of the Whiggish version of bourgeoisification, however, and chiefly the wish-fulfilling notions that some time during the eighteenth century there occurred the expiration of the aristocracy and the virtual elimination of any masters within British society capable of degrading middle-class aspirants to gentility.[9] What I am calling the reclassification of the picaresque is the return of the *pícaro* as aristocrat, which entails a return of the possibility of disintegration, this time emanating from the supposedly ideal type as though it were in fact a *living* corpse. This return of the historically and generically repressed is not a universal phenomenon. As far as I can tell, it is neither the effect of deep underlying causes nor the reflection of some prevailing tendency. It is more or less an accident. A monstrous accident.

II

The reviewer for the *British Critic* greeted the publication of *Don Juan* thus:

> Fearful indeed was the prodigy—a book without a bookseller; an advertisement without an advertiser—"a deed without a name." After all this portentous parturition, out creeps *Don Juan*—and, doubtless, much to the general disappointment of the town, as innocent of satire, as any other Don in the Spanish dominions.[10]

Despite its contempt, the *British Critic* does not put the poem down. That he cannot is a symptom of what a contemporary called "the contagion of Byronism." Observe its virulence. The reviewer poses the question, "If Don Juan then be not a satire—what is it?" He reflects that "a more perplexing question could not be put to the critical squad" and concludes that "as far therefore as we are enabled to give it any character at all, we should pronounce it a narrative of degrading debauchery in doggerel rhyme" (*RR B*, 1:297). Degrading whom? Lord Byron, certainly. But another victim announces himself in the reviewer's own doggerel alliteration. The reviewer is degraded to *Don Juan*'s level by his critical engagement with it. His degradation at magnifying the cultural phenomenon of Byronism by reviewing *Juan*—even though author and publisher fail to declare themselves, even though the poetry is morally and artistically reprehensible—

expresses his subjection to what, after Marx, we recognize as the dominant mode of literary production.

The reviewer has not read Marx. He understands his subjection as neither a structural predicament nor a historical necessity. He does not understand it at all. Rather he *experiences* his degradation as being forced, despite pretensions to professional disinterest and independence, into the service of a master. He learns the picaresque lesson that, in Chandler's words, "in order to live he must serve somebody," even though the code by which he pursues his livelihood promises an emancipation from servitude.[11] The reviewer experiences his subjection as dehumanizing, degrading. What makes this lesson picaresque is not only its content but its consequence: it will do him no good. He will have to learn it again and again, canto by canto. What makes this experience *disintegrative* is that the master cannot be located: that lord who would ideally heroically fill the bill is himself subject to the same degradation: master become writer, lord become *pícaro*.[12] The picaresque is the generic mediation of a subjection to the dominant mode of literary production, which cannot be understood or appreciated as such—a concealment for which the omission of the publisher's insignia from the title page of *Don Juan* is the apt index.

Whatever service formulas like the "dominant mode of literary production" provide at the level of the historical metanarrative, they do not really explain why any particular reviewer takes in his hands that which can only degrade him, why any freeborn Englishman would subject himself so slavishly. Why *would* anyone *buy* a book of bad verse?

That question is solicited by the *British*'s own dogged attempt to account for the strength of the negligible:

> The adventures which it recounts are of such a nature, and described in such language, as to forbid its entrance within the doors of any modest woman, or decent man. . . . Vice is here represented not merely in that grosser form which carries with it its own shame, and almost its own destruction, but in that alluring and sentimental shape, which captivates and corrupts. . . . But it is not, we trust . . . by the doggerel narrations of . . . the author of the poem before us, that the British nation is to be tricked out of unbending morality. (*RR* B, 1:299–300)

Whatever we think about the subversive potential of literature in general, this particular claim of degradation is convincing in light of an ambivalence so intense that within a few short sentences it produces the contradiction that *Don Juan* "*at once captivates and corrupts*" and yet fails to trick the British nation out of its "sturdy and unbending morality." Is there such a poetical magic? Has the British nation—and by synecdoche everything called "British," including the *British Critic* and *British Review*—been bent despite its posture of inviolate moral propriety?

In this instance, it is possible to specify what there is in the text that makes a reviewer "buy" it—proffer money or belief to it—even though it be "vile" and "trash." *Don Juan* is not bought because of the name Lord Byron, or John Murray, but because it calls the reviewer by name. Here is the lure that captivates the "British":

> The public approbation I expect
>   And beg they'll take my word about the moral,
> Which I with their amusement will connect
>   (So children cutting teeth receive a coral):
> Meantime they'll doubtless please to recollect
>   My epical pretensions to the laurel;
> For fear some prudish readers should grow skittish,
> I've bribed my grandmother's review—the British.
>
> I sent it in a letter to the Editor,
>   Who thank'd me duly by return of post—
> I'm for a handsome article his creditor;
>   Yet, if my gentle Muse he please to roast,
> And break a promise after having made it to her,
>   Denying the receipt of what it cost,
> And smear his page with gall instead of honey,
> All I can say is—that he had the money.
>
> (1:209–210)

Diabolically candid, the poet's tongue forks ambiguously. Two reviews speak as the "British": the *British Critic*, quoted previous, and the *British Review*. The *Critic* labeled the charge "facetious." The editor of the *British Review* did not laugh it off; he took it personally by identifying himself as that one named "British" and accused of receiving a bribe.

The *British Review*'s reply begins with the question, "Of a poem so flagitious that no bookseller has been willing to take upon himself the publication, though most of them disgrace themselves by selling it, what can the critic say?" Whatever "the critic" might say, *this* critic answers his own question by abandoning the pretense of a review in order to repudiate the charge. He challenges the evidence:

> If somebody personating the Editor of the *British Review* has received money from Lord Byron, or from any other person, by way of bribe to praise his compositions, the fraud might be traced by the production of the letter which the author states himself to have received in return. Surely then, if the author of this poem has any such letter, he will produce it for this purpose.... We really feel a sense of degradation as the idea of this odious imputation passes through our minds. (*RR* B, 1:477)

The reviewer protests too much. *Any* protest would be too much. The facts are known to both parties: Byron offered no bribe; the *British Review* accepted none. But, as Byron, under the *nom de plume* "Wortley Clutterbuck," points out in his wicked "Letter to the Editor of 'My Grandmother's Review,'" it is also a fact that the *British Review* has been at once captivated and corrupted. Enchanted by stanzas 209–10, the reviewer drops the pretense of criticism to entangle himself in self-defense; and in doing so he fulfills, despite himself and in the very denial of its existence, the terms of the imaginary obligation: "By the way," the pseudonymous Clutterbuck observes, "you don't say much about the poem, except that it is 'flagitious.' That is a pity—you should have cut it up; because, to say the truth, in not doing so, you somewhat assist any notions which the malignant might entertain on the score of the anonymous asseveration which has made you so angry."[13] The existence of a bribe would attest to an unseemly intimacy between writer and reviewer, but the roguish lord can more efficiently acquire the review he wants by trick than by trade—in Chandler's words, he wins "by wit or dexterity what others have wrought by labor or received by fortune."[14]

Having sprung the trap, Byron tosses off a bit of gratuitous economic instruction:

> You say, no bookseller "was willing to take upon himself the publication, though most of them disgrace themselves by selling it." Now, my dear friend, although we all know that those fellows will do any thing for money, methinks the disgrace is more with the purchasers; and some such, doubtless, there are, for there can be no very extensive selling ... without buying.[15]

The poem, its accusations, its libel, has no power of its own and would exert no force had not someone, despite the facts, *bought* it. Chief among those purchasers is the editor of the *British Review* himself, whose purchase (reviewers did not automatically receive complimentary copies) is exemplary because it exactly shows the coincidence of "buying" as putting money down for a commodity and tendering belief in a representation that, in this case, one knows to be false or "facetious." The libel is not nearly so degrading as the shameful fact that "I" *can* buy (psychologically speaking) and *must* buy (professionally speaking) that which says the worst imaginable things about "me"—that which violates both my personal and professional integrity. The "can" represents the psychological vulnerability into which the commercial imperative of the literary system bites. It is, in *Juan's* terms, this duplex of "buying," the coincidence of financial exchange and belief, which sorely pinches the *British Review.*

Clutterbuck goes so far as to theorize the rhetorical basis of the reviewer's social and psychological predicament: "The charge itself is of a solemn nature, and, although in verse, is couched in terms of such circumstantial gravity, as to induce a belief little short of that generally accorded to the thirty-nine articles."[16] "Circumstantial gravity" is the name for that which induces one to "buy" a poem, or a religion for that matter. Not context but the condition of context, "circumstantial gravity" can be concocted by calling a name: as in "British." The *British Review* answers to the call and buys *Don Juan*, even though, as the response of the *British Critic* (not to mention the histories of Wales, Scotland, and Ireland) proves, the "great name," "British," is "merely nominal." The name "British" does not acquire its circumstantial gravity from a proper correspondence with a particular reader or with some chronicled incident, but by its resemblance to many faces and facts and its capacity to simulate the precariousness of identity (personal, occupational, or national) as it prevails in the world at large.[17]

It is the corollary of its picaresqueness that *Don Juan* is not exempt from this precariousness. From the moment of its creeping forth, the life of *Don Juan* has been in doubt. From the very first, *Don Juan* acknowledges its vulnerability and allegorizes its written and unprotected inconsequence, its disintegrative tendency. This text imagines its death (a death that as text it cannot know) by a kind of prosopopoeia. It characterizes itself as "uncertain paper" (1:218), a letter signed, sealed, and delivered—whether it be the imaginary letter from the *British Review* accepting Lord Byron's bribe or, more conspicuously, as the epistle of the abandoned Donna Julia that brings canto 1 to its pathetic denouement.

Because paper is uncertain, letters, as both Donna Julia's and the *British* reviewer's experiences show, may come to bad ends.

His simply vanishes. Her note, sent from the convent where she will spend her life paying for her passion, a note exquisitely "written upon gilt-edged paper," finely sealed with a sunflower, and pathetically inscribed with the motto "Elle vous suit partout," suffers a more complicated, though equally disintegrative, fate. All that the narrative has figured in Julia's character—her sentimentality, her beauty, her vanity—is literalized in her letter. The letter, however, is also the performance of a promise: "she follows you everywhere"—she being the woman and *la lettre*, yoked in the metaphor of the sunflower. But the world is the arena where pretenses perish, correspondences fail, and seals are broken. Julia's attempt to master the future goes awry; the shipwreck episode in canto 2 realizes the nightmare of uncertainty, all to fungible paper. Julia's letter becomes the very token of chance.

> And when his comrade's thought each sufferer knew,
>   'Twas but his own, suppress'd till now, he found;
> And out they spoke of lots for flesh and blood,
> And who should die to be his fellow's food.
>
> But ere they came to this, they that day shared
>   Some leathern caps, and what remain'd of shoes;
> And then they look'd around them, and despair'd
>   And one to be the sacrifice would choose;
> At length the lots were torn up, and prepared,
>   But of materials that must shock the Muse—
> Having no paper, for the want of better,
> They took by force from Juan Julia's letter.
>
> Then lots were made, and mark'd, and mix'd, and handed
>   In silent horror, and their distribution
> Lull'd even the savage hunger which demanded,
>   Like the Promethean vulture, this pollution;
> None in particular had sought or plann'd it,
>   'Twas nature gnaw'd them to this resolution,
> By which none were permitted to be neuter—
> And the whole lot fell on Juan's luckless tutor.
>
>   (2:73–75)

The marked lot displaces the waxen sunflower. It seals the fate of Pedrillo, who, like Julia, is also a hostage to man's existence. Julia has been immured so that Juan may "range"; Pedrillo is killed that the crew may survive. But just as the seal is defaced and the letter torn, so is even the punctuality of the lot itself shattered by the convulsions of the men who, like reviewers of immoral verse, digest that which degrades them to the levels of animals:

> The consequence was awful in the extreme;
> For they, who were most ravenous in the act,
>   Went raging mad—Lord! how they did blaspheme.
> And foam, and roll, with strange convulsions rack'd,
>   Drinking salt-water like a mountain-stream;
> Tearing, and grinning, howling, screeching, swearing,
> And, with hyaena-laughter, died despairing.
>
> (2:79)

What moral might be taken from this picaresque sequence? *Cherchez la femme.* Julia might be blamed for trying to turn literary license into literal control. And from a certain distance (a few nautical miles) Julia's letter looks like one of those "oddities let loose" by a woman intent to "show (her) parts." Julia's commodified letter finds its ironically appropriate "mart" in the longboat, where the parts are parted again in order to separate the survivors into the disparate eaters and the dismembered eaten. If we may fault the woman, the grotesque disproportion of act and consequence (a gap that can only be crossed by moral convulsions) nonetheless dramatizes the inadequacy of the ethicojuridical format to come to terms with the disintegrative extremity of the picaresque. Indeed, to presume to offer a moral supposes the kind of distance that it is just the mission of the picaresque and just the effect of this powerful passage in the picaresque to collapse. Moreover, what makes this fully an *instance* of the picaresque rather than an *illustration* of the picaresque is the fact that Byron's book is prevented from moralizing the fate of Julia's letter because the fate of that book did not differ materially from the fate of hers.

Lord Byron chose to publish *Don Juan* anonymously, largely because he feared that a prosecution for blasphemy would result in the loss of paternal rights to his child. He could do so, however, confident that what makes books is not the name impressed on the title page but the power and right to copy. Since the appearance of *Childe Harold's Pilgrimage* in 1812, the phenomenon of "Byron" had been manufactured and managed by the publisher John Murray. Murray's admonition to his lordship (designed to dissuade him from continuing *Don Juan*) that "my name is connected to your Fame" is a reversible proposition;[18] the integrity of "Byron" depends on the willingness of the publishing house of John Murray to own him. Hence although Lord Byron's anonymity scarcely mattered, it was truly something new under the sun when *Don Juan* appeared in print without the publisher's name, a masterless poem.

The double eclipse of authorial sun and book-selling moon opened up an "interspersed vacancy" of law when *Don Juan* seemed to belong to no one. If like a freak it appeared to the *British Critic*, then like manna from heaven it came to the many publishers who made their living pirating best sellers, and like the loaves and fishes it multiplied in their cheap editions. Murray was in a ticklish position, losing money on a morally obnoxious poem that was a success in large part because of his refusal to admit he owned it. He sought legal advice as to whether a request for an injunction against the pirates would succeed or whether, as in the notorious case of the unauthorized publication of Southey's youthful, incendiary *Wat Tyler* (1794), the court would adjudge the poem seditious and therefore beyond the protection of copyright.[19] Murray's interests were equivocal. Although he was eager to prevent the pirates from profiting at his expense, his communications with his lawyer show that he was, if anything, more intent to stop Byron from writing any more shameful cantos of *Don Juan*. In his lawyer's eyes Murray was in a win-win situation: if he lost his appeal for an injunction, he could hope to get his advance back from Byron and deter the poet from his ruinous course. If the injunction were to be sustained, he would increase his profits and possess judicial confirmation that the poem was not seriously objectionable at all. The correspondence makes clear that all parties understood the copyright issue in the terms that a historian of English copyright would; copyright has no intrinsic tendency to increase the publication of books—its function is to keep others from publishing. In this case copyright is a weapon that the punitive publisher is attempting to turn against a stubbornly delinquent author. In this reasoning, Lord Byron has no more relation to his book than the next man. Indeed, for Murray the publisher, Byron the copyrighted author is always in danger of being degraded by that roguish lord—now identified by the title *Don Juan*—who *will* write as he pleases and whose best effects are picaresque, that is criminal thefts from the author whose work belongs to Murray, master publisher.

To the surprise of both publisher and attorney the judgment was returned that "the (contested) passages (in *Don Juan*) are not of such a nature as to overturn the property of it" and the injunction against piratical publication was conferred. The judgment gives the view of the law in all its purity and majesty. Observe how the question of copyright has become, by the most natural contraction in the world, the question of property rights itself; Byron's poetry maintains its property rights as long as it does not overturn property rights. The tautology defines what in the view of a law would constitute a revolutionary poem, one that overturned property rights—an act, however, that is by definition subject to the determination of the law. The tautology falls squarely in the grand tradition of English counterrevolutionary discourse; the revolution is identified as wholly conventional, as subject to identification and determination by the law. *Don Juan* is not the revolutionary poem that Murray feels it to be. The Murrayean connection between revolutionary and piracy hinges on Murray's mistaken and narcissistic notion that he is the master of the poem and that a challenge to his propertied dignity and rights subverts the order of things. The law pronounces the truth that *Don Juan* continually proves; the right of property is superior to the right of any individual to that property (even pirates, as Byron shows in canto 3, labor to the greater glory of property right); property right depends on mastery, but it is a mastery disintegrative of human individuals—the master is always elsewhere. The judicial pronouncement that *Juan* is not a revolutionary poem is, however, the proof that it is a picaresque one. By sustaining the injunction, the law protects Murray from his own scruples. The interest of property in general forces him to own that thing he would rather be without. This "win" did not feel like a victory. Murray, having already been put in the unseemly position of "pirating" his property had been further degraded by ratification of his connection with that which he felt to be immoral. The condition of his preeminence and wealth, Murray's subjection is also characteristic of every reader of *Don Juan* who answers to the name "British."

Perhaps the most salient consequence of the chancery opinion is the proof that a book has no more security than a letter and that any supposed superiority of Byron to Julia is therefore misconceived.[20] From the perspective of Julia the disintegration of her letter represents in the most lurid terms the fate of publication that the taboo of copyright pledges to prevent, or ought to prevent. For the lesson that Byron continues to learn is that taboos, like waxen seals, are made to be broken in one convenient extremity or another. No copyright can save the book from the depredations of pirates or publishers and from being cut up into brief extracts that are chewed over by the hungry savages of the culture industry, who are degraded by their employment and convulsed for their troubles—but, who, like the crew in the longboat, learn nothing from their experience. By the same token the fragmentation of the book that Byron fears—that cantos will be mutilated into "canticles,"[21] that pages will end up lining portmanteaus or wrapping fishes—does not exhaust its cultural effect. If *Don Juan* has any strength it is not as book but as *pícaro*. Not a novel, the poem inhabits no zone of propertied immunity where it can fantasize that it is the master of its fate. *Don Juan* disintegratively stages its own disintegration, and especially in the shipwreck scene—that episode of the poem which particularly disgusts reviewers who must, like the *British Review*, at their moral peril digest it for the sake of their professional survival. The shipwreck episode not only carries out the sentence of execution against Julia's letter, it represents the dismembering and digestion of *Juan* that occurs as the reviewers, slaves to an appetite that masters all aspirations to a civilized integrity, touch that which they know should not be touched, and represents also the way the dead thing touches back, the way it, shall we say, *publishes* convulsions among the custodians of culture, whose survival means the disintegration of the differences, natural and contrived, on which bourgeois—that is, a safely postpicaresque—society rests.

Notes

1. Harry Sieber, *The Picaresque* (London: Methuen, 1979), 57. Among those who might be aligned with Sieber as historicists of the picaresque, those whom I have found most instructive are Frank W. Chandler, *The Literature of Roguery*, 2 vols. in 1 (New York: Macmillan, 1899; repr., New York: Burt Franklin, 1974); Richard Bjornson, *The Picaresque Hero in European Fiction* (Madison: University of Wisconsin Press, 1977). The mythic position is represented by Claudio Guillén, "Toward a Definition of the Picaresque," in his *Literature as System: Essays toward the Theory of Literary History* (Princeton: Princeton University Press, 1971), 71–106; Ulrich Wicks, "The Nature of Picaresque Narrative: A Modal Approach," *PMLA* 89 (1974): 240–49 (which begins with a discussion of the "paradox in our usage of the term"); and Alexander Blackburn, *The Myth of the Pícaro* (Chapel Hill: University of North Carolina Press, 1979).

2. M. M. Bakhtin, "Epic and Novel: Toward a Methodology for the Study of the Novel," in *The Dialogic Imagination*, ed. Michael Holquist, trans. Caryl Emerson and Michael Holquist (Austin: University of Texas Press, 1981), 3–40. Hereafter references to this essay of Bakhtin's will appear in the text. The same characterization applies to Friedrich Schlegel's treatment of romantic irony—the model for Bakhtin's enterprise. See, for example, that moment in "On Com-

prehensibility" where Schlegel lets "irony go to the winds; and declares point-blank that in the dialect of the *Fragments* the word *(tendencies)* means that everything now is only a tendency, that the age is the Age of Tendencies" *(Friedrich Schlegel's Lucinde and the Fragments,* trans. Peter Firchow [Minneapolis: University of Minnesota Press, 1971], 264). Reading Schlegel's *History of Literature,* Byron comments, "He is not such a fool as I took him for, that is to say, when he speaks of the North. But still he speaks of things *all over the world* with a kind of authority that a philosopher would disdain, and a man of common sense, feeling, and knowledge of his own ignorance, would be ashamed of. The man is evidently wanting to make an impression ... like George in the vicar of Wakefield, who found out that all the good things had been said already on the right side, and therefore 'dressed up some paradoxes' upon the wrong side" *(Byron's Letters & Journals,* ed. Leslie A. Marchand [Cambridge: Harvard University Press, 1973–82], 8:38).

3. Lord Byron, *Childe Harold's Pilgrimage: Canto the Fourth* (1818), in *The Complete Poetical Works,* ed. Jerome J. McGann (Oxford: Oxford University Press, 1980–86), stanza 26. Quotations of Byron's poetry, identified by canto and stanza, are taken from this edition.

4. See Wicks, "Picaresque Narrative," 240.

5. Chandler, *Literature of Roguery,* 4; Bakhtin, "Epic and Novel," 19, 39.

6. Bakhtin, "Epic and Novel," 37.

7, Jacques Le Goff, *Medieval Civilization.* On the epic as a "walled" genre, see Bakhtin, "Epic and Novel," 16.

8. According to E. P. Thompson, eighteenth-century traditional culture "is picaresque not only in the obvious sense that more people are mobile, go to see, are carried off to wars, experience the hazards and adventures of the road. In more settled ambiences—in the growing areas of manufacture and of free labour—life itself proceeds along a road whose hazards and accidents cannot be prescribed or avoided by forethought: fluctuations in the incidence of mortality, of prices, of employment, are experienced as external accidents beyond any control ... ; in general, the populace has little predictive notation of time—they do not plan 'careers,' or see their lives in a given shape before them" ("Eighteenth-Century English Society: Class Struggle without Class?" *Social History* 3 [May 1978]: 157–58.) On the preprofessional character of the rogue, see Chandler, *Literature of Roguery,* 3.

9. See, for example, Lawrence Stone and Jeanne C. Fawtier Stone, *An Open Elite? England 1540–1880* (Oxford: Clarendon Press, 1984); J. C. D. Clark, *English Society 1688–1832* (Cambridge: Cambridge University Press, 1985); J. V. Beckett, *The Aristocracy in England 1660–1914* (Oxford: Basil Blackwell, 1986).

10. *The British Critic,* August 1819, in *The Romantics Reviewed,* ed. Donald A. Reiman (New York: Garland, 1972), B, 1:296 (hereafter cited in the text as *RR* by volume and page.

11. Chandler, *Literature of Roguery,* 2.

12. Indictments of Byron for degradation and perversion were frequent in reviews from fairly early in his career. For a discussion of this aspect of Byronism in relation to issues of gender and sexual object choice, see Jerome Christensen, "Perversion, Parody, and Cultural Hegemony," *South Atlantic Quarterly* (Summer 1989): 569–603.

13. Wortley Clutterbuck [Lord Byron], "A Letter to the Editor of 'My Grandmother's Review,'" *The Liberal* (London 1822), 1:43.

14. Chandler, *Literature of Roguery*, 4.
15. *The Liberal*, 1:43.
16. Ibid., 1:41.
17. Of emblematic significance is Lord Byron's family motto, inscribed on his crest: *Crede Byron*. As many tradesmen ruefully discovered, trusting Byron was practically synonymous with advancing credit to Byron. The degrading entanglement of the commercial economy with an aristocratic ethos is the inheritance that the lordly writer picaresquely performs.
18. Leslie A. Marchand, *Byron: A Biography* (New York: Alfred A. Knopf, 1957), 3:1040.
19. For Murray's letter informing Byron of the circumstances surrounding the publication of *Wat Tyler*, see Samuel Smiles, *A Publisher and His Friends: Memoirs and Correspondence of the Late John Murray* (London: John Murray, 1911), 1:383–84. The exchange between Murray and his attorney, Sharon Turner, is digested in 1:405–8.
20. In the best commentary on Donna Julia's letter, Lawrence Lipking discusses the identification of Lord Byron with the abandoned woman. See Lipking, *Abandoned Women and Poetic Tradition* (Chicago: University of Chicago Press, 1988), 41–47.
21. Marchand, *Byron*, 2:770.

The Brazilian Picaresque
MÁRIO M. GONZÁLEZ

The existence of a Brazilian picaresque supposes the definition of the picaresque novel I have formulated previously.[1] In "Picaresca," I argue that the picaresque novel is a narrative mode that, originating in sixteenth-century Spain, projects itself through the centuries in permanent transgression of previous modes, obeying historical circumstances that contextualize its different manifestations.

There is a clear, classic nucleus formed by *Lazarillo*, *Guzmán*, and *Buscón*, which function respectively as *germ*, *prototype* and *distortion* of the genre. After that, we have a well-known group of seventeenth-century Spanish novels. Next, there is a European expansion throughout the seventeenth and eighteenth centuries. In the nineteenth century, which was not favorable to picaresque antiheroes, the reappearance of this type of novel takes place in the Iberian American continent; on one hand, we have an American expansion that, in Mexico, means the survival of the Spanish model (adapted to new circumstances) in *El Periquillo Sarniento*; on the other, in Brazil a narrative model originates, without necessarily being conscious of the Peninsular model. In this model, the antihero feeds on a different reality and points to a production that, in the twentieth century, will assume its own characteristics and which I prefer to call neopicaresque.

In this group, the picaresque novel can be understood as a narrative, often pseudoautobiographical, whose protagonist is an antihero, marginalized from society; the narrative of his adventures is a critical synthesis of his attempts to ascend socially through trickery, while the *pícaro*'s social milieu is satirized. Several texts fall, more or less neatly, into the definition just set out. Therefore, we can talk not only of neopicaresque texts but also of parapicaresque or paraneopicaresque ones.

In the case of Brazil, the reappearance of the picaresque was favored perhaps by the preexistence of a social type equivalent to the historical *pícaro*, which was given a very specific name in sociological and anthropological studies—the crook (*malandro*).² The first manifestation of the literary crook is the protagonist of *Memórias de um Sargento de Milícias* by Manuel António de Almeida,³ a novel published as a "feuilleton" in *Pacotilha*, the Sunday supplement of *Correio Mercantil*, Rio de Janeiro, 73–131 (27 June 1852–31 July 1853). What are the picaresque traits of this novel?

In a well-known article,⁴ António Cândido argues—correctly, from my point of view—that Leonardo "is not a *pícaro* in the sense of the Spanish tradition." However, this does not mean that Leonardo cannot be clearly associated with the classic *pícaro*, as seems to be the intention of the critic.⁵ As far as I can see, Leonardo is the kind of crook who corresponds to what I call neo-*pícaro*, an antihero of a society very different from the Spanish society of the sixteenth and seventeenth centuries. The *pícaro* now appears as marginalized in relation to the bourgeoisie, a class absent in the Spanish Renaissance and Baroque. The realms of labour and nobility are not presented as referents, nor is the *pícaro* in the process of abandoning one to attain the other. But this antihero, besides having a series of analogies of varying degree with the traditional *pícaro*, moves in a world of characters who are sometimes more picaresque than he is. This intensifies the satire of his milieu, in which cunning allows him to survive without work until he settles down. Leonardo is an adventurer who cheats in a purely urban and, above all, labyrinthine way. The *pícaro* is now a sentimental being who, besides learning nothing from his experiences, is unable to think about his own acts. Perhaps here lies the reason for the third-person narrator. The narrative shapes itself as an explicitly serialized and transgressive discourse in relation to the romantic models in force at the time.⁶ This *pícaro* does not have the characteristic, personal project of the classic *pícaro*, although he does have some immediate or sentimental projects—like escape for escape's sake. If he goes against society, it is because he is a crook and nothing more than a crook; this fact brings him closer to the classic *pícaro*: his love for freedom. Once the Manichaean context of the Counter-Reformation is undone, the *pícaro* brings about the dialectical synthesis between order and disorder in a society wanting in contours.

One of the masterpieces of Brazilian literature—*Macunaíma, o herói sem nenhum caráter*,⁷ by Mário de Andrade—can be read as picaresque.⁸ Macunaíma, the protagonist, can be seen, without being reduced to this only, as a literary crook, a *neopícaro*, an observation already made by critics such as Cardozo, Fernandes, Cândido, and Bosi.[9]

However, the interpretation of Macunaíma by Gilda de Mello e Souza in her book *O Tupi e o Alaúde* deserves special consideration,[10] since it reads Mário de Andrade's rhapsody in the light of the picaresque. In chapter 3 of her work, the author shows the "strictly European" character of the central nucleus of Macunaíma, seen as a satire of the chivalric romance. Later on, she analyzes the parodic elements of Macunaíma, which, from my point of view, are also typical of the classic picaresque. Finally, she sees in Macunaíma a second degree parody of the chivalric romance, that is, a parody by atrophy of *Don Quixote*, which is, in turn, a parody by hypertrophy of the chivalric romance.

This critic, however, appears to overlook the fact that the chivalric romance had not one parody (*Don Quixote*) but two, Cervantes' work and the picaresque—the former, a hypertrophic parody, the latter, a parody by atrophy. Macunaíma is associated with the latter. However, this does not mean that, in Macunaíma, a view of reality characteristic of Don Quixote does not also persist. Thus, Macunaíma is not a parody but a parallel to Cervantes' text.

Macunaíma, then, is the crook who embodies the antithesis of the *pícaro*, Quixote, and by doing so brings together the two possible parodies of the classical hero. This trait will be common, in different ways, to the works I shall describe as picaresque in contemporary Brazilian literature.

Before considering the common traits between Macunaíma and the picaresque, I would like to recall a general analogy between the rhapsody and the Spanish genre, that is, the nature of "carnivalization of literature" present in both texts. This was the subject of a study of Maria Suzano Camargo.[11] Bakhtin himself mentions the picaresque as a carnivalized form.[12] In fact, the Spanish classic picaresque lasts exactly to the end of what Bakhtin calls carnivalization produced directly—the second half of the seventeenth century. From then on, the European picaresque will be carnivalization based on previously carnivalized literature.

This carnivalized picaresque is not absent from a revival of the genre in contemporary Brazil. On the contrary. In a culture in which carnival, far from being just an annual feast, is—as Bakhtin argues in the case of the Middle Ages—"a form of life itself," literature is once more carnivalized directly, especially after Macunaíma.

But this is not the only analogy. First of all, there is the rhapsodic nature of the picaresque, whether it refers to the procedure of accumulation or to the popular origins of the narrative in the larger text. It is unnecessary to emphasize the rhapsodic nature of *Macunaíma*, noted by the author himself in the subtitle, and thoroughly analyzed by Gilda de Mello e Souza.[13]

On the other hand, the parodic nature of *Macunaíma* is not restricted to the distant and involuntary satire of the classic hero; much livelier is the parody of romantic Indianism and of consumer society. In these aspects, *Macunaíma* reproduces the picaresque parody of the seventeenth-century idealistic narrative and of the "reputable man" of the time.

The protean nature, typical of the *pícaro*, characterizes Macunaíma, an Indian child who becomes a constellation later in life. At the same time, there is Macunaíma's wandering existence, reminiscent of the classic *pícaro*. He is also, like them, a permanent pretender. Last, common to the *pícaro* and Macunaíma is cunning, the only resource in the face of the hostile society they confront. In both cases, cunning does not prevent them from ending up as victims.

In Macunaíma's life story one can see some similarities with the *pícaro*'s: in regard to origin, departure, project, and conflict with society.

Whereas the *pícaro* degrades his origin by disqualifying his own parents, Macunaíma is born out of a process that clearly parodies the parthenogenesis myth. The *pícaro*'s denial of his family and departure for new horizons are symbolized by Macunaíma's assassination of the *viada parida* (a doe that had recently given birth), which turns out to be his own mother. The *pícaro*'s project of social ascent corresponds to the quest for the *muiraquita* (a greenish mineral charm worn by Amazon Indians). To realize their projects, both Macunaíma and the *pícaro* are constantly breaking codes, which causes them to confront their society. This clash, intensified when they get to São Paulo, is the source of intense satire, which, in the case of *Macunaíma*, covers ten of the seventeen chapters of the book.

In addition to the picaresque elements present in *Macunaíma*, however, it is also worth noting how other characteristics are recreated or transgressed—as in the best picaresque tradition—due to the historical differences of Mário de Andrade's rhapsody.

The first transgression, already mentioned, is the embodiment of the quixotic project together with that of the *pícaro*. Curiously enough, both projects are simultaneously symbolized in the *mui-*

raquitã. But this is not the only synthesis of opposing elements in *Macunaíma*. The rhapsody goes beyond the Manichaean dualism typical of the baroque picaresque.[14]

On the level of discourse, the autobiographical nature of the classic picaresque is surpassed by the adoption of another narrative device: the hero narrates his adventures to a parrot, which repeats them to the narrator of the rhapsody; thus, the latter inherits Macunaíma's *discours* and reproduces it in his *récit*, which results in the overlapping of mimesis and diegesis.[15]

Another trait of picaresque discourse—the stiffness of "realistic" chronology and geography—is surpassed in *Macunaíma* by the complete relativity of time and space, derived from the magic realm of myths. This results in a break in the linearity of the classic adventure; now, the hero without character easily loses sight of the larger project and is carried away by sidetracking adventures.

Finally, as a major consequence of the mythical realm it transfers, discourse in the rhapsody surpasses the predominance of the referential function of classic texts; Mário de Andrade uses language in this totality that is poetry, according to Eugenio Coseriu.[16] *Macunaíma* is a poetic text in the broadest sense of the word.

The protagonist, Macunaíma, differs from the classic *pícaro* in his "cunning for cunning's sake," typical, for António Cândido, of the Brazilian literary crook.[17] This quality drives him away from the classic *pícaro*'s pragmaticism at the same time as it gives him creativity. The pure comedy of the *Buscón* is surpassed by humor as a constant in the rhapsody.

Another innovation in *Macunaíma* breaks with the *pícaro*'s sexual self-repression, which, within the classic nucleus, evolves toward misogyny or implicit and explicit forms of proxenetism: it is unnecessary to detail the omnipresent and joyful eroticism of *Macunaíma*, unthinkable in the classic picaresque.

Last, the *pícaro* in the classic model rejects labor and sees it as a hindrance more than a step toward social ascent, nor does he present picaresque life as a social or political project. In *Macunaíma*, however, the protagonist's "ai, que preguiça!" ("gosh, am I lazy!") is a banner of rejection of industrial society in favor of a project ("utopia" in the eyes of colonizers and colonized) in which his similarity with Don Quixote, already pointed out, is further defined.

In short, it is possible to read *Macunaíma* in the light of the picaresque. This interpretation becomes more important since the Third World nature of the rhapsody echoes in a series of neopicaresque novels in Brazil in the 1970s and 1980s, which depart from the classic picaresque by embodying an alternative social project. These novels do not form a homogeneous whole. But it is possible to relate them to varying degrees with the picaresque, which, from my point of view, always refers to the major archetype represented by *Macunaíma*. All take place during the rise and fall of the so-called Brazilian economic miracle (a period coinciding with the military dictatorship that governed the country between 1964 and 1986).

It seems to me that the appearance of these novels is not foreign to the culmination of an economic system ("naive capitalism") whose most visible by-product is the widening of the base of the Brazilian socioeconomic pyramid and the creation of a void between the working class and the bourgeoisie, isolated in a tiny inaccessible summit. Labor, the best guarantee of permanence at the bottom strata of the social organization, begins to be rejected, as in *Macunaíma*. For the *neopícaro*, peripheral paths are the only valid key to social ascent.

Doubtless, the analogy with the Spanish society of the sixteenth and seventeenth centuries is unavoidable. In that society the ideological banishment of the bourgeoisie eliminated paths of ascent operative in the rest of Europe. The *pícaro* travels the guileful paths to attain the status of "reputable man." On this road, the importance of outward appearance induces the *pícaro* to constant pretense.

The selection of neopicaresque texts starts with *A Pedra do Reino*, by Ariano Suassuna in 1971.[18] Although I have no intention of reducing Suassuna's novel to its neopicaresque dimension, one can find in it characteristics of the genre—so much so that the author himself has called it a picaresque novel—namely, the traditional autobiography and antihero trait of the protagonist, marginalized by society. Curiously enough, his social climb has been transferred to the fictional realm of the epic, where he occupies the central position. This results in the *écriture* of the novel that realizes him as a writer. To face up to adversity along his adventurous route, he counts only on his own cunning and skill to cheat. A satire of Brazilian society is delineated, in which the protagonist ends up being the synthesis. There is also, if only implicit, a discussion of the worthlessness of work, the assertion of "honra-opinión," the "aristocratic" model defined by outward appearance, fiction within fiction, and a general prevalence of appearance over being.

Other possible comparisons with the picaresque derive from the serial aspect of the adventures, related to the "feuilleton" presentation, the connection with the rhapsodic, and the realistic motivation of the narrative.

On the whole, there is a rejection of the bourgeois model of social ascent and the suggestion of a leap that can take one from the underworld to aristocracy.

Galvez, imperador do Acre,[19] the best and most famous novel by the Amazonian writer Márcio de Souza, dates from 1976 and also fits very well the group of neopicaresque novels. The novel alludes to the historical character Luis Galvez de Aria, whose activities are fictionally transposed in serialized autobiographic form. Galvez, who leaves Belém in Northern Brazil for Acre in an enterprise related to independence, has adventures permeated by social satire. The protagonist's interests are solely materialistic, since he hopes to resume the aristocratic position once occupied by his family in Spain. His motivation contrasts with Joana's quixotic attitude: seduced by Galvez, she is a nun who believes in the enterprise and, in the role of guerilla, dies for an ideal that Galvez had communicated to her, without ever having himself believed it. The crook's cunning culminates in the parodic Empire of Acre, a mirror of Brazil in the 1960s, when a military revolt puts an end to Galvez's carnivalesque government, thanks to the pressures of some offended bigots.

The realistic motivation of the fiction, the presence of a pretender-protagonist, the company of a picaresque entourage are further traits of the classic picaresque mode. What is new, in terms of narration, is the presence of a third-person narrator who corrects the crook's unreliable narrative in the footnotes.

Last, it is also worth noting a difference between Galvez and his predecessor Macunaíma: unlike the latter, Galvez does not leave his conscience on the island of Marapatá, at the mouth of the Negro River. This attitude of getting rid of one's conscience is already present in *Guzmán de Alfarache*, as Heloisa Costa Milton's study demonstrates.

The third novel in the series is *Meu Tio Atahualpa* (1978), by Paulo de Carvalho Neto.[20] First published in Spanish in Mexico in 1972, the novel is set in Ecuador. The narrator (Atahualpa–the nephew) tells his story as well as his uncle's, a *pícaro* butler at an embassy, and Piter's, the ambassador's son. The nephew escapes being a shameless Indian ("índio sacana") like his uncle and ends up as a revolutionary side by side with Piter, now Pedro.

The uncle is a clear reissue of the classic *pícaro*: he denies his origins in search of easy social ascent as a manservant who ends up exercising some power at the embassy. His cunning prevails in his domestic adventures and he witnesses the corruption that rules the struggle for power, until he falls victim to this struggle by mistake. His nephew, who inherits his post, discovers everything and ends up in jail, where his process of awareness is completed. Rescued by Pedro, who has become a guerrilla himself, Atahualpa–the nephew goes to Cuba where he learns to write his stories.

The text is loaded with satire concerning means of social climbing among the dominating and dominated groups. These mechanisms exclude work and are based on outward appearance.

The quixotic realm permeates the narrative. The narrator, drunk and insane, turns the embassy into a chivalric world, characteristic of the popular stories he knows. However, when in jail, his quixotism assumes a revolutionary nature, which will make him accompany Pedro in his utopian project.

One year after the publication of Meu Tio Atahualpa, Os Voluntários by Moacyr Scliar was published.[21] The first-person narrative tells us the story of Paulo, a somewhat picaresque character. But his story is the nucleus of five other stories of picaresque characters who live near Voluntários de Pátria Street, in the southern Brazilian city of Porto Alegre. All are marginalized from society, and their personal projects collide with it. Nevertheless, all end up engaging in an enterprise completely foreign to their reality: to take the seriously ill Benjamin to Jerusalem in a tugboat so that he can make his dream of dying in that city come true. The quixotic enterprise fails from the very beginning and in the end the protagonist is back to mediocre reality, where there is no place either for the pícaro's hopes or for quixotic dreams.

In the same year as Os Voluntários, O Grande Mentecapto by Fernando Sabino was published in Rio de Janeiro,[22] and quickly ran through eleven editions. Although narrated in the third person, the autobiographic tendency of the text present in the intrusions by the implied author, and the protagonist's initial story can be compared with the picaresque. There is plenty of room for childish pique up to the moment of the protagonist's decision to leave home in quest of adventures. Later on, however, the character withdraws from consumer society, which is thus satirized. Viramundo's process of quixotism reaches its climax with a rebellion in a big city, Belo Horizonte. The wheel comes full circle with the protagonist's return to his place of birth, where he is killed by his brother without being recognized.

Viramundo's antiheroic attitude is the basis for a satire of the conservative society of Minas Gerais. But there is a passage from antiheroism to madness as Viramundo turns into a quixote who denounces society and its false values, like outward appearances that define the "reputable man" whom he does not intend to be mistaken for. Work is rejected, not in itself but for the alienation that goes with it.

Edward Lopes, a scholar of Spanish picaresque literature and author of the study, "Principios y funciones en la novela picaresca española" (1970), published his first novel *Travessias* in 1980.[23] Various elements relate E. Lopes's text with the classic picaresque: the first-person narrator, a servant to two successive masters, the wandering of the main characters, and social satire. Yet the narrator—reminiscent of Lazarillo—suffers passively all events. The protagonists of the events are the masters, true *pícaros* in the story and experts in cheating.

The picaresque formula is evident in the presentation of the book; in the first chapters, in which the child is given over as servant to a blind man who intends to bring him up; and even more so when hunger is present. Thus his wanderings begin with an undefined geography of Brazil and within a chronology removed from realism. Halfway through the book, the narrator changes masters—the blind man loses him to his youngest son, the black sheep of a family of farmers; the latter, who is "a famous drunk, gambler, and womanizer" is called "the angry master" in opposition to the blind man. In the end, both masters meet on their deathbed.

Throughout the text, the rhapsodic dimension of the picaresque is attained by means of the accumulation of adventures, anecdotes, and proverbs that are mingled with literary, linguistic, and philosophical reflections and quotations.

The end of the text clearly indicates the close of a picaresque cycle. However, the blind master calls all this "the beginning," thus keeping the narrative realm open. Coincidentally, this same author published his second novel *Lobos e Cordeiros* in 1983.[24] In this work, the utterly quixotic dimension of the protagonist of another story contrasts with the orthodox picaresque of the first.

In 1982, Haroldo Maranhão published *O tetraneto del-rei*, an excellent novel that can be read as a parody of the conquest of Brazil by the Portuguese.[25] It has other significant aspects, besides its possible connections with the picaresque, which the author did not intend. Nevertheless, it is impossible not to recall the *pícaro* in relation to the story of Torto, a fugitive from the court, incapable of heroism, who must survive by means of cunning all the drawbacks of an unintended adventure, especially after he is captured by Indians. Although the project of social climbing is lacking, the idea of getting richer is present in the third-person narrative that maintains the protagonist's point of view. When the first person is sometimes used, as in the letters to his beloved, we notice that he is an unreliable narrator, so that the feats he attributes to himself must be read in this light.

But Torto is not alone either. The group of conquerors constitutes a world of *pícaros* who form an infrahuman set and differ from him only in outward appearance, since they do not belong to the nobility. The importance of outward appearance is one of the aspects of the conquest caricatured by the author and presented as absurd and meaningless formulas; one scene, for example, reduces the fight against the Indians to a parodic sexual competition.

Torto's fate is to be devoured by the Indians. Yet he succeeds in inverting his fate by seducing Muira-Ubi, the Indian chief's daughter, whom he marries. Thus he wins his freedom back and that of the other captives, as well as the possibility of establishing a new society, the results of his rejection of all metropolitan residue and of his marriage to Muira-Ubi. The quixotic touch may be present in the project of the creation of a new world with which the novel seems to close.

Last, one should mention the excellent *O Cogitário* (1984) by Napoleão Sabóia.[26] This novel did not receive all the attention it deserves perhaps because of the complex treatment of time, which unfolds on three simultaneous planes, or perhaps because of the language, full of typically northeast Brazilian lexical, semantic, and syntatic peculiarities, so that it is less accessible to the wider Brazilian public.

Yet *O Cogitário* is a good example of the anthropophagic comeback of the picaresque, of which the author is clearly aware. This is the autobiographical story of Ampilóphio das Queimadas Canabrava, nicknamed Phipha, a northeastern Brazilian who struggles to survive in Europe on scholarships or by washing dishes at a second-rate restaurant in London. The crook, in this case, carries the burden of a chronic underdevelopment, which makes him lose out to his brother Jegue—who soon becomes lover to the queen's mare and starts to enjoy a lot of benefits. Jegue travels in Europe and becomes an interpreter for the

"North/South Mission in the Northeast of the Exclusive British Cooperation" and later "Exceptional Professor" at the Royal Academy of Letters for "au pair" mares of St. Columbia Gaelic, while Phipha struggles without managing to overcome the linguistic barrier of English. The parody of the relations between Brazil and the so-called developed countries is everywhere.

Phipha is the twice marginalized *pícaro*. He is from the poor Northeast of Brazil. He survives thanks to the cunning that makes him lie constantly and use escape as a last resort. His wits do not prevent him from being victimized by a hostile society. Thus he sees as more and more distant every possible realization of the impulse to social ascent that had brought him from the Northeast of Brazil. He writes his memoirs not to "vossa merce" (you) but to a girl in pajamas as befits his unbridled eroticism, characteristic of the transgression of the classic picaresque by a true descendant of Macunaíma.

Other topics, besides the treatment of time, go beyond the classic dimension of the picaresque: the fantastic (in the figure of Jegue) and the quixotic element. The latter involves to intertexts—Brazilian popular music seen as a condensation of national resistance and the literature of the marginalized and contesters, whose authors are brought together by Phipha in a football team captained by a certain Cervantes.

In conclusion, these texts—among possible others—suffice to show the symptomatic presence in contemporary Brazil of a narrative based on the antihero. The obstacles to social ascent, a result of the concentration of wealth and the loss of prestige of labor, impose marginalization and generate parody. The novelty in these neopicaresque works seems to lie in the relatively explicit formulation of alternative social projects that substitute for the contradictory eagerness, traditional in the classic picaresque, to integrate into the corrupt society being denounced.

Notes

1. Mário M. González, "Picaresca ¿historia o discurso? (Para una aproximación al pícaro en la literatura brasileña)," in *Actas del VIII Congreso de la Asociación Internacional de Hispanistas*, ed. David Kossoff et al. (Madrid: Istmo, 1986), 637–43; idem, *O romance picaresco* (São Paulo: Ática, 1988).

2. Roberto da Matta, *Carnaval, malandros e heróis*, 3d ed. (Rio de Janeiro: Zahar, 1981).

3. Manuel António de Almeida, *Memórias de um Sargento de Milícias*, ed. crítica de Cecilia de Lara, com estudos críticos, documentos e ilustrações (Rio de Janeiro/São Paulo: LTC, 1979).

4. António Cândido, "Dialética da malandragem (Caracterização das *Memórias de um sargento de milícias*)," *Revista do Instituto de Estudos Brasileiros* (Universidade de São Paulo) 8 (1970): 67–89.

5. For a good counterargument, see Rubia Prates Goldoni, "Galvez, o pícaro nos trópicos" (M.A. diss., Universidade de São Paulo, 1989).

6. *Lazarillo* is implicitly serialized, to the extent of having been the first text to be published serially in France, some years after *Memórias*.

7. The best critical edition of *Macunaíma* is Telê Porto Ancona Lopes, ed. (Paris/São Paulo: UNESCO/CNPq, 1988).

8. See Heloisa Costa Milton, "A picaresca espanhola e *Macunaíma* de Mário de Andrade" (M.A. diss., Universidade de São Paulo, 1987). Her careful study is useful, though I do not completely share the author's point of view.

9. See Joaquim Cardozo, "Macunaíma," in *Folha Carioca*, Rio de Janeiro, 18/01/45. In this article, the author intends to show *Macunaíma* as a symbol in a time of few symbols, a situation he attributes to the lack of the creativity typical of Spain's Golden Age. He thinks that we should read *Macunaíma* in the context of the picaresque novels of that age, exemplified by *Celestina*, *Don Quixote*, and *Marcos de Obregón*. Leaving aside this flexible and even mistaken concept of what a picaresque novel is, I would like to call attention to the fact that he refers to the genre stimulated by the reading of *Macunaíma*. Cardozo sees the protagonist as halfway between Don Quixote and Obregón, a buffoon distant from the model of the classic nucleus. He represents neither Quixote's defeat nor Obregón's victory, but something in between: the true *pícaro* the author does not know how to define with precision. Florestan Fernandes, "Mário de Andrade e o folclore brasileiro," *Revista do Arquivo Municipal* (São Paulo) 12, no. 106 (1946): 123–58. For the author, *Macunaíma* is a synthesis of Brazilian folklore realized in the form of picaresque novel. Fernandes emphasizes the importance of the "formal" aspect in the relation he establishes as a reader. In his article on *Memórias* (71), Cândido characterizes Leonardo as the "first crook to appear in Brazilian novels, a crook who was to become a symbol in Mário de Andrade's *Macunaíma*." See *História concisa da literatura brasileira* (São Paulo: Cultrix, 1970), 398. The author describes *Macunaíma* as "half epic, half picaresque."

10. Gilda de Mello e Souza, *O Tupi e o Alaúde: Uma interpretação de "Macunaíma"* (São Paulo: Duas Cidades, 1979).

11. Maria Suzano Camargo, *Macunaíma, ruptura e tradição* (São Paulo: Massão Ohno/João Farkas, 1977).

12. Mikhail Bakhtin, *Problemas da poética de Dostoievski* (Rio de Janeiro: Forense-Universitária, 1981), 105–18, 136–37.

13. *O tupi*, 9–33.

14. Haroldo de Campos, *Morfologia do Macunaíma* (São Paulo: Perspectiva, 1973), 113–14.

15. Gérard Genette, "Frontières du récit," *Communications* 8 (1966): 152–63.

16. Eugenio Coseriu, "Tesis sobre el tema 'lenguaje y poesia.'" *El hombre y su lenguaje* (Madrid: Gredos, 1977), 201–7.

17. Cândido, "Dialetica da malandragem," 71.

18. Ariano Suassuna, *A pedra do reino* (Rio de Janeiro: José Olympio, 1971).

19. Márcio Souza, *Galvez, imperador do Acre* (Manaus: Fundação Cultural do Amazonas, 1976). This novel's similarity with the picaresque was analyzed by Rubia Prates Goldoni in her dissertation "Galvez, o pícaro nos trópicos."

20. Paulo de Carvalho-Neto, *Meu tio Atahualpa*, trans. Remy Gorga Filho

(Rio de Janeiro: Salamandra, 1978). The original version appeared in Mexico in 1972, published by Siglo XXI. This novel was analyzed by Maria Teresa Cristófani de Souza Barreto, "*Mi Tio Atahualpa:* A sagração do herói na terra do carnaval" (M.A. diss., University of São Paulo, 1987).

21. Moacyr Soliar, *Os voluntários* (Porto Alegre: L&MP, 1979).
22. Fernando Sabino, *O grande mentecapto* (Rio de Janeiro: Record, 1980).
23. Edward Lopes, *Travessias* (São Paulo: Moderna, 1980).
24. Edward Lopes, *Lobos e cordeiros* (São Paulo: Moderna, 1983).
25. Haroldo Maranhão, *O tetraneto del-rei* (Rio de Janeiro: Francisco Alves, 1982).
26. Napoleão Sabóia, *O cogitário* (Porto Alegre: Mercado Aberto, 1984).

Notes on Contributors

MICHAEL O. ZAPPALA A graduate from Harvard University (1975) he specialized in Spanish Golden Age literature and classical languages. Dr. Zappala taught at several universities—Harvard, Brandeis, Saint Lawrence, and Maryland. He published articles dedicated to Cervantes, López de Cortegana, Alfonso de Valdés, Juan Luis Vives, and the Picaresque. He also wrote *Lucian in the Two Hesperias: An Essay in Literary and Cultural Translation* (1991).

CARMEN BENITO-VESSELS A graduate of the University of Salamanca (1977), the University of Lisbon (1979), and the University of California-Santa Barbara (1988), Dr. Benito-Vessels has published several articles and essays on Spanish Medieval historiography and the interaction of medieval literary genres. She has also written [forthcoming] *Don Juan Manuel: recepción y escritura de la historia*.

JERRY C. BEASLEY is professor of English at the University of Delaware. He has published several books on eighteenth-century British literature, including *A Check List of Prose Fiction Published in England, 1740–1749* (1972) and *Novels of the 1740s* (1982). He is general editor of *The Works of Tobias Smollett*, currently in progress.

MARINA SCORDILIS BROWNLEE is the Class of 1963 College of Women Professor of Romance Languages at the University of Pennsylvania. She has published on a variety of Medieval and Golden Age topics and is the author of *The Poetics of Literary Theory: Lope's 'Novelas a Marcia Leonarda' and Their Cervantine Context* (1981), *The Status of the Reading Subject in the 'Libro de buen amor'* (1985), and *The Severed Word: Ovid's 'Heroides' and the 'Novela Sentimental'* (1990).

NOTES ON CONTRIBUTORS

JEROME CHRISTENSEN teaches in the English department at Johns Hopkins University. He is the author of *Coleridge's Blessed Machine of Language* (1981), *Practicing Enlightenment: Hume and the Formation of a Literary Career* (1987), and *Lord Byron's Strength: Romantic Writing and Commercial Society* (1992).

BRUNO M. DAMIANI is professor of Romance Languages and Literatures at the Catholic University of America. He has written numerous articles on Petrarch, Quevedo, Aretino, Malon de Chaide, Cervantes, *Lazarillo de Tormes*, and *La lozana andaluza*. He has also published editions of *La lozana andaluza* (1967 and 1979), *La Celestina* (1974), and *La pícara Justina* (1982).

GERALD GILLESPIE has taught at the University of Southern California, SUNY-Binghamton, and—since 1975—at Stanford. He has held guest professorships or research fellowships at Penn, NYU, Pittsburgh, Munich, Paris, Minnesota, Cambridge, Peking, and East Anglia, and he twice served as secretary general of the International Comparative Literature Association. He has published widely as a comparatist on European Renaissance, Romantic, and Modern literature. Among his more recent studies and edited collections are *Garden and Labyrinth of Time* (1988), *Littérature comparée/littérature mondiale* (1991), *German Theater before 1750* (1992), *Romantic Drama* (1993), and *Visions in History* (1993).

MÁRIO M. GONZÁLEZ is a Brazilian born in Córdoba, Argentina—where he graduated with a degree in Spanish. Assistant professor of Spanish Literature at the University of São Paulo, where he received his M.A. and Ph.D., he is the author of *El conflicto dramático en "Bodas de sangre"* and *O romance picaresco*.

RANDOLPH D. POPE is professor of Spanish and Comparative Literature at Washington University in St. Louis. He is the editor of *Revista de Estudios Hispánicos*. Among his publications are two books, *La autobiografía española hasta Torres Villarroel* and *Novela de emergencia: España, 1939–1954*. He has written several articles about autobiography in Spain and Latin America. In 1991 he taught an NEH Summer Seminar for College Teachers on "Spanish Autobiography in the European Context."

JOSEPH V. RICAPITO is professor of Spanish and Comparative Literature at the Louisiana State University at Baton Rouge. He has published several books on Spanish works of the Golden Age and numerous articles on Spanish, Italian, and Comparative Literatures. He is also a published poet and short story writer. Currently, he is writing a critical study of Cervantes' *Novelas ejemplares*.

NANCY VOGELEY is professor of Spanish and Spanish American Literatures at the University of San Francisco. At the time of the picaresque symposium, she was visiting at Duke University. Her publications include articles in *Hispania, Dieciocho, PMLA, Ideologies and Literature,* and *Dispositio*.

CALHOUN WINTON received his bachelor's degree at Sewanee (the University of the South), a master's at Vanderbilt, and a master's and Ph.D. at Princeton. He has taught at Dartmouth College, Virginia, Delaware, and South Carolina, and is currently at the University of Maryland. He has published widely in eighteenth-century literary and cultural history, his most recent book being *John Gay and the London Theatre* (forthcoming).

Selected Bibliography

Alewyn, Richard. *Deutsche Barockforschung: Dokumentation einer Epoch.* Cologne: Kipenheuer & Witsch, 1965.

Alfaro, Gustavo. "El despertar del pícaro." *Romanische Forschungen* 80 (1968): 44–52.

———. *La estructura de la novela picaresca.* Bogotá: Instituto Caro y Cuervo, 1977.

Alter, Robert. *Rogue's Progress: Studies in the Picaresque Novel.* Cambridge: Harvard University Press, 1964.

Avalle-Arce, Juan Bautista. "Tres comienzos de novela (Cervantes y la tradición literaria. Primera perspectiva)." In *Nuevos deslindes cervantinos,* 213–45. Barcelona: Editorial Ariel, 1975.

Bakhtin, M. M. *The Dialogic Imagination.* Translated by Caryl Emerson and Michael Holquist. Austin: University of Texas Press, 1981.

———. *Rabelais and His World.* Translated by Helena Iswolsky. Cambridge: MIT Press, 1968.

Bancroft, Robert L. "El 'Periquillo Sarniento' and 'Don Catrín de la Fachenda': Which Is the Masterpiece?" *Revista Hispánica Moderna* 34 (1968): 533–38.

Bataillon, Marcel. *Le roman picaresque: Introduction et notes.* Paris: Le Renaissance du Livre, 1931.

Blanco Aguinaga, Carlos. "Picaresca española, picaresca inglesa: Sobre las determinaciones del género." *Edad de Oro* 2 (1982–83): 49–65.

Beasley, Jerry C. "*Roderick Random*: The Picaresque Transformed." *College Literature* 6 (1979): 211–20.

Benjamin, Walter. *The Origin of German Tragic Drama.* Translated by John Osborne. London: NLB, 1977.

Bernard, G. *Les modèles castillans de nos grands écrivains français: Études et analyse.* Paris: Ficker, 1910.

Berrettini, Celia. "El primer asomo de la picaresca en la literatura brasileña." *Sin Nombre* 13 (1983): 59–66.

Bjornson, Richard. *The Picaresque Hero in European Fiction.* Madison: University of Wisconsin Press, 1977.

Blackburn, Alexander. *The Myth of the Picaro: Continuity and Transformation of the Picaresque Novel 1554–1954.* Chapel Hill: University of North Carolina Press, 1979.

Brakhage, Pamela S. *The Theology of "La Lozana andaluza."* Potomac, MD: Scripta Humanistica, 1986.

Cabrera, Rosa M. "El pícaro en las literaturas hispánicas." In *Actas del Tercer Congreso Internacional de Hispanistas,* edited by Carlos H. Magis, 163–73. Mexico: El Colegio de México, 1969.

———. "La feria de Juan José Arreola: La picaresca como manifestación colectiva." In *Actas del Sexto Congreso de la Asociación Internacional de Hispanistas*, edited by Alan M. Gordon and Evelyn Rugg, 136–38. Toronto: Department of Spanish and Portuguese, University of Toronto, 1980.

Campbell, Glen. "The Search for Equality of Lesage's Picaresque Heroes." In *L'Egalité*, edited by Leon Ingber, 136–43. Brussels: Bruyland, 1984.

Casas de Faunce, María. *La novela picaresca latino-americana*. Madrid: Cupsa, Planeta, Universidad de Puerto Rico, 1977.

Castro, Américo. "Perspectiva de la novela picaresca." In *Hacia Cervantes*, 83–105. Madrid: Taurus, 1957.

Cela, Camilo José. "Pícaros, clérigos, caballeros y otras falacias y su reflejo literario en los siglos XVI y XVII." *Edad de Oro* 4 (1985): 33–45.

Chandler, Frank W. *Romances of Roguery: An Episode in the History of the Novel*. New York: Macmillan, 1899.

———. *The Literature of Roguery*. 2 vols. Boston: Houghton Mifflin, 1907.

Colomer, José Luis. "Translation and Imitation: Amplificatio as a Means of Adapting the Spanish Picaresque Novel." *Revue de Littérature Comparée* 63 (1989): 369–76.

Costa Milton, Heloisa. "A picaresca espanhola e *Macunaíma* de Mário de Andrade." Ph.D. diss., Universidade de São Paulo, 1987.

Criado del Val, Joaquín. *Novela picaresca*. Madrid: Taurus, 1960.

Cros, Edmond. *L'aristocrate et le carnaval des gueux*. Montpellier: Université Paul Valéry, 1975.

———. *Ideología y genética textual. El caso del "Buscón."* Madrid: Cupsa, 1980.

Cruz, Anne J. "Sexual Enclosure, Textual Escape: The Pícara as Prostitute in the Spanish Female Picaresque Novel." In *Seeking the Woman in Late Medieval and Renaissance Writings: Essays in Feminist Contextual Criticism*, edited by Sheila Fisher and Janet E. Halley, 135–59. Knoxville: University of Tennessee Press, 1989.

Damiani, Bruno M. *Francisco Delicado*. New York: Twayne, 1974.

———. *Francisco López de Úbeda*. Boston: Twayne, 1977.

Debaisieux, Martine. *Le procès du roman: Écriture et contrefaçon chez Charles Sorel*. Saratoga, CA: Anma Libri, 1989.

Earle, Peter G. "De Lazarillo a Eva Luna: Metamorfósis de la picaresca." *Nueva Revista de Filología Hispánica* 36 (1988): 987–96.

Eisenberg, Daniel. "Does the Picaresque Novel Exist?" *Kentucky Romance Quarterly* 26 (1979): 201–19.

Faller, Lincoln B. *Turned to Account: The Forms and Functions of Criminal Biography in Late Seventeenth- and Early Eighteenth-Century England*. Cambridge: Cambridge University Press, 1987.

Forstreuter, Karl. *Die deutsche Icherzählung: Eine Studie zu ihrer Geschichte und Technik*. Berlin: Ebering, 1924.

Francis, Alan. *Picaresca, decadencia, historia*. Madrid: Gredos, 1978.

Friedman, Edward. *The Antiheroine's Voice: Narrative Discourse and the Transformation of the Picaresque*. Columbia: University of Missouri Press, 1987.

---. "The Picaresque as Autobiography: Story and History." In *Autobiography in Early Modern Spain*, edited by Nicholas Spadaccini and Jenaro Taléns, 119–29. Minneapolis: Prisma Institute, 1988.
Frye, Northrop. *The Great Code: The Bible and Literature*. New York: Harcourt Brace Jovanovich, 1982.
Gillespie, Gerald. *Garden and Labyrinth of Time: Studies in Renaissance and Baroque Literature*. New York: Peter Lang, 1988.
Gómez Bedate, P. "João António y la picaresca paulista." *Cuadernos Hispano Americanos* 61 (1965): 177–80.
Gómez-Moriana, Antonio. "Intertextualidad, interdiscursividad y parodia: Sobre los orígenes de la forma narrativa en la novela picaresca." *Dispositio* 8 (1983): 123–44.
González, Mário M. "Picaresca ¿historia o discurso? (Para una aproximación al pícaro en la literatura brasileña)." In *Actas del VIII Congreso de la Asociación Internacional de Hispanistas*, edited by A. David Kossoff, José Amor y Vázquez, Ruth H. Kossoff, and Geoffrey W. Ribbans, 637–43. Madrid: Istmo, 1986.
---. *O romance picaresco*. São Paulo: Atica, 1988.
Gorp, Hendrik van. "Traductions et evolution d'un genre litteraire: Le Roman picaresque en Europe aux 17ème et 18ème siècles." *Poetics Today* 2 (1981): 209–19.
Goytisolo, Juan. "La picaresca, ejemplo nacional" and "La herencia picaresca." In *Problemas de la novela*, 87–94, 95–106. Barcelona: Seix Barral, 1959.
Grimmelshausen, Johann Jakob Christoffel von. *Der Abenteuerliche Simplicissimus*. Edited by Alfred Kelletat. Munich: Winkler-Verlag, 1956.
Guenther, Hans. "La novela picaresca y de aventuras en la literatura alemana contemporánea." *Boletín de Estudios Germánicos* 4 (1960): 76–84.
Guillén, Claudio. "Toward a Definition of the Picaresque." In *Literature as System: Essays toward the Theory of Literary History*, 71–106. Princeton: Princeton University Press, 1971.
---. *Anatomies of Roguery: A Comparative Study in the Origins and Nature of Picaresque Literature*. New York: Garland, 1987.
Haberkam, Klaus. *"Sensus Astrologicus": Zum Verhältnis von Literatur und Astrologie in Renaissance und Barock*. Bonn: Bouvier, 1972.
Hogan, Margarita B. "Picaresque Literature in Spanish America." Ph.D. diss., Columbia University, 1953.
Iffland, James. *Quevedo and the Grotesque*. London: Tamesis Books, 1982.
Jacobs, Jürgen. "Bildungsroman und Pikaroroman: Versuch einer Abgrenzung." *Amsterdamer Beiträge zur neueren Germanistik* 20 (1986): 9–18.
Jaen, Didier T. "La neopicaresca en México: Elena Poniatowska y Luis Zapata." *Tinta* 1 (1987): 23–29.
Jung, C. G. "Zur Psychologie der Schelmenfigur." In *Picarische Welt: Schriften zum europäischen Schelmenroman*, edited by Helmut Heidenreuch, 245–54. Darmstadt: Wissenschaftliche Buchgesellschaft, 1969.
Kermode, Frank. *The Sense of an Ending: Studies in the Theory of Fiction*. London: Oxford University Press, 1968.
Knight, Kenneth. "German Satire in European Context." *University of Leeds Review* 24 (1981): 135–52.

Koopmann, Helmut. "Pikaro in der Romantik? Eine Spurensuche." *Amsterdamer Beiträge zur neueren Germanistik* 20 (1986): 19–36.

Koschlig, Manfred. *Das Ingenium Grimmelshausens und das Kollektiv: Studien zur Enststehungs- und Wirkungsgeschichte des Werkes.* Munich: Hanser, 1977.

Krebs, Jean-Daniel. "La pícara, l'aventurière, la pionnière: Fonctions de l'héroine picaresque à travers les figures de Justina, Courage et Moll Arcadia." *Zeitschrift für vergleichende Literaturwissenschaft* 24 (1989): 239–52.

Laighton, Joseph. "Courasche and Moll Flanders: Roguery and Morality." In *Festschrift für Blake Lee Spahr: Barocker Lust-Spiegel: Studien zur Literatur des Barock*, edited by Martin Bircher et al., 295–310. Amsterdam: Rodopi, 1984.

Lasarte, Pedro. "Don Catrín, Don Quijote y la picaresca." *Revista de Estudios Hispánicos* 23 (1989): 101–12.

Laurenti, Joseph L. *Ensayo de una bibliografía de la novela picaresca española.* Madrid: Consejo Superior de Investigaciones Científicas, 1968.

Lázaro Carreter, Fernando. "Para una revisión del concepto 'novela picaresca.'" In *Actas del Tercer Congreso Internacional de Hispanistas*, edited by Carlos H. Magis, 27–45. Mexico: El Colegio de México, 1970.

Leal, Luis. "Picaresca hispano-americana: De Oquendo a Lizardi." In *Estudios de literatura hispanoamericana en honor a José Juan Arrom*, edited by Andrew P. Debicki and Enrique Pupo-Walker, 47–58. Chapel Hill: University of North Carolina Press, 1974.

Márquez Villanueva, F. *Espiritualidad y Literatura en el siglo XVI*, 30–38, 67–137. Madrid: Alfaguara, 1968.

Martini, Fritz. "Der Bildungsroman: Zur Geschichte des Wortes und der Theorie." *Deutsche Vierteljahrsschrift für Literaturwissenschaft und Geistesgeschichte* 35 (1961): 44–63.

Matta, Roberto da. *Carnaval, malandros e herdis.* 3d ed. Rio de Janeiro: Zahar, 1981.

McKeon, Michael. *The Origins of the English Novel 1600–1740.* Baltimore: Johns Hopkins University Press, 1987.

Menhennet, Alan. "Grimmelshausen, the Picaresque and the Large Loose Baggy Monster." *Seventeenth Century* 1 (1986): 11–126.

Meyer, Herman. *The Poetics of Quotation in the European Novel.* Translated by Theodore and Yetta Ziolkowski. Princeton: Princeton University Press, 1968.

Miller, Stuart. *The Picaresque Novel.* Cleveland: Case Western Reserve University Press, 1967.

Misch, Georg. *Geschichte der Autobiographie.* Leipzig: Teubner, 1907.

Mish, Charles C. *English Prose Fiction, 1600–1700: A Chronological Checklist.* Charlottesville: Bibliographical Society of the University of Virginia, 1967.

Molho, Maurice. "Le roman familial du pícaro." In *Estudios de literatura española y francesa: Siglos XVI y XVII. Homenaje a Horst Baader*, edited by Frauke Gewecke, 141–48. Barcelona: Hogar del Libro, 1984.

Monte, Alberto del. *Itinerario de la novela picaresca española.* Translated by Enrique Sordo. Barcelona: Lumen, 1971.

Pages Larraya, A. "Tradición e innovación en la picaresca: Matices de *El casamiento de Laucha.*" *Cuadernos Hispano Americanos* 75 (1968): 649–74.

Palma Ferreira, João. *Do pícaro na literatura portuguesa.* Lisbon: Biblioteca Breve, 1981.

Parker, Alexander A. *Literature and the Delinquent: A Study of the Picaresque Novel in Spain.* Edinburgh: University Press, 1967.

Pastalosky, Rosa. *Henry Fielding y la tradición picaresca.* Buenos Aires: Solar, 1970.

Pawlowski, John. "'Periquillo' and 'Catrín': Comparison and Contrast." *Hispania* 58 (1975): 830–42.

Petriconi, Helmut. "Zur Chronologie und Verbreitung des spanischen Schelmenromans." *Volkstum und Kultur der Romanen* 1 (1928): 324–42.

Preiser, W. *Spitzbuben und Vagabunden: Eine Blütenlese aus dem spanischen Schelmenroman.* Leipzig: H. Koch, 1956.

Rauhut, Franz. "La picaresca española en la literatura alemana." *Revista de Filología Hispánica* 1 (1939): 237–56.

Reynier, Gustave. *Le roman réaliste au dix-septième siècle.* Paris: Hachette, 1914.

Ricapito, Joseph V. *Bibliografía razonada y anotada de las obras maestras de la picaresca española.* Madrid: Castalia, 1980.

Rico, Francisco. *La novela picaresca española,* Vol. 1. Barcelona: Planeta, 1967.

———. *La novela picaresca y el punto de vista.* Barcelona: Seix Barral, 1970.

Roger, Paul Patrick. "Spanish Influence on the Literature of France." *Hispania* 9 (1926): 205–35.

Rötzer, Hans Gerd. *Picaro—Landstötzer—Simplicius: Studien zum niederen Roman in Spanien und Deutschland.* Darmstadt: Wissenschaftliche Buchgesellschaft, 1972.

Roubaud, Sylvia. "Cartas son cartas: Apuntes sobre la carta fuera del género epistolar." *Criticón* 30 (1985): 103–25.

Sánchez, Francisco, and Nicholas Spadaccini. "Maravall y el estudio de la picaresca." *Cuadernos Hispano Americanos* 477–78 (1990): 323–35.

Saraiva, António J. *Fernão Mendes Pinto; ou a sátira picaresca na ideologia senhorial.* Lisbon: Jornal do Foro, 1961.

Schleussner, B. *Der neopikareske Roman: Pikareske Elemente in der Struktur moderner englischer Romane: 1950–1960.* Bonn: Bouvier, 1969.

Shinagel, Michael. *The English Rogue.* Boston: New Frontiers Press, 1961.

Sieber, Harry. *The Picaresque.* London: Methuen, 1977.

Smith, Paul J. "The Rhetoric of Representation in Picaresque Narrative." In *Writing in the Margin: Spanish Literature of the Golden Age,* 78–127. Oxford: Clarendon Press, 1988.

Spell, Jefferson R. "The Intellectual Background of Lizardi as Reflected in *El Periquillo Sarniento.*" *Publications of the Modern Language Association* 71 (1956): 414–32.

Taléns, Jenaro. *Novela picaresca y práctica de la transgresión.* Madrid: Ediciones Júcar, 1975.

Trullemans, Ulla M. *Huellas de la picaresca en Portugal.* Madrid: Instituto Ibero-Americano Gotemburgo, Sweden, 1968.

Walty, Ivete Lara Camargos. "O Piolho Viajante: Literatura Picaresca." *Minas Gerais, Suplemento Literário* 15, no. 799 (1982): 3–4.

Warburg, Aby. *Heidnisch-antike Weissagung in Wort und Bild zu Luthers Zeiten*. Heidelburg: Carl Winter, 1920. Reprinted in: *Ausgewählte Schriften und Würdigungen*. Edited by Dieter Wuttke. Baden Baden: Valentin Koerner, 1979.

Weydt, Günther. *Nachahmung und Schöpfung im Barock: Studien um Grimmelshausen*. Berne: Francke, 1968.

Whitbourn, Christine J. *Knaves and Swindlers: Essays on the Picaresque Novel in Europe*. London: Oxford University Press, 1974.

Wicks, Ulrich. "Picaro, Picaresque: The Picaresque in Literary Scholarship." *Genre* 5 (1972): 153–216.

———. "The Nature of Picaresque Narrative." *Publications of the Modern Language Association* 89 (1974): 240–49.

———. *Picaresque Narrative, Picaresque Fictions: A Theory and Research Guide*. Westport, Conn.: Greenwood Press, 1989.

Wiles, Roy M. *Serial Publication in England before 1750*. Cambridge: Cambridge University Press, 1957.

Zahareas, Anthony. "The Historical Function of Picaresque Autobiographies: Toward a History of Social Offenders." In *Autobiography in Early Modern Spain*, edited by Nicholas Spadaccini and Jenaro Taléns, 129–62. Minneapolis: Prisma Institute, 1988.

Zamora Vicente, Alonso. *¿Qué es la novela picaresca?* Buenos Aires: Columba, 1962.

Index

Abencerraje, El, 31
Abenteuerliche Simplicius Simplicissimus, Der (Grimmelshausen): autobiography in, 16, 107, 116; closure in, 117; confession in, 118, 119; deceptions in, 112, 113; episodic form of, 111; frontispiece emblem for, 108–9; as German picaresque, 15–16, 20, 96, 107–22; irony in, 113; modeled on Guzmán de Alfarache, 108; protagonist of, 109; quester fool in, 110; quest for home in, 28
Adams, Percy G., 80
Addison, Joseph, 20, 85, 87
Adventures tragicomiques du Chevalier de la Gaillardise, Les (Préfontaine), 16
Aeneid (Virgil), 94
Albertus Magnus, Saint, 131
Alemán, Mateo, 13, 63, 69, 70, 77, 97
All for Love (Dryden), 97
Almeida, Manuel Antônio de, 15, 164
Alonso mozo de muchos amos (Yáñez), 14
Alter, Robert, 98, 99
Andrade, Mário de, 15, 164–65, 167
Andreae, Johann Valentin, 115
Anthony and Cleopatra (Shakespeare), 97
A Pedra do Reino (Suassuna), 168–69
Apuleius, Lucius, 27, 71
Aristotle, 25
Astrology, 114–16
Aubrey, John, 82, 87
Auerbach, Erich, 63
August, Bille, 72
Augustine, Saint, 29–30, 33, 71
Autobiography, 11, 13, 19, 29, 69–78, 101, 104, 163, 167

Avalle-Arce, Juan Bautista, 12
Aventuras del bachiller Trapaza (Castillo Solórzano), 14

Bagby, Ian, 59
Bakhtin, Mikhail, 27, 33, 34, 117, 147, 148, 165
Baldwin, Barry, 19
Barbadillo, Salas, 60
Batallon, Marcel, 65
Battestin, Martin, 90
Beasley, Jerry, 16, 19, 79, 99
Beggar's Opera, The (Gay), 90
Bélic, Oldrich, 58
Bell, Aubrey, 71
Benjamin, Walter, 115
Bildungsroman, 111, 114
Bjornson, Richard, 1–4, 80, 83, 98, 99, 100
Blackburn, Alexander, 99, 104
Blum, Carol, 123
Boasting (bragging), 84
Boileau, Nicolas, 25
Booth, Wayne, 87
Bosi, Alfredo, 165
Bourgeoisie, emergence of, 150–51, 164, 168
Brant, Sebastian, 107, 110, 114
Brémond, 97, 98
Brownlee, Marina, 13, 19
Brunet, J. Ch., 37
Buñuel, Luis, 72
Bunyan, John, 16, 17
Burlesque, 64
Buscón, El (Quevedo): autobiography in, 70, 73, 76; and conversion, 29; cruelty in, 72, 74; deceptions in, 43; as parodic of picaresque, 13, 25–26, 163; popularity of, 14, 96; satire in, 101, 167; translations of, 16, 97, 98; vengeance in, 48

Byron, George Gordon (Lord Byron), 20, 147, 148

Cabral, M. Silva, 15
Camargo, Maria Suzano, 165
Cândido, António, 164, 165, 167
Cardozo, Joaquim, 165
Carreter, Lázaro, 70, 71
Castigo de la miseria, El (Zayas y Sotomayor), 14
Castillo Solórzano, Alonso de, 14, 60
Castro, Américo, 65, 71
Castro e Vasconcelos, Felix Machado da Silva, 15
Celetina, La (Barbadillo). See *Hija de la Celestina, La* (Barbadillo)
Cervantes, Miguel de, 26, 63, 107, 108, 112, 148
Chandler, Frank W., 98, 148, 152, 154
Chapbooks, 84, 86, 90
Chapelain, Jean, 97
Charles V (king of Spain), 36
Chemical Wedding of Christian Rosenkreuz, The (Andreae), 115
Chettle, Henry, 16
Childe Harold's Pilgrimage (Byron), 147, 148–50, 157
Chivalric romances, 11–12, 27, 28, 31–32, 62, 150, 165
Christensen, Jerome, 20
Clareo y Florisea, 31
Clarissa (Richardson), 91, 104
Cobos, Francisco de los, 36
Colman, George, 87
Colonel Jacque (Defoe), 103
Comedy. See Satire
Complaisant Companion, or New Jests (Head), 84, 85, 90
Confessions (Augustine), 29, 71
Conrad, Joseph, 99
Converso issue: in *Buscón*, 76; in English picaresque, 103; in Spain, 65
Corneille, Pierre, 107
Cortés de Tolosa, Juan, 14, 33
Coseriu, Eugenio, 167
Country Wife, The, 83
Courtly literature, 62
Criminal biographies, 16, 17, 80, 90
Criticón, El (Gracián), 26, 111

Croce, B., 44
Cros, Edmond, 26

Damiani, Bruno, 12, 19
Dante Alighieri, 110
Defoe, Daniel, 90, 96, 102, 103, 123
Delicado, Francisco, 57, 63, 64
Diana, La, 31
Discourse, 26–27, 30, 33
Discourse on the Arts and Sciences (Rousseau), 137
Don Catrín de la Facenda (Lizardi): irony in, 126–27; morality in, 14–15, 20, 125–26, 130, 133–34, 135; protagonist of, 128–29, 130–31, 135; publication of, 126, 138, 140; satire in, 130
Don Juan (Byron): influence of Cervantes in, 148; morality in, 152–53, 157, 160; as a picaresque work, 20; publication of, 151, 157–59; reviews of, 151–55, 160; satire in, 151
Don Quijote (Quixote) (Cervantes), 30, 107, 112, 128, 165, 167
Don Quixote (Smollett, trans.), 95
Dreams (Quevedo), 74
Dryden, John, 94, 97
Dunciad (Pope), 104

Eisenberg, Daniel, 26
English Rogue described in the Life of Meriton Latroon, The (Head): autobiography in, 81–83; censorship of, 87; as imitation of earlier works, 96; popularity of, 82, 84, 90; publication of, 17, 20, 80, 82, 83, 87
Epics, 27, 117, 147–50
Epistolary novels, 30
Erasmus, Desiderius, 13, 37, 110
Espinel, Vicente, 14
Estebanillo (González), 72, 73
Evans, James E., 85

Faustus (chapbook), 107
Ferdinand Count Fathom, 102
Ferdinand VII (king of Spain), 131
Fernandes, Florestan, 165
Fernández Retamar, Roberto, 135, 136

Ferreira, João Palma, 15
Fielding, Henry, 90, 102, 103
Finley, M. I., 44
Fortunate Country Maid, The (anon.), 95
Foucault, Michel, 31, 32
Francis, Alan, 18
Freemasonry, 131
Friedman, Edward, 13, 28
Frye, Northrop, 117
Fuentes, Carlos, 95
Furetière, Antoine, 16

Galvez, imperador do Acre (Souza), 169
Galvez de Aria, Luis, 169
García, Francisco Javier, 36
Garduña de Sevilla (Castillo Solórzano), 14
Garzoni, Thomas, 116
Gay, John, 90
Genre, 25, 26–27, 30, 33–34
Giaour, The (Byron), 150
Gillespie, Gerald, 20
Gilman, Stephen, 57
Giolito, Gabriel, 36
Godwin, William, 103
Gogol, Nikolay Vasilyevich, 99
Golden Ass, The (Apuleius), 71
Gómez, António Enrique, 15
González, Estebanillo, 70
González, Mário M., 15, 20
González, Palencia A., 36
Gracián, Baltasar, 26, 111
Grant, Damian, 102
Greuze, Jean-Bapiste, 123–24
Grimmelshausen, Johann Jakob Christoffel von, 16, 20, 96, 107–22
Guillén, Claudio, 17, 31, 59, 73–74, 99, 104
Gulliver's Travels (Swift), 104
Guzmán de Alfarache (Alemán): autobiography in, 14, 70–77; compared to *La Lozana andaluza*, 62, 63; conscience in, 169; and conversion, 29; decadence in, 63, 73; deceptions in, 43; edification in, 27; nature in, 110–11; as paradigmatic of picaresque, 13–14, 25, 26, 163; popularity of, 25, 31; publication of, 25, 30, 69; quest for home in, 28; realism in, 63; relationship to *Lazarillo*, 70; satire in, 101; translations of, 14, 16–17, 96, 97–98, 100; tropes of, 18; vengeance in, 48
Gypsies, 82

Haywood, Eliza, 94–95
Head, Richard, 17, 19–20, 80–83, 84, 85, 86–87, 96
Hidalgo y Costilla, Miguel, 133, 134
Hija de la Celestina, La (Barbadillo), 19, 57, 60
Histoire comique de Francion (Sorel), 16, 107–8, 112
Histoire de Gil Blas de Santillane (Lesage), 16, 79, 95–96, 99–102, 123
Hogarth, William, 123
Holcroft, Thomas, 103
Homer, 94
Horace, 69, 70
Hume, David, 103, 123

Iffland, James, 72
Illusion comique, L' (Corneille), 107
Inkle and Yarico, tale of, 87–89
Interpolated narratives, 84
Iriarte, Tomás de, 36

Jarvis, Charles, 95
Jauss, Hans-Robert, 29, 71
Jenny, Laurent, 32
Jews, in Spain, 65
Jonathan Wild (Fielding), 90, 102, 103
Joseph Andrews (Fielding), 81, 84, 90, 103
Joyce, James, 99
Jung, Carl Gustav, 77

Kermode, Frank, 117
King Lear (Shakespeare), 97
King Lear (Tate), 97
Kirkman, Francis, 17, 82, 96
Knight, Charles A., 89

Laclos, Pierre, 103
La Geneste, Sieur de, 16, 97, 98, 111
Landstörtzerin Courasche, Die (Grimmelshausen), 15–16
Lazarillo de Manzanares (Cortés de Tolosa), 14, 33

Lazarillo de Tormes: antithetical tropes in, 18; autobiography in, 70, 73, 76; compared to *La Lozana andaluza*, 58, 59, 61, 62; compared to *Odyssey*, 37–49; and conversion, 29; cruelty in, 72; deceptions in, 43–44, 48, 74; edification in, 27; editions of, 13, 14, 37, 69; as the "epic of hunger," 44–45, 46–47, 49; episodic fragmentation of, 12; kinship in, 40–42; language in, 30; model texts for, 27; popularity of, 30–32; as protopicaresque, 25, 26, 70, 163; publication of, 31, 37, 48; quest for home in, 28; satire in, 101; social prejudice in, 65; suffering hero of, 38–40; translations of, 96, 97; vengeance in, 48
Le Goff, Jacques, 149
Leibniz, Gottfried Wilhelm, 107
Lesage, Alain-René, 16, 95–96, 97, 98, 100, 101, 102, 123
Liber vagatorum, 11
Libro de buen amor, 28–29
Life and Death of Mr. Badman, The (Bunyan), 16, 17
Life on the Mississippi (Twain), 84
Ligon, Richard, 87, 88
Lizardi, José Joaquín Fernández de, 20, 125–46
Lobos e Cordeiros (Lopes), 171
Lopes, Edward, 171
Lozana andaluza, La (Delicado): humor in, 63–66; as precursor of the picaresque, 12, 19, 57–68; protagonist of, 57–62; publication of, 57; realism in, 62–63, 66
Lucian, 27, 33, 74–75
Lukàcs, Georgy, 31
Luna, Juan de, 14, 33
Luther, Martin, 114–15

Mabbe, James, 16, 80, 96
Machiavelli, Niccolò, 20, 131–32
Machiavellian Moment, The (Pocock), 132
Macunaíma o herói sem nenhum caráter (Andrade), 15, 21, 164–68
Males de la desunión, y utilidades que debe producir la confraternidad (pamphlet), 132

Mann, Thomas, 99, 113
Mannerism, 109
Man of Mode, The, 83
Maranhão, Haroldo, 171
Marasso, Arturo, 43
Marivaux, Pierre Carlet de Chamblain de, 94
Marx, Karl, 152
McKenzie, Donald F., 80
McKeon, Michael, 80, 81, 108
Mello e Souza, Gilda de, 165, 166
Melville, Herman, 99
Memórias de um Sargento de Milícias (Almeida), 15, 164
Menéndez y Pelayo, M., 36
Mermall, Thomas, 18
Meu Tio Atahualpa (Neto), 169–70
Meyer, Herman, 117
Miller, Stuart, 18, 61, 98, 99
Milton, Heloisa Costa, 169
Mise en abime, 109
Mish, Charles, 84
Molho, Maurice, 13
Moll Flanders (Defoe), 17, 90, 96, 102, 103
Monte, Alberto del, 11, 14
Montesinos, José, 26
Morelos y Pavón, José María, 133
Moscherosch, Hans Michael, 111
Motteux, Peter, 95
Mouhy, Charles de fieux chavalier de, 94, 95
Murray, John, 157–59
Myth of the Picaro, The (Blackburn), 99

Nair, Mira, 72
Napoleon Bonaparte, 149
Nashe, Thomas, 16, 79–80
Neoclassicism, 97
Neoplatonism, 48
Neostoicism, 48
Neto, Paulo de Carvalho, 169
New Art of Making Plays (Vega), 115
Nicholson, Jack, 86
Nobili, Giacinto, 11
Novels, 33–34, 147–48, 149–50
Nugget fictions, 20, 84–86, 90

O Cognitário (Sabóia), 21, 172–73
O desgraciado amante Peralvilho (Rebelo), 15

Odyssey (Homer), 36–49
O Grande Mentecapto (Sabino), 170–71
"Olvidados, Los" (film, Buñuel), 72
Os Voluntários (Scliar), 170
O tetraneto del-rei (Maranhão), 171–72
Ozell, John, 95

Palazzo del Te, 109
Pamela, or Virtue Rewarded (Richardson), 94, 150
Parker, Alexander A., 11, 16, 26, 63, 71, 97, 98, 99, 123
Parker, William Riley, 83
Parmigianino (Girolamo Mazzola), 109
Parzival (Wolfram), 110
Pastoral writings, 31, 62
Paysanne parvenue, La (Marivaux), 94
"Pelle the Conqueror" (film, August), 72
Pencz, Georg, 115
Penzol, Pedro, 58
Peregrine Pickle, 102
Pérez, Antonio, 36
Pérez, Gonzalo, 19, 36, 49
Periguillo Sarniento, El (Lizardi), 14–15, 125, 163
Petriconi, Helmut, 26
Petronius, 19, 71
Phillip II (king of Spain), 36
Piazza Universale (Garzoni), 116
Pícara Justina, La (Ubeda): morality in, 61; as a picaresque novel, 14, 110; satire in, 65–66; translations of, 97
Picaresque: as autobiographical, 11, 13, 19, 29, 69–78, 101, 104, 163, 167; classical models for, 71; confession in, 13, 29, 71, 74; deception in, 12, 43–44, 48, 59, 70, 85–86, 163; English versions of, 20, 79–93; episodic form of, 12, 66, 82, 98, 103, 111; eroticism in, 167; impact of Enlightenment on, 20, 123, 124, 127, 129, 132–33, 135, 136; journey in, 58, 61, 80–81, 166; in Latin America, 20–21, 124–46, 163–75; as a mode, 163; models for, 27–30; morality in, 59–61, 66, 80, 98, 123–25; mythology of, 99, 104–5, 147; and neopicaresque, 15, 20–21, 163, 168, 173; origins of, 11, 13, 17, 18; paradigmatic, 13–14, 25, 26, 163; parodies of, 13, 25–26, 163; popularity of, 96; and protopicaresque, 25, 26, 70, 163; realism in, 12, 62–63, 66, 98, 167; relationship to the novel, 147–48; satire (humor) in, 27–28, 63–66, 89, 101, 108, 130, 151, 163, 167; skepticism in, 61; translation of, 19, 94–106; as travel literature, 80–81
Pícaro na literatura portuguesa, Do (Ferreira), 15
Pícaros (rogues): as antiheroes, 164, 173; as aristocrats, 151; as avengers, 48; definitions of, 11, 123, 131; dishonorable background of, 11, 57, 60, 81, 166; as hermits, 61; life course of, 58, 61; morality of, 59–61, 83; origin of the word, 47; physical appearance of, 47–48; sarcasm (humor) of, 72; skepticism of, 61; social stature of, 11, 59, 60, 83, 108, 163; as storytellers, 73, 77; survival of, 58, 59, 71
Pícaros en la literatura española, Los (Parker), 11
Piers Plinnes Seaven Yeres Prentiship (Chettle), 16
"Pixote" (film), 72
Pocahontas, 88
Pocock, J. G. A., 132
Poe, Edgar Allan, 81
Polyandre (Sorel), 96
Pope, Alexander, 94, 104
Pope, Randolph, 19
Portinariis, Andrea de, 36
Praise of Folly (Erasmus), 110
Préfontaine, Oudin, 16
Processo de cartas, 30
Proteo de Madrid, El (Castillo Solórzano), 14

Quevedo, Francisco de, 14, 62, 63, 74, 97

Rabelais, François, 108, 117
Rampazeto, Francesco, 36

Rapin-Thoyras, Paul de, 97
Realism, 12, 62–63, 66, 98, 167
Rebelo, Father Gaspar Pires, 15
Reed, Walter, 33–34
Restoration comedies, 83
Retrato de la Lozana andaluza, El (Delicado). See *Lozana andaluza, La* (Delicado)
Rhapsody, 165–68
Ricapito, Joseph, 19
Richardson, Samuel, 91, 94, 95
Rico, Francisco, 17, 26, 33, 37, 72
Robinson Crusoe (Defoe), 104, 120
Roderick Random (Smollett), 96, 98–100, 101–3, 104, 147
Rogue, The (Mabbe), 16–17, 96
Rogue's Progress (Alter), 98
Roman bourgeois (Furetière), 16
Romance. See Chivalric romance
Roman comique (Scarron), 16, 96
Romano, Giulio, 109
Rousseau, Jean-Jacques, 137
Roxana (Defoe), 103
Rymer, Thomas, 97

Sabino, Fernando, 170
Sabóia, Napoleão, 172
"Salaam Bombay" (film, Nair), 72
Satire: and nationalism, 89–90; in picaresque, 27–28, 63–66, 89, 101, 108, 130, 151, 163, 167
Satyricon (Petronius), 63, 71
Scarron, Paul, 16, 96
Scholes, Robert, 27
Scliar, Moacyr, 170
Segre, Cesare, 25
Segunda parte del Lazarillo (anon., 1555), 31, 32–33
Segunda parte del Lazarillo (Luna, 1620), 14, 33
Self-portrait in a Convex Mirror (Parmigianino), 109
Seltsame Springinsfeld, Der (Grimmelshausen), 15–16
Sentimental writings, 62, 102
Ship of Fools (Brant), 107, 110, 114
Sieber, Harry, 19, 30, 147
Smith, John, 88
Smith, Paul Julian, 12, 14, 17, 79
Smollett, Tobias, 95–96, 98–99, 101–3, 147

Sorel, Charles, 16, 96, 107–8, 112
Southey, Robert, 158
Souza, Márcio de, 169
Spectator, 85, 87–90
Spell, Jefferson Rea, 140
Spufford, Margaret, 86
Steele, Richard, 20, 85, 87, 88, 89–90
Stelsio, Juan (Jan Steels), 36
Sterne, Laurence, 117, 120
Suassuna, Ariano, 168
Sueños (Quevedo), 111
Swift, Jonathan, 104

Tacitus, 69, 70
Tate, Nahum, 97
Tatler, 85
Tercera parte de Guzmán de Alfarache (Castro e Vasconcelos), 15
Tesauro, Emanuele Conte, 111
Thousand and One Nights, A, 43
Tom Jones (Fielding), 81, 84, 90, 102, 103, 104
Tovar, María, 36
Translation, 19, 94–106
Travel literature, 80–81
Travessias (Lopes), 171
Tristram Shandy (Sterne), 117, 120
True History (Lucian), 27
Twain, Mark, 84, 99

Ubeda, Francisco López de, 14, 65, 97
Ulyxea, La (Pérez): deceptions in, 42–44, 48, 49; food and hospitality in, 44–47, 49; kinship in, 40–42; profit from reading of, 37–38; publication of, 36–37; relationship to *Lazarillo*, 19, 37; suffering hero of, 38–40; vengeance in, 48
Unfortunate Traveller, or the Life of Jack Wilton (Nashe), 16, 80
Updike, John, 86

Vagabondo, Il (Nobili), 11
Valdés, Alfonso de, 36
Vance, Eugene, 30
Vega, Lope de, 115
Vida de Dom Gregório Guadanha (Gómez), 15
Vida de Marcos de Obregóon, La (Espinel), 14

Vida de Peralvilho de Córdoba (Cabral), 15
Virtuous Villager, or Virgin's Victory (Haywood), 94–95
Vogeley, Nancy, 14–15, 20

Wall, John N., Jr., 85
Warburg, Aby, 114
Wat Tyler (Southey), 158
Weydt, Günther, 115, 116
Wicks, Ulrich, 28
Winstanley, William, 83, 86, 87
Winton, Calhoun, 16, 19–20
Witches of Eastwick, The (Updike), 86
Wolfram von Eschenbach, 110
Wollstonecraft, Mary, 103
Wonderful Life, Prophecies, and Death of Mother Shipton, the Female Merlin (Head), 86
Wondrous and Veracious Visions of Philander von Sittewald (Moscherosch), 111

Yáñez, Jerónimo Alcalá, 14

Zappala, Michael, 17
Zayas y Sotomayor, María de, 14